SHAKESPEARE AND VICTORIAN WOMEN

Much has been written on the cultural significance of Shakespeare, his influence on particular periods, and his appropriation and subsequent transformation. However, no book until now has specifically addressed the nature of the relationship between Shakespeare and Victorian women. Gail Marshall gives an account of the actresses who played an essential part in redeeming Shakespeare for the Victorian stage, the writers who embraced him as part of the texture of their own writing as well as of their personal lives, and those women readers who, educated to be alert to the female voices of Shakespeare, often went on to re-read Shakespeare for their own ends. Dr Marshall argues that women form a fundamental part of the narrative of how the Victorian Shakespeare was made, and that translation, rather than terms such as 'appropriation' or 'adaptation', is the most pertinent metaphor for understanding the symbiosis between Shakespeare and Victorian women.

GAIL MARSHALL is Reader in Nineteenth-century Literature at the Department of English, Oxford Brookes University.

CAMBRIDGE STUDIES IN NINETEENTH-CENTURY
LITERATURE AND CULTURE

General editor
Gillian Beer, *University of Cambridge*

Editorial board
Isobel Armstrong, *Birkbeck, University of London*
Kate Flint, *Rutgers University*
Catherine Gallagher, *University of California, Berkeley*
D. A. Miller, *University of California, Berkeley*
J. Hillis Miller, *University of California, Irvine*
Daniel Pick, *Birkbeck, University of London*
Mary Poovey, *New York University*
Sally Shuttleworth, University of Oxford
Herbert Tucker, *University of Virginia*

Nineteenth-century British literature and culture have been rich fields for
interdisciplinary studies. Since the turn of the twentieth century, scholars and
critics have tracked the intersections and tensions between Victorian literature
and the visual arts, politics, social organization, economic life, technical
innovations, scientific thought – in short, culture in its broadest sense. In
recent years, theoretical challenges and historiographical shifts have unsettled
the assumptions of previous scholarly synthesis and called into question the
terms of older debates. Whereas the tendency in much past literary critical
interpretation was to use the metaphor of culture as 'background', feminist,
Foucauldian, and other analyses have employed more dynamic models that
raise questions of power and of circulation. Such developments have reani-
mated the field. This series aims to accommodate and promote the most
interesting work being undertaken on the frontiers of the field of nineteenth-
century literary studies: work which intersects fruitfully with other fields of
study such as history, or literary theory, or the history of science. Comparative
as well as interdisciplinary approaches are welcomed.

A complete list of titles published will be found at the end of the book.

SHAKESPEARE AND VICTORIAN WOMEN

GAIL MARSHALL

CAMBRIDGE
UNIVERSITY PRESS

CAMBRIDGE UNIVERSITY PRESS
Cambridge, New York, Melbourne, Madrid, Cape Town, Singapore, São Paulo, Delhi

Cambridge University Press
The Edinburgh Building, Cambridge CB2 8RU, UK

Published in the United States of America by Cambridge University Press, New York

www.cambridge.org
Information on this title: www.cambridge.org/9780521515238

First published 2009

Printed in the United Kingdom at the University Press, Cambridge

A catalogue record for this publication is available from the British Library

ISBN 978-0-521-51523-8 hardback

For Rosa with much love,
and in fond memory of Inga-Stina Ewbank

Contents

List of illustrations	*page* viii	
Acknowledgements	ix	
Introduction	1	
1 Shakespeare and Victorian girls' education	13	
2 Elizabeth Barrett Browning and Shakespeare: translating the language of intimacy	45	
3 'She had made him, as it were, the air she lived in': Shakespeare, Helen Faucit and Fanny Kemble	72	
4 George Eliot and Shakespeare: defamiliarising 'second nature'	99	
5 Socialism, nationalism and Stratford: Shakespeare and the New Woman at the *fin de siècle*	128	
6 Shakespeare and the actress in the 1890s	153	
Notes	178	
Bibliography	194	
Index	204	

Illustrations

1 Ford Madox Brown, *Romeo and Juliet* (1870). Reproduced by kind permission of the Delaware Art Museum, Samuel and Mary R. Bancroft Memorial, 1935. *page* 32

2 Gordon Browne, illustration of *Romeo and Juliet*, V.ii, Irving edition of Shakespeare (1888). 33

3 Lucy Madox Brown, *Romeo and Juliet in the Tomb* (1870). Reproduced by kind permission of the National Trust. Photograph by permission of Cliff Guttridge and Angela Thirlwell. 43

4 'Great Attraction', *Punch*, 31 May 1899, p. 258. 174

5 'Fashion à la Shakspeare', *Punch*, 11 September 1897, p. 110. 175

Acknowledgements

Over the time it's taken to write this book, old friendships have endured and new ones have been made, sometimes through the means of the book itself, which has introduced me to many new scholars in the field of Shakespeare studies. Colleagues in the School of English at the University of Leeds, and in the English department at Oxford Brookes University have been central to my work on this project, as have the following friends, whose support and inspiration, both domestic and professional, has been crucial: Bridget Bennett, Tom Betteridge, Elleke Boehmer, Marian Boyle, Martin Butler, Shirley Chew, Denise Chmelova, Phillipa Davies, Phil Davis, Pip Deacon, Richard Foulkes, Fiona Green, Tracy Hargreaves, Tom Healy, Juliet John, David Lindley, Steve Matthews, Gordon McMullan, Mark Robson, Yvonne Savage, Jessica Sharkey, John Stokes, Marion Thain, Ann Thompson, Shearer West, Jane Wood and Katharine Woodcock. I am grateful to Dinah Birch, Elisabeth Jay and Kate Newey for reading parts of this book, and especially to Adrian Poole for his support over the last twenty years, for his own inspiring work on Victorian Shakespeare, and for reading several chapters in manuscript.

I am grateful to the British Academy for a grant which enabled me to visit the Folger Shakespeare Library in Washington DC, to the School of English at Leeds for study leave to work on this book, and to the School of Arts and Humanities at Oxford Brookes for help with the costs of illustrations; to the staff of the libraries in which I have worked, principally the Bodleian Library, the British Library, Cambridge University Library, and the Folger, where I was especially pleased to be able to benefit from the expertise of Georgianna Ziegler; to the Folger Shakespeare Library and The Cheltenham Ladie's College for permission to quote from manuscript material in their possession; and to the editors of *Nineteenth-Century Gender Studies* and *Victorian Poetry* for permission to use material in the chapters on George Eliot and Elizabeth Barrett Browning which first appeared in their publications. I am grateful too to Angela Thirlwell and Cliff Guttridge for their generous permission to reproduce the Lucy Madox Brown painting which is on the cover of this book. My thanks too to Gillian Beer and Linda Bree for their support of this project, and to Jo Bottrill, Wendy Toole, Maartje Scheltens and Tom O'Reilly for all their help.

My final thanks go to my family: to my parents and brother for sustained support, and to my Mum in particular for first taking me to Stratford to watch Shakespeare; to Andy for his enthusiasm and patient help with computing matters; and to Lily for being such fun, and for her early enthusiasm for Shakespeare – who could resist a play with a character called Bottom? The book is dedicated to two important people: to the memory of Inga-Stina Ewbank, whose own example of expansive and scholarly achievement was the biggest inspiration behind it, and whose friendship I so valued; and to Rosa, born into the midst of Shakespeare's women, and who embodies their most gorgeous charm and not a little of Puck's mischief.

Introduction

In 1895, Kathleen Knox wrote the article 'On the Study of Shakespeare for Girls' in the guise of a letter to her young friend Dorothy. Dorothy had begun to study Shakespeare at school, and was not enjoying it:

I. You have recently been moved up into the 'Senior Cambridge' form, and, therefore, been obliged to take their studies, one of which is the systematic reading of a play of Shakespeare's, with the laborious study and committing to memory of many notes, and you have found the occupation dry, difficult, and uninteresting.
II. You want to know why what was meant for a pleasure in one generation should be a pain and grief to another.
III. You want to know what there is in Shakespeare to make people rave about him as they do.
IV. You have a lurking suspicion that the fault is in yourself, and you want to be told the remedy.
V. In short, why should one 'learn Shakespeare' at all?[1]

Knox's response is practical and briskly admonitory, initially citing Dorothy's taste for the reading of contemporary weekly newspapers and magazines, supplemented by the fiction of 'Conan Doyle, Rider Haggard, Stanley Weyman, or Anthony Hope' (p. 222), as part of her problem. The dangers of such a state of affairs cannot be overstated:

it is as certain now as it was in the days of the Renaissance that, if we habitually saturate our minds in mediocre or commonplace literature, they will sink below even the level of what we read, and that, unless we strenuously seek and study the best and highest in art and literature, we shall remain weak, childish, puerile, ignoble, and, therefore, less fitted to do a noble work in the world. (p. 222)

Arnoldian concepts of culture are invoked as a mainstay against the decline represented and facilitated by an immersion in popular culture, and specifically in the culture of the present day and its alleged advances: 'the best kind of literature has no affinity with bicycles and telephones!' (p. 222).

I

It soon becomes clear, however, that Knox's aim for Dorothy, and indeed for Shakespeare, is rather more specific than her cultural framework might have suggested. The specific moment of 1895 is giving Knox serious cause for concern, representing as it does the proliferation of the 'new woman' movement in literature and politics. Whilst not precisely condemning the new woman, she is nonetheless emphatic that her example and activities will be destructive unless leavened by the lessons of Shakespeare. Precisely what those lessons are is initially unclear:

in this age of feminine eagerness and prominence, when everything in life, literature and science is being attempted by women, and often – as must infallibly be the case at the beginning of every great movement – with woful lack of judgment, it will be well to have such a standard of sanity, moderation, and harmony as is presented to us by Shakespeare's world, where the men, even, fail when they are immoderate, violent or unbalanced in character or aim. I would have every would-be 'new woman' before she begins her crusade against this wicked world, especially if the pen be her weapon, study and lay to heart the lessons contained in 'King Lear', 'Hamlet', 'Macbeth' or 'Julius Caesar'. (p. 223)

This list of plays is intriguing, containing as it does no single discernible pedagogic aim, and an extraordinary range of female characters not usually noted for their didactic functions, moral or otherwise. The lack of a unitary lesson within these plays suggests that Knox intends that the plays should stand synecdochically for all that Shakespeare is deemed able to teach, or, as she puts it, 'all the human wisdom that is to be found in Shakespeare', and which Dorothy can 'imbibe unconsciously to bear fruit in the woman's life [she] will have to lead hereafter' (p. 223). This, then, is Dorothy's part of the inheritance of the English reader who is privileged by birth to come into close connection with Shakespeare, representative of 'the best that has been thought and said in the world', as Knox quotes from Matthew Arnold's *Culture and Anarchy* (1869).[2]

Should all this prove 'too deep' for Dorothy, however, Knox ends by suggesting a further reason for her continuing her study of Shakespeare: his standing 'pre-eminent in the creation of lovely women – lovely in body and soul' (p. 223). By imbibing his lessons on this subject, Knox suggests, Dorothy will not only achieve loveliness herself, but will also be able to moderate the impulses of the late-Victorian period which seem to threaten those qualities most prized in Shakespeare, or at least in Knox's reading of him:

The nineteenth century has given education, enlightenment, and freedom, the twentieth century will, it is to be hoped, temper these somewhat stormy elements into a serene and harmonious whole, but what is it all without what the sixteenth century has said first? If for no other reason, my dear Dorothy, than your own embellishment, study Shakespeare's women, and be assured that without the deep heart of Cordelia, the devotion of Imogen, the patience of Hermione, the generosity of Portia, the gentleness of Desdemona, the joyousness of Rosalind, and the grace of Perdita, all the enlightenment and freedom of the nineteenth century will but serve to make you a byword in your generation. (p. 223)

The strength and terms of the admonition are startling, and signal both all that Knox feels about the advances of the 1890s, and how important Shakespeare might be in the attempt to counter the threats of contemporary culture and specifically of contemporary women. She ends by enjoining Dorothy, 'while yet in [her] "teens", to be a "Shakespeare woman"' (p. 223), studying him exhaustively, learning his lessons, and only then adding what modern civilisation has to offer.

The thrust of her comments is undoubtedly conservative, both culturally and politically, as well as in terms of women's aspirations, in advocating that Dorothy's relationship with the heroines primarily be one of emulation, and in finding in those heroines a form of apparently timeless and morally exemplary femininity. Knox is far from alone in her approach, with John Ruskin simply the best known of the many writers who, as we will see, would hold up Shakespeare's heroines as an example to their countrywomen. In *Sesame and Lilies* (1865), he seeks to consult the greatest men of the past as to their testimony 'respecting what they held to be the true dignity of woman, and her mode of help to man'. He begins with Shakespeare:

¤:56. Note broadly in the outset, Shakespeare has no heroes; – he has only heroines … Whereas there is hardly a play that has not a perfect woman in it, steadfast in grave hope and errorless purpose: Cordelia, Desdemona, Isabella, Hermione, Imogen, Queen Catherine, Perdita, Sylvia, Viola, Rosalind, Helena, and last, and perhaps loveliest, Virgilia, are all faultless; conceived in the highest heroic type of humanity.
¤:57. Then observe, secondly, The catastrophe of every play is caused always by the folly or fault of a man; the redemption, if there be any, is by the wisdom and virtue of a woman, and, failing that, there is none.[3]

He goes on to exemplify this view with considerations of *King Lear*, *Othello*, *Romeo and Juliet*, *Cymbeline*, *Measure for Measure*, *Coriolanus*, *All's Well That Ends Well* and *Much Ado About Nothing* before turning to Portia, the 'unlessoned girl' (*Merchant of Venice*, III.ii.160):

who appears among the helplessness, the blindness, and the vindictive passions of men, as a gentle angel, bringing courage and safety by her presence, and defeating the worst malignities of crime by what women are fancied most to fail in, – precision and accuracy of thought. (¤57)

He proceeds via a brief view of Ophelia, the 'only weak woman' in Shakespeare, and Lady Macbeth, Goneral and Regan – 'frightful exceptions to the ordinary laws of life, fatal in their influence also, in proportion to the power for good which they have abandoned' (¤58) – to conclude:

Such, in broad light, is Shakespeare's testimony to the position and character of women in human life. He represents them as infallibly faithful and wise counsellors, – incorruptibly just and pure examples – strong always to sanctify, even when they cannot save. (¤58)

Thus is Shakespeare enrolled by Ruskin in his attempts to articulate the 'guiding function of the woman' (¤67).

Both Knox and Ruskin, however, belie the evidence of the enormous variety of ways in which Victorian women read, quoted, responded to, argued with and countered Shakespeare in their work, conversations, letters, education and performances. Far from the inert presence Knox and Ruskin would make of him in their attempts to create generations of 'Shakespeare women', the playwright inhabits a space in Victorian women's culture which, as we will see in the body of this book, is characterised by a discursive, interrogative energy. Indeed, even when a woman takes on the mantle of the ideal figure that Knox and Ruskin extract from Shakespeare, as Helen Faucit arguably does in her stage performances, and in her subsequent book on Shakespeare's heroines,[4] the resulting figure is far from the simple icon that the commentators envisage. As far as Faucit is concerned, Shakespeare enables her to support a career, first as an actress and then as an author, which won for her a considerable measure of fame and financial reward, and a degree of influence which went far beyond Knox's and Ruskin's visions.

To say all of this is, of course, to recognise how Victorian women's responses to Shakespeare have helped to shape current critical opinion on Shakespeare's Victorian position and significance. No longer content unthinkingly to accept the accuracy of the Carlylean 'King Shakespeare', recent scholars have done much to uncover the influence of one 'whose voice', according to Adrian Poole, 'is not singular but carnival, teeming, multitudinous'.[5] Far from imbibing his influence unconsciously, as Knox suggested they might do, absorbing him passively as part of the culture of their country, the women dealt with here, from the schoolgirls learning about Shakespeare at Cheltenham Ladies College to the most eminent women writers of the period, are all engaged in debating Shakespeare's cultural capital, in investigating his various legacies for them, and in seeking to realise his influence upon them. Even those who are most intimate with him, those writers whose language is infiltrated to its core by Shakespeare's linguistic and literary legacy, are concerned to penetrate the nature of his hold over them and their century, and to contest that legacy where necessary. George Eliot's work as a novelist is shot through with her reading of Shakespeare, but her relationship with him is in no way complicit, and neither is her sense of how her century has itself remade Shakespeare's legacy.

These women read, argue with, 'talk back'[6] to Shakespeare, both in his works and also in his guise as metonym for a form of institutionalised power, what Christy Desmet engagingly terms the 'Big-time Shakespeare', who 'serves corporate goals, entrenched power structures, and conservative cultural ideologies'.[7] But women's negotiations with Shakespeare occupy other arenas too, most notably the domestic spaces where they grew up and where many of them first encountered Shakespeare, and where adult relationships subsequently evolve through the language and structures provided by Shakespeare. To draw attention to this aspect of women's links with Shakespeare is not to try to insist on autobiographical readings of their work, but rather to assert the importance of the genealogy of their relationship with Shakespeare, and to demonstrate his position as a writer who can mediate, uniquely perhaps, between private and public, personal and professional. To suggest this is not to seek to instantiate a gap between public and private spheres, a notion which anyway seems to hold increasingly less validity as a tool for modelling the Victorians, but rather to stress how readily Shakespeare inhabits both spaces, mediating public words with the intimacies of the romantic and family relationships through which he is often best made known, and which colour his afterlife. His is a language which is spoken on stage, quoted in novels, and appropriated for advertising in this most commercial of ages,[8] but he also slips almost unnoticed into love letters and the textures of everyday life. This book seeks to address the particularities of such private moments, as well as some of the cultural dynamics of women's public engagement with Shakespeare, and in doing so makes clear that their private use of Shakespeare far exceeds the terms of the ideal of the 'Shakespeare woman'.

The very possibility of this ideal rests upon the unexamined assumption of its timelessness in the works of writers and artists such as Ruskin and Knox, the actress Helen Faucit, and artists such as those gathered together by Charles Heath for his successful collections of portraits of Shakespeare's women, which appeared in 1836 and 1848. Each of these commentators upon Shakespeare's women was concerned to emphasise the timelessness of the ideal Shakespeare woman and of her attributes. There is no hint in

Ruskin's work, for instance, of the financial and class status which enables Portia's education and underpins her successful functioning in Venice, and which indeed makes it possible for her to travel independently to Venice in the first place. Such an observation would be completely out of line with an agenda that seeks to elevate even the most modest of women into a Shakespearean pantheon that is simultaneously deemed to denote the best of Victorian womanhood. The rhetoric of timeless femininity works to deny the agency of history and contingency within a profoundly aspirational ethic, and consequently makes synonymous Shakespearean and Victorian feminine ideals.

However, the concept of the timelessly ideal feminine is, of course, deeply problematic as applied to Victorian gender ideology, confident though both Ruskin and Knox are that they are able to articulate that notion through Shakespeare's women. Questions of its precise constitution apart, the very possibility of such an ideal demands further interrogation, for it is deeply oxymoronic: it is both timeless, eternal, and hence other in historical terms; and also ever-present, ever relevant, and available to be incorporated within the terms of contemporary culture. In theoretical terms, Shakespeare's women and their qualities, and indeed the playwright himself, are thus both in the realm of the semiotic, the transcendent, beyond history; and yet are also expected to operate within the symbolic order, inscribed and incorporated as they are within institutional frameworks and apparatuses. This fissure lies at the heart of the variety of ways in which Shakespeare and his women were celebrated throughout the Victorian period, and their assessment and negotiation of it defines Victorian women's relationships with Shakespeare.

Throughout this book, I will argue, we see women variously negotiating their Shakespearean legacy and attempting to plot its meaning for themselves and for their culture along the temporal and ideological axes I've outlined. Women negotiate their political, personal and professional relationships with Shakespeare and his women via this matrix, whereby, broadly speaking, an historicist attentiveness to the cultural situation of the playwright and his women generally signals a recognition of Shakespeare as fundamentally, and often liberatingly, non-Victorian. This is certainly the case in Anna Jameson's work on Shakespeare's heroines, which was published in 1832 as *Characteristics of Women, Moral, Poetical, and Historical,* and which came to be known in later editions as *Shakespeare's Heroines.* This gallery of portraits, as we will see, recognises the crucial, determining impact of historical contingency on characterisation, an aspect of the work which, as Anne E. Russell notes, becomes submerged in its later title.[9] Jameson emphasises that Portia is, like other characters, 'individualised by qualities peculiar to herself; by her high mental powers, her enthusiasm of temperament, her decision of purpose, and her buoyancy of spirit. These are innate; she has other distinguishing qualities more external, and which are the result of the circumstances in which she is placed.'[10] More controversially, she suggests that such a heroine

constituted like Portia, and placed in this age, and in the actual state of society, would find society arm'd against her; and instead of being like Portia, a gracious, happy, beloved, and loving creature, would be a victim, immolated in fire to that multitudinous Moloch termed Opinion. With her the world without would be at war with the world within; in the perpetual strife, either her nature would 'be subdued to the element it worked in', and bending it to a necessity it could neither escape nor approve, lose at last something of its original brightness; or otherwise – a perpetual spirit of resistance, cherished as a safeguard, might perhaps in the end destroy the equipoise; firmness would become pride and self-assurance, and the soft sweet, feminine texture of the mind settle into rigidity. Is there then no sanctuary for such a mind? – Where shall it find a refuge from the world? – Where seek for strength against itself? Where, but in Heaven? (pp. 92–3)

Unlike Ruskin, Jameson finds herself defeated by the imaginative effort to situate such a woman within the nineteenth century, and is indeed confident that she could not survive its prejudices. As we will see, George Eliot and Eleanor Marx share Jameson's sense of the affront that, correctly interpreted, Shakespeare's women offer to the Victorians. They stand in stark contrast to Faucit's and Marie Corelli's enrolling the heroines within an aspirational rhetoric designed to appeal to their contemporaries. There are of course ironies within this model, which mean for instance that Corelli's championing of Shakespeare and his women earned political recognition for her as well as the popular status as a novelist for which she is best known.

This book does not claim to be exhaustive, but proceeds through broadly chronological chapters to deal with a number of women whose lives were shaped by their reading, viewing and acting Shakespeare. It begins with an examination of some of the ways in which Shakespeare was introduced to the Victorian girl through education or childhood reading, and of the implications of that early immersion in Shakespeare, and argues that despite the best efforts of their educators, Victorian girls – and women – found in Shakespeare an energy and vigour which operated beyond the parameters prescribed for Shakespeare's influence on them. In this opening chapter too, I draw on the visual arts as a context which both complements the more prescriptive side of girls' education, and offers scope for women's more liberal and inquiring engagement with their Shakespearean sources.

The next three chapters examine the lives and works of individual women and their relationships with Shakespeare. Helen Faucit and Fanny Kemble were close contemporaries whose lives demonstrated remarkable superficial similarities, and a fundamental difference in the uses to which Shakespeare was put in their careers. In their differences, the pair illuminate the practical distinctions between the semiotic and symbolic Shakespeares outlined above, and provide models against which their contemporaries may be read. In the case of Faucit, it is crucial to recognise the essentially self-conscious impulse of her work, and of her desire to represent one of the Shakespeare women celebrated by Knox and Ruskin, for in such a deliberate cultural identification we can find the roots of an aspiration to be culturally determining. By contrast, Kemble eschews such spheres, remaining instead within a childhood-inspired love of Shakespeare which continually reiterates the terms of her first engagement with him.

Chapters on Elizabeth Barrett Browning and George Eliot examine the presence of Shakespeare and his words in the lives and works of these two authors, in their letters and journals as well as in their printed work, and suggest that Barrett Browning finds in Shakespeare a language of intimacy not otherwise available in the Victorian period. For Eliot, Shakespeare was of the essence of her relationship with G. H. Lewes, as he was of her professional life, threaded through as her novels are with references to him, as Marianne Novy has so amply demonstrated elsewhere.[11] However, I want to suggest that Eliot is also concerned, as a fellow author, with the Victorians' tendency to co-opt Shakespeare for contemporary purposes, and specifically to use his women rather reductively as markers of modern femininity.

In the last two chapters of the book, the narrative moves on to the late Victorian period, as we examine first the unlikely congruence of the socialist radicals Eleanor Marx and Mathilde Blind, and the novelist Marie Corelli at Stratford in the 1890s. For all three women, Shakespeare represented something pre-lapsarian, essentially non-Victorian, and hence fundamentally enabling to them in their very varied ideologies. The chapter also shows how important it is to all three women to contest the commodification of Shakespeare within the tourist industry based in Stratford. In the last chapter, we return to the stage, and to the theatres of London in the 1890s. It was a decade initiated by the debates over Ibsen, but in which Shakespeare enjoyed a continuous presence. We will examine the impact of new theatrical and cultural conditions on the century's most pre-eminent Shakespeare actress, Ellen Terry, and how the new theatre's influence is manifested in actresses' performances in Shakespeare. We will end by considering responses to Sarah Bernhardt's 1899 Hamlet, a performance which insisted upon the strength and vitality, the Protean aspects, of the ongoing relationship between Shakespeare and Victorian women, a relationship which was constantly being recalibrated in order to accommodate the new conditions of the century.

How then should we speak of the processes by which Shakespeare is both known and made known by the Victorian period and its women? A host of tropes and metaphors describe how subsequent generations produce and reproduce Shakespeare: appropriation, engagement, re-visioning, reconstruction, reinventing, mythologising, to name but a few.[12] These terms do not, however, necessarily accommodate the intimacy of the relationships struck up between women and Shakespeare, nor do they emphasise that what is being built here is precisely a relationship. Neither do they necessarily convey the kind of mutuality which seems to me to be at the heart of the relationship between Shakespeare and the Victorian women whom I discuss here, for as surely as they accrue cultural status, an enriched language, and psychological insights from him, so is he indebted to them for their ongoing recognition of him and the considerable extent to which their witness of his acuity and complexity, their appreciation of his wisdom, actively contribute to his status in the nineteenth century. We have need also of a term that articulates the chronological difference and distance between Shakespeare and the Victorians, for a recognition of that distance is, as I have argued above, central to the way in which Victorian women were able to make use of Shakespeare. And finally, it needs to connote the vitality of the relationship, the extent to which Victorian women give Shakespeare's language and characters new life beyond the moments of their initial delivery or inscription.

The term which most comprehensively embraces all these attributes is 'translation', and it is that which I would suggest is the most appropriate metaphor or mechanism through which to speak of the relationship between Shakespeare and Victorian women. Translation was arguably of the essence of the Shakespeare experienced by the Victorians. Their theatres hosted German, Italian and French touring companies, whose repertoire would often include Shakespeare in translation. Tommaso Salvini, Ernesto Rossi, Adelaide Ristori, Eleanora Duse, Sarah Bernhardt, Charles Fechter, and the Duke of Saxe Meiningen's company are simply the best known names of a century's intensive European fertilisation of Britain's Shakespearean theatre.[13] Though a handful of performers attempted English versions of Shakespeare, most notably Ristori, who played Lady Macbeth in English in 1882 after several seasons of playing the role in an Italian version, and the Polish Helena Modjeska whose 1881 Juliet fell foul of critics who were protective of the character as something of a national icon, most actors performed in their own languages, watched by audiences prepared to bring along play scripts to help them through the evening. And as it happens, four of the women on whom I concentrate in the body of this book (Barrett Browning, Eliot, Marx and Blind) are also notable translators, for whom this mode of work was simply another part of the varied literary portfolio typical of the Victorian woman of letters.

However, I would want to argue here that translation is not simply a matter of moving between languages, important though that is to Victorian theatrical and literary culture. Rather it is of the essence of the transactions between Shakespeare and Victorian women, as it is, according to George Steiner, of 'any thorough reading of a text out of the past of one's own language and literature'.[14] Steiner's sensitivity to the historical aspect of translation and interpretation is crucial to the relationships I'm positing here, and indeed, as I will go on to argue, to the Victorian women I write about, but I would want to develop further his sense that 'When using a word we wake into resonance, as it were, its entire previous history', and that 'To read fully is to restore all that one can of the immediacies of value and intent in which speech actually occurs' (p. 24). That emphasis on restoration and rediscovery is crucial, but we need to go beyond it to highlight also the additional value accrued to the source text by the work of the translator, and the way in which the translator enables the 'growth of the original, which will complete itself *in* enlarging itself'.[15] This insight recognises the capacity for texts to renew themselves through what Kurt Mueller-Vollmer and Michael Irmscher describe as 'a complex practice of cultural transfer'[16] and subsequently then to become 'a simultaneous network of reciprocal relationships',[17] between translators and text, between old texts and new contexts, between the imagined persona of the writer of the source text and the translator. Appropriately, given the translator's power to create a new moment of origin for the source, contemporary translation theory gives prominence to the person responsible for the process of translation, a prominence which Barbara Godard capitalises upon in the case of the feminist translator, arguing that she 'flaunts the signs of her manipulation of the text', of her active participation 'in the creation of meaning' (Godard, p. 94). In this creation of course, the credibility of the source text's 'production of a singular truth and meaning [is] suspended' (p. 90), if not wholly abandoned, as emphasis shifts instead to the possibilities opened up by the relationship between translator and text.

Victorian women who write of, quote, act and variously re-present Shakespeare to their contemporaries are all, I would argue, involved in the process of translation, of interpreting Shakespeare for their age. The ways in which they do so are extraordinarily varied, as one would expect, and range from attempts to make Shakespeare into an exemplary Victorian, to responses which value most his ability to shock the Victorian period into a sense of its own insularities and limitations. What the model of translation specifically enables is an emphasis on the person and practice of the translator as being crucial to the proliferation of the source, a recognition of the importance of those who translate and transmit the source. This is of course a useful conceit in a book whose emphasis is on the particularity of named women's relationships with Shakespeare, but to the extent to which those women are also some of those primarily responsible for the proliferation and popularisation of Shakespeare in the Victorian period, it underlines the precise nature of their agency.

The objection might be raised of course that, unlike in translation as traditionally conceived, source and target language are generally the same: Shakespeare's words are still recognisably his. But the source and target contexts are entirely different, and Shakespeare's words are edited, re-shaped, spoken afresh in spaces which transform them. Sarah Bernhardt is the one woman with whom I deal in detail here for whom Shakespeare was linguistically translated. But that fact should not override the extent to which she too was involved in the sort of cultural translation which characterised the work of her English counterparts. As we will see, she was part of a tradition of Hamlet performances to which she added by trying to recapture the youthful vitality of Hamlet as a Renaissance hero, thereby eschewing the Romantic Hamlets of her French and English contemporaries.[18] She sought connection with Shakespeare and his times in her conception of the role, rather than being bound by contemporary theatrical parameters. Shakespeare's works are being translated into shapes appropriate to their new setting, and to the uses conceived for them by his female 'translators'. What distinguishes these processes from other forms of re-working or appropriation is, however, that Shakespeare is always present within the translated form, always immanent in the shape his words take, as Victorian women variously actuate his status, his historical distance, or his presence as interlocutor. This is not the case, for instance, in Ruskin's use of the heroines. In his text they rather act inertly as symbols of an extant, wholly known ideological framework, whose parameters have already been decided by Ruskin. Shakespeare here has simply been conscripted into a Victorian setting, uprooted from his origin, and rendered devoid of agency within the driving exigencies of Ruskin's programme. Far different, I would suggest, are the relationships described below, which are more actively 'relationships' in the fullest sense of that lambent, evolving, insecure word.

Finally, we might ask, given that the act of translation always presupposes an already receptive audience, for whom Shakespeare is being translated. Audiences range from the public of the actresses to the intimate spaces between correspondents who might be close friends or lovers. The nature of this set of relationships needs to be taken into account as another of the layers which make up the translator's act, and as something which contributes to the dynamism of the translation model. This is particularly the case with friendship: it is both secured and articulated in Eliot's early correspondence with Sarah Hennell by her references to *As You Like It*, and her likening of herself and her correspondent to Rosalind and Celia (see Novy, *Engaging with Shakespeare*, p. 47); Barrett Browning cements her friendship with Mary Russell Mitford through rueful reference to *King Lear*, and a shared recognition of the demands of difficult fathers; and Ellen Terry, reflecting on a lifetime of acting Shakespeare, stresses in her lectures on Shakespeare's plays the importance of friendship between female characters, and implicitly the importance of her own friends. Kathleen Knox too writes of friendship in advocating a scheme of study for the recalcitrant Dorothy. Seeking to sugar the pill of hard study, she advises:

some sunshiny spring or summer Saturday, go out into a garden, or into the woods, ask your best school friend to go with you, and take a volume of Shakespeare – the 'Midsummer Night's Dream' for instance ... [Take] the prettiest volume you can find, ... and lay in it a sprig of scented geranium or verbena, to mark the place and be a pleasure to the sense ...

Do not stay to puzzle over words and sentences of Elizabethan English, but read for the story and the charm of the wood, if you can find it. Talk about Helena and Hermia, settle which is the prettiest, speculate as to their school days, and what their lovers were like, think of Bottom in his ass's head, and imagine the beauty of Titania, try to realise Theseus, that most noble Athenian hero and perfect gentleman, and next Shakespeare day in class, I think, some breath of the summer wood and the scent of the geranium will blow on your Clarendon Press edition. (p. 222)

Knox effectively recommends that Dorothy and her friend perform an act of imaginative identification which translates Shakespeare's Athens via their own romantic fantasies. This transaction is complex, relational, fundamentally unpredictable. Filtered through friendship, and across time, it promises outcomes beyond Knox's predictions, and as such reflects the vitality and energy of the relationships discussed in the rest of this volume.

CHAPTER I

Shakespeare and Victorian girls' education

An obvious way to begin a study of Victorian women and Shakespeare is to ask how women came to know about Shakespeare, how they first came across his name and those of his characters, and what those names meant in a century which witnessed the increasing popularity and proliferation of Shakespeare's work and reputation. Just as the century saw an increase in Shakespeare's renown, so it also saw an increase in the availability and extent of women's and girls' education. Were the two phenomena linked, and if so how, and to what effect? To what extent was an educated female audience necessary to the promulgation of Shakespeare's cultural significance in the nineteenth century? And conversely, to what extent did an educated female readership need the guiding example of Shakespeare and his women in order to use its new opportunities and responsibilities wisely? The relationship between the growth of Shakespeare's significance and of women's literacy is deeply embedded in Victorian culture, as we will see, and in the variety of that culture's aspirations for women's education.

Broadly speaking, girls first come to know about Shakespeare either through the home or, particularly later in the century, through formal education. Rarely, if ever, except in the case of girls from theatrical families, do they discover Shakespeare first through the theatre. Some of the volumes through which girls encounter Shakespeare might of course straddle home and school, but the space itself carries determining resonances. Shakespeare was far from being imbibed osmotically as part of the 'gradual unforced acquisition'[1] of desirable social endowments for boys and girls, men and women, as some commentators seem to suppose. Rather, he is always somehow introduced into a girl's life, and the form of that introduction does much to determine his future connection with, and usefulness to, the girl. This chapter will look at how girls read Shakespeare and at the contexts and needs which conditioned their reading, and will set those individual experiences alongside contemporary education theory. The broader connotations of that theory are exemplified through reference to depictions of some of Shakespeare's women in the visual arts, which show traces of the ideological foundations of girls' education and demonstrate the pervasiveness and significance of the educational aspirations being inculcated.

'A NET OF DANGEROUS FASCINATION'

In a carefully orchestrated setting, Shakespeare could be a source of great pleasure and a strengthening element within the family. Eleanor Marx was brought up in a household which rang with Shakespearean cadences and resonances. In his biography of Karl Marx, Isaiah Berlin writes that Marx's

admiration for Shakespeare was limitless, and the whole household was brought up on him: he was read aloud, acted, discussed constantly. Whatever Marx did, he did methodically. Finding on arrival that his English was inadequate, he set himself to improve it by making a list of Shakespeare's turns of phrase: these he then learnt by heart.[2]

Mrs Marx was herself brought up in a Shakespeare-loving household, and wrote a number of articles on Shakespeare and the London stage for the *Frankfurter Zeitung* in the 1870s. According to Mrs Marx, her eldest daughter Jenny's room was 'a sort of Shakespeare museum'.[3] Eleanor's own participation in the family's worship of Shakespeare was precocious. Chushuchi Tsuzuki writes that Eleanor knew whole passages from the plays by the time she was three or four years old. At the age of ten, she admitted in the game of 'Confession' that Shakespeare was her favourite poet.[4] Eleanor herself writes vividly to Karl Kautsky forty years later (in January 1898) of this period in her life, and of Shakespeare's part in it. She writes that his works were 'the bible of our house, seldom out of our hands or mouths', and that her 'favourite scenes were the soliloquy of Richard III ("I can smile and smile and be a villain", which I *know* I loved because I had to have a knife in my hand to say it!) and the scene between Hamlet and his mother!' (Tsuzuki, p. 12). She recollects that at the line 'Mother, you have my father much offended', she used to look 'very pointedly' at her father. Arguably, Eleanor Marx's lifelong admiration of Shakespeare always carried within it, implicitly, its roots in this close family setting.

A similarly strong paternal figure is at the heart of the early Shakespeare memories of the popular novelist Annie S. Swan. In her autobiography, she wrote of the reading culture in the Scottish farmhouse in which she grew up in the 1860s. Books were scarce, she recalls, which was 'possibly the reason why our hunger [for reading], always unappeased, was frequently acute'.[5] The principal item of the bookcase was the eighteen-volume *Penny*

Encyclopaedia, left by an uncle who had been a tutor in 'noble families', 'some bound volumes of sound magazines, such as *Good Words*, *Chambers*, and the *Sunday Magazine*. Then, to crown all, there was Shakespeare!' (p. 27). The exclamation mark seems initially to recognise ironically the banality of the crowning metaphor, the emptiness of the popular novelist's plea for the greater cultural status that might accrue from the association with Shakespeare. Yet, in the following paragraph, a more localised and unaggrandising understanding is conveyed, which locates the exuberance of that exclamation mark back in the enthusiasms of childhood, when Shakespeare was first known, rather than within the cultural anxieties of the literary market place, and the author's concern for her own reputation:

The first Shakespeare Society I ever heard of was in our own home at Mountskip. The members consisted of the whole family, except my mother, who, sitting in the chimney corner with the work from which her hands never rested, composed the audience. We had a parrot, who sometimes interpolated a remark here and there, on occasion singularly appropriate … We used to act the plays, without scenery or equipment, of course. It was actually a reading circle, with the parts in the plays apportioned as seemed most fit. I see my father now as Shylock, standing at the table, declaiming at the top of his voice. I can't remember about Portia or the others. His personality and voice in my memory dominate the scene. (p. 27)

Swan's memory is typical of many mid-Victorian girls' accounts of coming to Shakespeare for the first time: it happens in the midst of a warm and loving family circle; the plays are acted out, or at least read aloud; and the father features most strongly at the heart of the play or reading.

This last detail seems crucial to a productive engagement with Shakespeare in the home, and also colours the early encounters between Shakespeare and Molly Vivian Hughes, whose account of growing up in London in the 1870s and 1880s was published as *A London Family* in 1946. In that book she recalls long walks over Hampstead Heath with her mother, during which she learnt of the stories of Shakespeare's plays, along with the plots of contemporary novels, but it is the Sunday evening family performances of Shakespeare that are most vividly remembered:

My father's Sunday efforts weakened towards evening, and after tea he liked to read aloud to us from books that sounded quite well, but afforded some chance of frivolity. Of course Shakespeare is Shakespeare, but we got boisterous joy out of Falstaff and his men in buckram, out of Hotspur's contempt for Glendower, and Fluellen's brush with Pistol over the leek.[6]

There is within this account a double consciousness of the term 'Shakespeare' which makes a precise resonance difficult to pin down. 'Shakespeare is

Shakespeare' seems to denote the casual recognition of a given status, a certain weightiness which is so readily known that it needs no further acknowledgement. In this instance, however, that status as recognised public good, as one of the 'books that sounded well', effects Shakespeare's subversive infiltration of Sunday evenings and his subsequently providing a 'boisterous joy' to Molly Hughes and her brothers.

Hughes's terms recognise Shakespeare's fundamentally fluid status as a Protean writer whose work could be put to a variety of acceptable as well as more edgy uses. But the unresolved and mild unease of Hughes's account sounds only as the slightest echo of a dissonant strain which permeates more strongly other accounts of the relationship between girls and Shakespeare, and its management, throughout the century. The ever-vigilant Sarah Stickney Ellis writes in *The Young Ladies' Reader* of 1845 of the 'prudent and judicious mother' who might, if she were a good reader, and one 'thoroughly imbibed with a sense of the beautiful and the pure, read passages from Shakespeare to her family … to improve the taste of those around her, and to raise their estimate of what is great and good'.[7] In that instruction is sounded out an anxiety about the extent to which the use of Shakespeare needs to be carefully managed. The mother needs not only to be a good reader, presumably in a technical sense, but also to have a sense of beauty and purity, the better to point out those qualities to her children and perhaps to edit passages which did not contain them. Suitably mediated then, Shakespeare might improve taste and provide the foundation of concepts of greatness and goodness; whether in literary or moral terms is not specified, but probably both are indicated in this typically vague aspiration. However, Ellis goes on, the mother should not allow 'unrestrained and private' reading lest the good of her mediating influence be undone.

Shakespeare is not then unequivocally a source of good, but one needing careful management, as Harriet Martineau implies in her 1877 autobiography. She recalls how, at the onset of her deafness in childhood, Shakespeare provided a welcome, though also a slightly illicit, form of solace:

My beloved hour of the day was when the cloth was drawn, and I stole away from the dessert, and read Shakspere by firelight in winter in the drawing-room. My mother was kind enough to allow this breach of good family manners; and again at a subsequent time when I took to newspaper reading very heartily. I have often thanked her for this forbearance since. I was conscious of my bad manners in keeping the newspaper on my chair all dinner-time, and stealing away with it as soon as grace was said; and of sticking to my Shakspere, happen what might, till the tea was poured out: but I could not forego those indulgences, and I went on to enjoy them uneasily.[8]

The solace afforded prefigures the isolation from family which her deafness would confer, and takes her out of that family unit which had effectually guaranteed Shakespeare's good.

This unease is conveyed even more forcefully in the account of the novelist Charlotte Elizabeth Tonna, who writes:

One evening my brother was taken to the theatre, while I, on account of a cold, had to stay at home. To compensate for this, I was permitted to read the play to him; and that play was *The Merchant of Venice*. I will not dwell upon the effect: I had already become fond of such theatrical spectacles as were considered suitable for children – pantomime and broad farce – and like a child I gazed upon the glitter, and enjoyed the bustle: but now, seated in a corner, all quiet about me, and nothing to interfere with the mental world, I drank a cup of intoxication under which my brain reeled for many a year. The character of Shylock burst upon me, even as Shakespeare had conceived it. I revelled in the terrible excitement that it gave rise to; page after page was stereotyped upon a most retentive memory, without an effort, and during a sleepless night I feasted on the pernicious sweets thus hoarded in my brain.

Pernicious indeed they were, for from that hour my diligence in study, my docility of conduct, every thing that is usually regarded as praiseworthy in a child sprung from a new motive. I wanted to earn a reward, and that was no longer a sweet story from the Bible, but permission to carry into my retreat a volume of Shakespeare. A taste so unusual at my age was hailed with applause; visitors questioned me on the different plays, to ascertain my intimate acquaintance with the characters … Reality became insipid, almost hateful to me … Oh, how many wasted hours, how much of unprofitable labour, what wrong to my fellow-creatures, what robbery of God must I refer to this ensnaring book. My mind became unnerved, my judgment perverted, my estimate of people and things wholly falsified, and my soul wrapped in the vain solace of unsubstantial enjoyments during years of sorrow, when but for this I might have early-sought the consolations of the gospel.[9]

For the lone reader, Shylock becomes a figure of terror, or rather of 'terrible excitement', one of the oxymoronic formulations which litter Tonna's troubled account. Isolated as she is, rather than fully integrated within the family, she feels Shylock's capacity to terrorise, unlike in Swan's household, where children safely enjoy both their father's virtuosity, and Shakespeare's creativity. In Tonna's account, the initial motif of illness is maintained and developed into the abiding metaphor for speaking of Shakespeare as a playwright ultimately harmful to moral and religious well-being.

That sense of danger may have a fear of exposure to specific issues, such as sexuality, at its root, but it is articulated here as a fear of reading and its effects: its engendering an anti-social approach, its disruption of the family unit, and its exempting the girl from the normal round of female duties. How then was Shakespeare rescued from this position of moral obloquy? By mid-century he was, for some, a guarantor of appropriate femininity, and specifically a safeguard against inappropriate reading habits. We need to examine the processes of that transition, whilst bearing in mind that that strand of increasing cultural valency does represent only one part of Shakespeare's configuration at the time.

FORMING A 'SHAKESPEARE FOR GIRLS'

The trajectory travelled by Shakespeare over the nineteenth century is quite extraordinary in terms of his relationship with girl readers, and is, I would argue, echoed in more muted form by his achievement of greater cultural and social pre-eminence over the same period. The reasons, and the means, behind the progression of Shakespeare from source of girlhood trauma to guarantor of sanctioned intellectual activity and moral guidance are multiple, and of course partly dependent upon that parallel narrative of broad cultural esteem, but they also rely heavily on two material factors: developments in formal education for girls, and the increased availability of forms of Shakespeare made appropriate to the young female reader. The best-known example of such a work is Charles and Mary Lamb's prose *Tales from Shakespear* (1807), editions of which proliferated, with seventy-four published before the end of the century. This provided not only an amenable first introduction to Shakespeare for children, but also a persistent way of framing and conducting subsequent readings which enabled readers more readily to place Shakespeare within a set of reading practices condoned by their own century, rather than have to confront a set of ideological matrices from the Renaissance, which were beyond the experience of the nineteenth-century child, and specifically of the girl who was the principal reader of the *Tales*. As Mary Lamb wrote in her preface to the *Tales* (to which she contributed the bulk of the versions, with her brother Charles writing up only *King Lear*, *Macbeth*, *Hamlet*, *Romeo and Juliet* and *Othello*),[10] the volume was written chiefly for 'young ladies'

because boys being generally permitted the use of their fathers' libraries at a much earlier age than girls are, they frequently have the best scenes of Shakespeare by heart, before their sisters are permitted to look into this manly book; and, therefore, instead of recommending these Tales to the perusal of young gentlemen who can read them so much better in the originals, their kind assistance is rather requested in explaining to their sisters such parts as are hardest for them to understand.[11]

Within the *Tales* themselves, few parts would need explanation as the plots are lucidly simplified, and such terrors as Shylock, for instance, represents are greatly diminished. Indeed, in *The Merchant of Venice*, Shylock takes a secondary place in a narrative of fraternal and marital love, and his terrifying language of religious hatred and vengeance is mostly omitted.

Also in 1807, Henrietta Bowdler's *Family Shakespeare* appeared, in which the anonymous editor, the first woman to edit Shakespeare, sought to expunge the indelicacies of his age. The edition in no way seeks to be complete, and happily advertises its partial status as the only safe way in which Shakespeare can be consumed by the young. It is the editor's wish to produce an edition for those guardians who 'wish to make the young reader acquainted with the various beauties of this writer, unmixed with any thing that can raise a blush on the cheek of modesty' (quoted in Thompson and Roberts, p. 47). The number of plays is severely curtailed in this edition, which comprises *The Tempest, A Midsummer Night's Dream, Much Ado About Nothing, As You Like It* and *The Merchant of Venice* (volume 1); *Twelfth Night, The Winter's Tale, King John, Richard II* and *Henry IV, part 1* (volume 2); *Henry IV, part 2, Henry V, Richard II, Henry VIII* and *Julius Caesar* (volume 3); and *Macbeth, Cymbeline, King Lear, Hamlet* and *Othello* (volume 4). A similarly curtailed version of Shakespeare was produced in 1828 by Caroline Maxwell, whose *The Juvenile Edition of Shakespeare: Adapted to the Capacities of Youth* presented parents and guardians concerned for both the education and the morality of their charges with a volume of prose versions of some of the plays which could safely educate without being morally compromising. In her preface, Maxwell states that polite education cannot be complete without a knowledge of Shakespeare, but that his unexpurgated plays would not be appropriate for the young, recognising both the desirability of exposure to Shakespeare, and the necessity for his mediation.

The negotiation of these two factors determines the writing of arguably the most influential mediator, or translator, of Shakespeare for young women, Mary Cowden Clarke. Cowden Clarke's literary career was deeply involved with Shakespeare, whom she edited by herself in 1860 and again with her husband in 1865. She also produced a Shakespeare concordance in 1844–5, which took her sixteen years to prepare, and which confirmed her place as the pre-eminent female Shakespeare scholar of the century. She was herself introduced to Shakespeare by her father's gift of the Lambs' *Tales from Shakespear*, which he went on to discuss with her (Thompson and Roberts, p. 81). But Cowden Clarke is particularly interesting in citing her mother as a crucial influence, writing in a note to the Preface to her

Complete Concordance to Shakspere that it was 'she who forms the glory and happiness of her children, she who first inspired me with a love of all that is good and beautiful, and who therefore may well be said to have originated my devotion to Shakspere'.[12] This comment embeds her understanding and reading of Shakespeare within not just an enabling and domestic literary and cultural set of practices, which went on to be developed further in the marital and literary collaboration she enjoyed with her husband Charles, but more particularly within a maternally derived aesthetic which shapes the moral judgements and aspirations of many of the accounts in Cowden Clarke's popular *The Girlhood of Shakespeare's Heroines* (1850–2). This text was a significant presence in Shakespeare reception throughout the second half of the century, with an abridged version prepared by Mary's sister appearing in 1879, and a new edition of the whole text in 1892 (Thompson and Roberts, p. 82). The fifteen tales which make up the *Girlhood* give a novelistic account of the pre-history of some of Shakespeare's heroines, anticipating both in minute details and in broader emotional impulses the fate that awaits them in the plays. The tales attest both to Cowden Clarke's intimacy with Shakespeare, and to a form of moral pedagogy, enabled perhaps by the adoption of the form of fiction, which she uses to convey to her juvenile readers the moral of her heroines' upbringing, more often than not by morally incompetent parents. In an essay in the popular and respectable *Girls' Own Paper*[13] of 1887, which preceded the magazine's essay-writing competition on 'My Favourite Shakespeare Heroine', Cowden Clarke describes thus the way in which Shakespeare might provide a better form of parenting:

To the young girl, emerging from childhood and taking her first steps into the more active and self-dependent career of woman-life, Shakespeare's vital precepts and models render him essentially a helping friend … She can take her own disposition in hand, as it were, and endeavour to mould and form it into the best perfection of which it is capable, by carefully observing the women drawn by Shakespeare.[14]

She goes on to enumerate the different ways in which girls can learn from Shakespeare, and his specific utility for them:

For moral introspection and self culture Shakespeare is a grand aid, as well as for mutual discipline; and, perhaps, peculiarly so, as regards women: since he, the most manly thinker and most virile writer that ever put pen to paper, had likewise something essentially feminine in his nature, which enabled him to discern with sympathy the innermost core of woman's heart. (p. 562)

These suggestions are embedded within an explicitly conjured lifelong love of and relationship with Shakespeare which reiterates the playwright's affiliations with specifically maternal wisdom:

Happy she who at eight or nine years old has a copy of *Lamb's Tales from Shakespeare* given to her, opening a vista of even then understandable interest and enjoyment! Happy she who at twelve or thirteen has Shakespeare's works themselves read to her by her mother, with loving selection of fittest plays and passages! Happy they who in maturer years have the good taste and good sense to read aright the pages of Shakespeare, and gather thence wholesomest lessons and choicest delights! (p. 564)

It is tempting to insert the *Girlhood* within this trajectory of increasing maturity at the moment of maternal intervention. The girl in early adolescence would seem to be the reader at whom Cowden Clarke was aiming, and who was perhaps most in need of guidance at that critical stage of life, and hence Shakespeare and the figure of the mother combine to try to produce the young woman of good taste and good sense of whom Cowden Clarke writes. Some critics, most notably George C. Gross, have found in Cowden Clarke an explicitly moralistic writer, one concerned to use the plays for her own ends:

After carefully working in a few names, dates and allusions which are given some sanction in the plays, she allows her imagination free rein in developing such incidents as might explain the characters she conceives Shakespeare's women to be. She goes far beyond the requirements of such a goal to invent other characters and incidents which seem to be included for the express purpose of teaching lessons about the sexual snares that lie along the virginal path to honest wedlock.[15]

Cowden Clarke is far from being either as prescriptive or as narrow-minded as Gross suggests, though it is obviously possible to perceive a pedagogical imperative in some of her imaginative reconstructions, an imperative which she clearly felt was present in Shakespeare's writings themselves.[16]

But there persists alongside this sense of variety, and lively moral and intellectual engagement, a strain which seeks to control and harness that reading vitality, whether for domestic, moral or various pedagogic ends. Shakespeare is too potentially explosive – and useful – an author to be left unedited, unmediated, unexplained, as is evidenced in the versions of Shakespeare aimed explicitly at girls which proliferated throughout the century, and which carry their pedagogic and ideological colours in full view. This is well illustrated by Adelaide C. Gordon Sim's *Phoebe's Shakespeare, arranged for children* (1894) and Edith Nesbit's *The Children's Shakespeare* (1897) which both contain versions of *The Taming of the Shrew* which specifically posit responses to the dangerous anti-marriage tendencies of the contemporary new woman. Sim ends her account by discussing Katharine's advice to Bianca in V.ii.137ff on the duties of good wives:

I don't know if Bianca and her friends took Katharina's advice; but if they did not they were very foolish, for if women are gentle, and sweet, and loving, they get all their own way in the world, and men are ready to work and do everything to protect and help them. But if they are rough and ill-tempered, and want what they call their rights, they will always find that men are the stronger, as did Katharina the Shrew.[17]

Nesbit is even more explicit in extrapolating a coercive message from the play: 'So Petruchio won his wager, and had in Katharina always a loving wife and a true, and now he had broken her proud and angry spirit he loved her well, and there was nothing ever but love between these two. And so they lived happily ever afterwards.'[18]

SHAKESPEARE AT SCHOOL

There is an effort throughout the century to embed Shakespeare within the rhetoric and canon of girls' reading, as, for instance, Nesbit demonstrates in lifting the language of the fairy tale. We need to be aware of this canonisation as working alongside both the increasingly central cultural position of Shakespeare in the Victorian period, and the potentially more engaging, and far from idiosyncratic, stories of girls imbibing Shakespeare through radical and forward-thinking parents like Karl Marx and the father of Molly Hughes. And we need further to note how Shakespeare works within the burgeoning educational establishment. For, as well as being read at home, Shakespeare increasingly played a part in the more formal education of Victorian girls, information about which may be gleaned from first-hand accounts of Victorian schoolgirls, 'readers' of material graded to help teach literacy, and the writings of some of the numerous educational reformers and reform groups dedicated to promoting women's education. A range of motivations determining Shakespeare's presence in girls' school rooms emerges in this material: the pedagogic ambitions which sought to allow girls to emulate their male counterparts as far as possible; the notion that Shakespeare was ineluctably a part of a Victorian cultural inheritance; and the less articulable but nonetheless absolutely pervasive sense that Shakespeare could educate for female citizenship in the nineteenth century. We also see Shakespeare range across a number of educational settings, from pioneering schools, through governesses and other forms of home education, to the new colleges of higher education, and the provision of adult education for late-Victorian women through evening classes and correspondence courses in the later part of the century.

During the years 1850–1900, when the debates over women's education were most vociferous, the recurring theme of the domestic, which, as we have seen, provided Shakespeare's initial context for many women readers, is still prevalent, as educationalists strive both to articulate appropriate motives for improving the education of women of all classes, and to design appropriate models and curricula whereby those ends might be attained. As the *Quarterly Review* observes, a domestically derived motivation for education was not a good solely to those women who would become mothers and who would be responsible in turn for the education of their children, but to all women:

In each sphere, if she realises her mission, she has it in her power to be 'vainqueur des vainqueurs de la terre'; the more cultivated her mind and heart, the more complete her spell in whatsoever state of life she finds herself occupying under the allotments of Providence. The childless wife, if highly educated, has the greater power to solace her husband's regret at lack of offspring by being all in all to him herself; the maiden lady, whose youthful training has ministered to her the essentials for becoming, if need be, agreeable company to herself, is the more likely to be welcome in society, because she brings to it the grace of contentment with her lot, and the power and will to contribute to it additional ornament and brightness. It is the lack of sound early education and intelligent preparation for life which makes the dissatisfied old maid, no less than the silly wife, and the weak incompetent mother. ('Female Education', p. 500)

David Vincent writes of the ways in which women's experience of Victorian education is determined by the evolving relationship between the 'domestic and [the] official curriculum in nineteenth-century England'.[19] The domestic curriculum was associated most strongly with imaginative reading and the imbibing of morality, but it was both 'a rich and complex and at the same time a limited and incomplete programme of learning ... [based in] the memories and behaviour of those with whom they lived and worked' (p. 171). The place of literature in general, and of Shakespeare in particular, is interesting in this respect, being a medium which could, and did, mediate between the two fields, being both a force for good domestically and bringing publicly conferred cultural authority into the home, as Ruskin's *Sesame and Lilies* exemplifies. Simultaneously, however, literature is naturally also a realm in which the tensions between the two curricula might be made manifest.

Those tensions are most evident in the range of motives given by educationalists advocating the extension of girls' and women's education. Information about part of this provision can be found in the scrupulous records kept by the National Union for Improving the Education of Women of All Classes, an upper- and middle-class group whose president was the Princess Louise, and whose committee members numbered among them Leslie Stephen and Mrs Baden-Powell, aristocrats, clergy and educationalists.

The National Union is best known for establishing the Girls' Public Day School company in 1872, which provided the impetus and means behind the establishment of many of the country's leading girls' independent schools. However, even more importantly, the work of the institutions affiliated to the national grouping was promulgated through the *Journal of the Women's Education Union*, edited by Shirreff and George C. T. Bentley, thus offering an essential means of advertising the crucial work being done to improve the education of thousands of women in extension schemes throughout the country. Within these schemes – whether the correspondence system 'conducted by members of the University of Cambridge', or the courses of lectures given under the auspices of the Liverpool Ladies' Educational Association – literature figured largely in the offering to women, some of whom might already have been teachers but who seem for the most part simply to have been women working independently to improve their education, with little thought of achieving qualifications.[20] Over three hundred women in Liverpool were attending the course on literature being given by Professor Morley (exceeding the average attendance at lectures of 195), and over sixty wrote essays each week on either Shakespeare, Milton, Spenser or the poets of their own century which were being covered by Morley. Likewise at the Windsor and Eton Association for the Education of Women, literature was by far the most popular subject.[21]

There is, however, as Rosemary O'Day suggests, little sense of the development of a consensus about the motives for women's education at this time[22] and, concomitantly, little evidence of the evolution of more intellectual or professional motivations out of a period in which the domestic predominated. Rather, the two were in a constant, mutually defining relationship. It should be said, of course, that much of what follows applies primarily to middle-class girls and readers, those for whom Emily Shirreff's recommendation that they learn at least two foreign languages through the attendance of appropriate foreign staff, ideally a maid and a governess, and Lucy Soulsby's recognition that in adulthood they might 'lead the social and intellectual energies of their neighbourhood', might be realisable ambitions.[23] For these girls, the figure of God is frequently invoked in justifying their recourse to education, insofar as that might be a means of 'drawing out and strengthening all the faculties which God has implanted in the soul'.[24] More pragmatically, Soulsby, headmistress of Oxford Girls High School from 1887 to 1897, claims that 'in every half-hour of study, in every effort to be thorough and to look things out, you are, so far as in you lies, working for what should be the object of all advancement of learning, "the glory of God and the relief of man's estate"'.[25] That same half-hour will also hone a girl's moral qualities (p. 12). In more radical vein, Maria G. Grey uses the argument from God to argue for women's equal right to education, suggesting that 'if [education] were understood to mean the drawing out and cultivation of all the faculties with which it has pleased God to endow his human creatures ... it would be at once seen that education is as important to women as to men'. It can also, she goes on, perhaps in more placatory mode, strengthen women's 'moral discipline'.[26]

The God-inspired argument is closely tied up with that which suggests that education is good for both an individual's and the nation's morals. Emily Shirreff, an educational reformer, and the sister of Maria G. Grey, writes that 'education, apart from all secondary objects (that is, all objects which have reference to peculiar circumstances or positions), has one and the same purpose for every human being; and this purpose is the systematic and harmonious development of his whole moral and intellectual nature' (Shirreff, *Intellectual Education*, p. 7). Shirreff argues that 'making love of knowledge for its own sake the very spring of their intellectual life' will give girls good habits of 'mental exertion' which will counteract the dangers of leisure and the 'narrowing tendencies of small cares and occupations amidst which women must unavoidably live' (pp. 28, 29). Education may then be a bulwark against the enervation of the domestic, as well as, in Lucy Soulsby's view, offering a means of disciplining the girl for that home life that requires 'more saintliness, more self-discipline, than the easy task of any definite outside work, such as a profession' (Soulsby, *Use of Leisure*, p. 11). Even Dorothea Beale, arguably one of the century's leading and most prolific educational theorists on girls' education, in *On the Education of Girls* is relatively conservative, suggesting that as all has been created for a use, so women's 'mental and moral capacities ... should be cultivated and improved "for the glory of the Creator and the relief of man's estate"'.[27] And she continues that she seeks 'simply to say what seems to be the right means of training girls, so that they may best perform that subordinate part in the world, to which I believe they have been called' (p. 1). In opposition to Shirreff, she explicitly cites education as a means, with 'moral training' and the production of a 'meek and quiet spirit' its unequivocal ends (pp. 13, 14). Given O'Day's suggestion that 'At this time tremendous persistence was required from women to obtain an academic education. Women educationalists were independent, creative rebels, the products to a great extent of self-education' (O'Day, p. 95), Beale's insistence throughout her career on the assimilative product of education is interesting, and only partially answered by O'Day's suggestion that 'the gendered perspective upon what is educationally acceptable ... led women to mimic male

educational forms and lament their own deprivation' (p. 96). These
Victorian educationalists' writings seem rather to be making a virtue of
women's distinctive needs and approaches.

Whatever the particular orientation of the commentators, literature is
one of the subjects deemed appropriate to, even desirable within, girls'
education, which prompts the question of how literature in general, and
Shakespeare in particular, contributes to the moral and intellectual forms of
education variously espoused. In some instances, 'Literature' might operate
as a corrective to the effects of unsupervised reading of sensation fiction, or
'the revelations of domestic life in the newspapers' (Beale, *On the Education
of Girls*, p. 14), another illicit form of reading. Though fears about such
influences were most strongly articulated in the 1860s and 1870s – the high
point of sensation fiction – as early as 1850 Grey and Shirreff were expressing
concerns about the peculiar dangers of popular fiction for women readers:
'For there is in their quiet, inactive existence no scope for the love of
excitement and of strong emotion fostered by such reading, and no corrective for the overworking of the imagination, no wholesome toil to engross
the mind and restore its tone and sobriety' (Grey and Shirreff, II, 226).
Instead, the reader should turn to poetry, to 'Shakespeare or Milton [who]
may be the companions of each solitary hour snatched from wearing cares,
or household occupations' (p. 226). It would seem that the form of poetry
enacts its ability to discipline the excesses of the female imagination. A little
later, the even more prescriptive Dorothea Beale bemoaned 'the injurious
excitement, which is merely passive' and which was caused by the reading of
'light' literature. She goes on:

The reading of good imaginative literature in prose and verse is a necessary and
valuable part of education, but a good selection should be made, and a limited time
allowed … It would, indeed, be well if headaches and nervous exhaustion were
always traced up to the true cause, instead of being hastily attributed to over-work.
Some doctors would then prescribe abstinence from novels, instead of lessons.[28]

Beale wrote from personal experience of a childhood which benefited from
the management of reading that she describes, in the form of the presence
of a highly literate father whose Shakespeare readings were part of the
'early reading practices' which, as Kate Flint argues, 'formed the foundation of later educational policy'.[29] Isabella Tod and Shirreff also both
suggest the importance of knowing the literature of one's own country, as
if, through that means, an appropriate education in citizenship might be
gleaned. Tod writes that 'The literature of our own language has been too
little studied at school', perhaps because the predominant model in many

schools was the classically dominated one of the extant boys' schools, and continues:

It should certainly be so examined as to awaken an appreciative love for it. The field is too vast for more to be attempted than a sketch of its history and development, with its divisions and their characteristics, and the thorough study of some one or two representative authors. This will stimulate the spirit of self-culture in after years; a thing of unspeakable importance to women, whose often uneventful lives render them peculiarly susceptible to the influence of the books they read. (Tod, pp. 22–3)

Again, the vulnerability of women's imaginations needs to be managed and safeguarded, here within an explicitly national, even nationalist, context.

Shirreff proposes a scheme of reading and study for different age groups, envisaging that even a child of twelve might be in love with Shakespeare. Amy Lumby's chapter on English Literature in *Work and Play in Girls' Schools* (1898) similarly promotes a reading regime, and suggests that a girl who had followed it 'would have a fair all-round acquaintance with the best kind of literature by the time she was eighteen'. As we can see, she, like Shirreff, has girls reading Shakespeare from age twelve:

Age

10–12 Macaulay's 'Lays'; 'Marmion'; Kingsley's 'Heroes'; Keary's 'Heroes of Asgard'.
    'Evangeline' and 'Hiawatha'; 'Enoch Arden'; 'Ancient Mariner'; Lamb's 'Tales from Shakspere'; 'Ivanhoe'.
12–14 'Midsummer Night's Dream'; 'Lady of the Lake'; 'Deserted Village'; 'Gulliver's Travels'; 'Kenilworth'.
    'Merchant of Venice'; 'Childe Harold'; 'Morte d'Arthur'; 'Vicar Of Wakefield'; Essays from the 'Spectator'.
14–16 'As You Like It'; 'Henry V'; Gray's 'Elegy'; 'The Princess'; 'Esmond'; some of the 'essays of Elia'.
    'Fairie Queene' book 1; 'Julius Caesar'; Milton's 'Minor Poems'; Macaulay's Essays on 'Clive' and on 'Mme. d'Arblay'; Ruskin's 'Sesame and Lilies'.
16–18 'Macbeth'; 'Paradise Lost' books i and ii; 'The Holy Grail'; 'Areopagitica'; Burke's 'speeches on America'.
    'Hamlet'; 'Essay on Man'; 'Selections from Wordsworth'; Bacon's 'Essays'; 'Rasselas'; Carlyle, 'The Hero as Poet and the Hero as Man of Letters'.[30]

Within the body of her chapter, Lumby establishes the study of Shakespeare as epitomising the benefits of studying literature, namely that such an experience would counter the taint of the reading of 'trivial literature and comic papers' (p. 192), and would instead 'inspire delight and at the same time ... impart wisdom' (p. 192). The principal emphasis which emerges here is upon the plays as examples of moral laws, and more specifically on the characters as exemplars of how 'persons develop and change under the stress of circumstances and according to the absolute decrees of the moral law' (p. 197). The concept of character is something to be taught, primarily in an effort to develop the young readers' sense of their own characters, to rouse 'their consciousness to realise what their own moral experience has been, so that they look into themselves for confirmation of the facts with which the play deals' (p. 196). One of the most transparent ways of trying to teach character was through the use of 'gobbets'. Deemed counter to the cultivation of proper reading habits by some,[31] brief extracts from writers were packaged in texts such as J. S. Laurie's *Graduated Series of Reading Lesson Books*, E. T. Stevens and Reverend C. Hoole's *Grade Lesson Books in Six Standards* and the popular series of Nelson's *Royal Readers*. In the *Royal Readers* Shakespeare dominates the books' collection of 'Choice Quotations – To be written from memory'. Taken from a wide range of plays and poems, the quotations are arranged under a series of headings such as Conscience, Content, The Blessings of a Low Station, Character, Prudence, Submission to Heaven our Duty, The Cares of Greatness, and Self-Respect. They are geared primarily to the importance of knowing one's place. The book's preface suggests that this series has, initially at least, a primarily male audience in mind, as it takes some of its material from civil service examination papers, but the continuity of an essentially character-forming ethos across the sexes in the teaching of Shakespeare is interesting, suggesting as it does that the nineteenth century looks back to the Renaissance for instruction in how best to be Victorian.

One of the most detailed sources of information we have about the teaching of Shakespeare to Victorian girls relates to Cheltenham Ladies' College, founded in 1854, and headed from 1858 until her death in 1906, by Dorothea Beale. Beale's pedagogic approach was one not overtly concerned with exams, but rather with teaching girls good methods, leading them 'to observe and think for [themselves]', in order that they turn into good, responsible members of society.[32] Growing up herself in a literate household, she sought to reproduce some of her early opportunities for the girls at Cheltenham, which involved her in giving an annual lecture to the girls of the first class on one of Shakespeare's plays. According to her biographer, this usually stressed the importance of knowledge of character, especially in the arena of marriage:

Ophelia, to take an instance, was for all the generations of girls who read *Hamlet* at Cheltenham the woman who failed a man because she could not dare to be true. A matter like this was vital to Miss Beale … Desdemona, again, was always marked as the wife who not unnaturally roused the suspicions of a jealous-minded husband, because he knew that in marrying him she deceived her father.[33]

Sadly, little of Beale's teaching material has survived, though an essay of hers, which, like the account above, focuses on extrapolating truths of human character from Shakespeare, was published in the College's magazine in 1881. According to Rachel Roberts, the College archivist, the magazine, which was begun in 1880, was intended primarily for the benefit of old girls wishing to keep in touch with their school and each other as they pursued their interests and careers in all reaches of the Empire. The magazine seems to have become effectively an extension of the College's preparing its girls for life, but its medium was intellectual, rather than social. A paragraph in the *Girls' Own Paper* for 1887 thanks Beale and others for sending in a prospectus of the Guild of Cheltenham Ladies' College, 'the object of which is to give information to its old pupils and others, of essay, reading, and other societies, so as to help in their own self-improvement and in work for others'.[34] In her essay, '*King Lear:* a Study', Beale locates her reading in the light of Coleridge's Shakespeare criticism before going on to treat the play as one 'unrivalled' in Shakespeare's canon 'for its subtle analysis of feeling'.[35] She begins with an examination of the play's opening consideration of the forms that love might take, and situates the drama alongside Milton, Scott and George Eliot in its analysis of the 'petty selfishness' of love which '[lays] waste noble lives' (p. 36). She particularly considers the relative demands on Cordelia of Lear and France, father and husband, and how those demands could best be satisfied. She goes on methodically, character by character, examining unblinkingly each one's capacity for love, giving subtle analyses of the different ways in which Goneril and Regan use love as a weapon, and not shrinking from admitting that even Edgar could love and inspire love. It is a thoughtful piece which nonetheless carries its pedagogic purpose in full view, particularly in its abrupt ending, when it concludes with a reminder of the wisdom that the play has passed down to its readers:

> This play has supplied many saws with which we are familiar – best known of all,

'A dog's obeyed in office.'
And 'Truth's a dog must to kennel.'
'Speak less than thou knowest.'
'Fortune ne'er turns the key to the poor.'
'We'll set thee to school to an ant, to teach thee.'
There's no labouring in the winter.'
'Let go thy hold, when a great wheel runs down a hill, but the great one that goes upward, let him draw thee after.'

'He that hath and a little think wit
Must make content with his fortunes fit.'
'Striving to better, oft we mar, what's well.'

The aim of these saws, largely unfamiliar though they may be to modern readers, is to teach, both their morals and the derivation of this wisdom. The purpose of the whole piece is to instruct, not only specifically about *King Lear*; it is also to show that moral instruction might be derived from any text or situation if the properly trained girl or woman has the ability to seek it out and learn from it. In the previous year, a similar approach was to be found in 'The Ladies in "Coriolanus"' by Alice Greenwood, then approaching the end of her time at the College, before going on to Somerville in 1886, and later co-editing the *Cambridge History of English Literature*. Like Beale, she moves easily between Shakespeare's invocation of Rome and her own time, suggesting that although Volumnia's 'overbearing pride and manly behaviour are repulsive to the modern ideal of feminine character[, y]et there are women who resemble her in her aristocratic pride, her belief in her own powers, and her love for her son, more pride in his fame and courage than affection'.[36] Again the emphasis is on domestic affections, and on women's duty to love with responsibility, with due awareness of the implications of that love for friends, family and country. The tone of both pieces is admonitory and aggrandising, and finds through a scholarly attention to women's conventional domestic roles the key to their influence.

Taken together then, girls' formal education and the editions of Shakespeare prepared specifically for them conjoin to produce a framework for studying Shakespeare which has a number of effects. It can make Shakespeare 'acceptable' and thus enable girls to participate in the cultural citizenship that Shakespeare represents. It could also work to control and appropriately to modulate girls' desire to read, for lurking beneath the surface of much writing about girls and literature in the nineteenth century is the fear that they are what they read. As James Mason writes in the *Girls' Own Paper*, 'A girl becomes a reflection of the graces of her favourite authors, and though she may have no wealthy or aristocratic friends, if she moves at home in the society of Shakespeare and Milton, she can never be commonplace, and will always make herself respected.'[37] Mason thus articulates how far an education in Shakespeare in fact resulted in an education in appropriate femininity, in becoming the 'Shakespeare woman' advocated by Knox.

This is a form of education which is both aspirational and potentially punitive. In his survey article 'What Girls Read', Salmon notes the prevalent tendency of 'the literature which is published exclusively for girls' to be predominantly 'undoubtedly sad' (p. 521). He sees this as deriving from a laudable attempt to 'avoid the absurdities of extremes' in moral issues (p. 521), whereby previous generations of girls had been taught that virtue regularly triumphed over vice. In present times he suggests, in response to this fairy tale aspect of children's stories:

the teaching which comes of girls' books practically amounts to this. If you are wicked you must reform, and when you have reformed you will die! Good young people are not allowed to see many years of life. It is an uncompromisingly severe rendering of the classic axiom 'whom the gods love die young.' (pp. 521–2)

This is a striking reading, and if applied to Shakespeare suggests that, in parallel with his use as an advocate and champion of women, Shakespeare was also being used as a pedagogically and morally punitive force.

This is made particularly clear in the case of Juliet, the pre-eminent juvenile Shakespeare role for women on the nineteenth-century stage. The English actresses Fanny Kemble and Helen Faucit both debuted in the role (see chapter 3), as did the popular American actress Mary Anderson, who made such a hit in Britain in the 1880s. Kemble and Faucit are both keen to stress the young age at which they made their premieres, and indeed go on to suggest that Juliet's youthful unconsciousness determines the parameters of their performances. However, alongside this cultural awareness of youth sits a more dissonant awareness of sexuality, which can only be countered and controlled by its subject's death. This is particularly apparent if we consider briefly the realm of the visual arts, which offers a commentary on the reception of stage Juliets, an insight into the more punitive incorporation of Shakespeare into Victorian culture, and a sense of how broadly embedded within forms of that culture is the need to find ways of guiding appropriate responses to Shakespeare's women.

The production of Victorian images of the play is dominated by two scenes, each of which is regularly reproduced in the numerous illustrated editions of the plays, in texts about them, and in independent paintings. These are Romeo and Juliet's second balcony scene, in III.v, where the lovers take their leave of each other after spending a night together, and the crypt scene. Some depictions of the former scene can be quite chaste, such as that from the Irving edition of 1888, and Sir John Gilbert's image for Howard Staunton's popular edition of *The Works of Shakespeare*, published in three volumes from 1858 to 1860, an image which found a new life in the late 1870s as it was recycled in a new edition of the Lambs' *Tales from Shakespeare*. More typical of depictions of this moment, however, are paintings by Anselm Feuerbach, *Romeo and Juliet* from 1864, and Francesco

1 Ford Madox Brown, *Romeo and Juliet* (1870). Reproduced by kind permission of the
Delaware Art Museum, Samuel and Mary R. Bancroft Memorial, 1935.

Hayez, *The Last Farewell of Romeo and Juliet* (1833), which show the
yearning lovers parting in a lingering embrace whose physical intimacy
sustains a post-coital moment. The most sensually explicit of all is the
image by Ford Madox Brown, from 1870, whose voluptuous Juliet leaves
the viewer in no uncertainty about what has just occurred (illustration 1).
The physicality of these scenes anticipates that of the crypt scene, perhaps
containing within its specific echo of Juliet's clinging to Romeo the root of
their troubles.

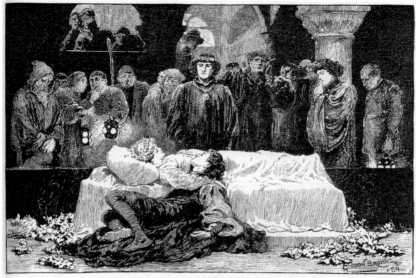

Prince. For never was a story of more woe
Than this of Juliet and her Romeo.

2 Gordon Browne, illustration of *Romeo and Juliet*, V.ii, Irving edition
of Shakespeare (1888).

The central focus of the crypt scene is, of course, the lovers at the centre of
the images, whether arranged for public view and public instruction, as
in Henry Irving's edition of *Romeo and Juliet* (illustration 2), which was
specifically targeted at schools, or in the immediate aftermath of their deaths,
as in Frederic Leighton's striking painting of 1853–5. Painted by Leighton in
Rome when he was in his early twenties, this is an extraordinary image,
and quite at odds with the often marmoreal or waxen images of his later and
more famous works. The sumptuous trademark fluidity and textures of his
fabrics are there, but dominating the composition is the slight, pure, white,
graceful shape of Juliet, resting on her Romeo, and unsullied by the blood
she must have shed in stabbing herself. The voluptuous merging of their
two bodies is one of the most intimate images in Victorian art, as Juliet's
embrace of Romeo sustains the moment of intimacy beyond sex and indeed
beyond death. What makes their intimacy all the more stunning of course,
is its publicity and the extent of the business around them: the figure of
Juliet's grieving mother; Friar Laurence's beseeching heaven for forgiveness
for his role in the tragedy and for the souls of Romeo and Juliet; and the
business of the reconciliation of the Montague and Capulet families over

the bodies of their children. There is, I think, in this image a sense of outraged intimacy not unlike the similarly rather visceral shock experienced on first seeing *Dejeuner sur l'herbe*. That shock is of course quickly mediated in Manet by the eye contact of the female nude, as the image becomes even more confrontational. In Leighton's picture, we seek in vain for a similar recognition of complicity with the viewer, as we remain forever beyond that possibility, beyond the range of those dead eyes. The deathbed scene is the easiest way in which we gain entrance to the Victorian bedroom, and Romeo and Juliet's deaths gain us a similarly rare access to the sight of a mediated form of sexual intimacy. In this scene, the pleasures of the death scene, which Regina Barreca argues is of peculiar relish for the Victorians,[38] is used to enable the punitive connection of sex and death which is so prominent in Victorian culture.

The *Theatre* illustration of Clement Scott's review of the Lyceum's 1882 production of the play, with Ellen Terry as Juliet, nicely points up the dynamic of responses to the play. In it we see the head of Juliet reclining with loose hair and a peaceful smile on her lips. We do not know if Juliet is dead or merely sleeping, but it confirms her availability to be viewed whilst not herself looking out. We are forced, in pairing the illustrations of the crypt and the second balcony scenes, retrospectively to view the causes of death as emanating from the clinging of Juliet which in the crypt signals her death. In that last moment, we see that clinging as only ever having signalled imminent death, and not a passion which had the potential for life. The images thus, in typically Victorian fashion, both capitalise upon and are condemnatory of Juliet's sexuality. They demonstrate the dual ways in which Shakespeare might be read as a writer concerned to bring to the surface, in a bid to control, unruly passions.

'GIRLS' OWN' READING

The final section of this chapter will deal with some of the counter-institutional readings proposed by a variety of girls and women within an educational discourse. The first thing to note is that many of their more radical ways of using Shakespeare were not concerned with sexuality but with professional, intellectual and emotional autonomy. The counter movement arguably begins with Anna Jameson's 1832 study, *Characteristics of Women, Moral, Poetical, and Historical*, which was more aptly renamed *Shakespeare's Heroines* in 1879. Jameson's work is a series of contemplations of twenty-three of Shakespeare's heroines, grouped under the headings of 'Characters of Intellect', of 'Passion and Imagination', of 'the Affections', and 'Historical Characters'. Jameson's introduction, in the form of a spirited dialogue between the purported author, 'Alda', and a slightly sceptical male admirer, 'Medon', which one critic has suggested resembles the exchanges of a Shakespearean hero and heroine,[39] sets out her purpose in writing and her justification for using the characters of Shakespeare rather than figures from history in her work. Rejecting Medon's suggestions that she has written to 'maintain the superiority of your sex over ours' or 'to make [women] better', Alda explains that she has

> endeavoured to illustrate the various modifications of which the female character is susceptible, with their causes and results … It appears to me that the condition of women in society, as at present constituted, is false in itself, and injurious to them, that the education of women, as at present conducted, is founded in mistaken principles, and tends to increase fearfully the sum of misery and error in both sexes; but I do not choose presumptuously to fling these opinions in the face of the world, in the form of essays on morality and treatises on education. I have rather chosen to illustrate certain positions by examples, and leave my readers to deduce the moral themselves, and draw their own inferences. (Jameson, pp. 48, 49–50)

The text is thus situated in the midst of a discussion of female education, in which Shakespeare is invoked as both matter and remedy. In the introduction's discussion of the characters of passion and imagination, Jameson's diatribe against early Victorian education for girls is made more explicit as she critiques the hothousing of girls which produces 'the strange anomalies of artificial society – girls of sixteen who are models of manner, miracles of prudence, marvels of learning, who sneer at sentiment, and laugh at the Juliets and the Imogens' (p. 66), girls who are victims to 'that imperfect education which at once cultivates and enslaves the intellect, and loads the memory while it fetters the judgement' (p. 67). Shakespeare's heroines of passion and imagination appear in this section of the introduction to act implicitly as correctives to this vision and experience of contemporary young womanhood, to counter Alda and Medon's belief that, 'in this selfish and calculating age', in which 'the heartless system of expediency … is the favourite philosophy of the day', young people need little warning against 'an excess of sentiment and imagination' (p. 65).

The argument of the introduction at this point is quite contorted. Through the person of Alda, Jameson baldly asserts that the characters of imagination are meant to serve as 'warnings' (p. 65) for the youth of her time, but it is Medon who tries and fails to explicate that warning: 'Against the dangers of romance? but where are they?' He then leads off a joint diatribe against the spirit of the young people of the age, leaving the reader to ponder exactly how Shakespeare's characters can act as warnings. The women of this section of the book are far from unequivocally admonitory examples; as well as Juliet and Ophelia, they include Perdita, Miranda and Viola, all of whom arguably end their plays happily, though in thrall to the romances which have dominated their stories. It seems unlikely that Jameson is arguing against passion and imagination per se, but, in her ensuing comments on the partial and splintered nature of the current provision of girls' education, she seems implicitly to be arguing that an appropriate form of education that could unite an education of the mind with the proper exercise of judgement would temper women's vulnerability to the dependence on emotion which they now experience, and against which their current educational experiences offer no bulwark. If Juliet and Imogen were not laughed at, something might perhaps be learnt to prevent even the best-educated girls from perpetuating their mistakes. Shakespeare is then being used by Jameson in radical, counter-institutional ways to insist upon the importance of women's being able to think beyond their emotions. Victims of an education which 'cultivates and enslaves the intellect, and loads the memory while it fetters the judgment', they are deemed by Alda to be incapable of reasoning, or generalising, and condemned always to be 'political through their affections, their prejudices, their personal *liaisons*, their hopes, their fears' (p. 67). Or at least so it seems, for Jameson's reasoning and her writing here are curiously elided, evasive and oblique; her claim that some of Shakespeare's most popular heroines might act as warnings to young girls left vulnerable to their emotions is muted almost to the point of silence, as she seems unable finally to articulate the need for women's intellectual independence any more explicitly. In a sense the whole text is her response and argument, her assertion that women are more and better than they are currently believed or allowed to be, and that Shakespeare has long been witness to women's capabilities.

As a number of recent critics have variously pointed out, Jameson intervenes strongly in the practice of contemporary Shakespeare critics in the interests of both women characters and women readers, exemplifying in her own person the benefits that might accrue from a close study of Shakespeare's women.[40] The body of the text speaks to, of and for women in its efforts to complicate conventional expectations of the women of whom she writes, to create an additional dimension to 'that admirable picture gallery of the sex', which, according to the *Monthly Review*, Shakespeare had created.[41] The reference to the visual arts is telling, as just a few years later, in 1836, Charles Heath would publish the first of his two collections of engravings of Shakespeare's heroines, suggesting that there was a popular appetite for the range of Shakespeare's women. It was entitled *The Shakespeare Gallery, containing the Principal Female Characters in the Plays of the Great Poet. Engraved in the most highly-finished manner, from drawings by the first artists, under the direction and superintendence of Mr. Charles Heath*. The publishing venture obviously proved lucrative, for Heath followed it up twelve years later with a book depicting exactly the same heroines, albeit in a markedly different manner.

Heath's address to the 1836 volume suggests that his book will fill an inexplicable void of which he has recently become aware:

The vast number of female portraits which have recently been published in illustration of the productions of our modern authors, naturally excite, in the least reflective mind the very obvious question, Wherefore have the sweet and beautiful characters of our great Poet – of the great Poet – of him with whose exquisite creations our imaginations have been familiarized from our earliest infancy, been neglected by the modern artist? Why has he, whose writings contain the most gorgeous and endless mine of lovely subjects for the pencil, been unheeded and forgotten, while the more material heroines of authors compara-tively circumscribed and secondary, have been presented, and re-presented to us, under every form and aspect almost *usque ad nauseam*?[42]

Heath is of course, on one level, being deeply disingenuous: Shakespeare's plays had long been a popular subject for artists, as is evidenced most famously by the Alderman John Boydell's Shakespeare Gallery, which opened in Pall Mall in 1789 and which ran with considerable success until early in the nineteenth century, as well as by the annual shows of the Royal Academy.[43] On the other hand, there had not yet been a series dedicated to Shakespeare's heroines.

Quite what the volume was to achieve is debatable. Camouflaged behind the easily adopted tones of the Bardolatrist is the voice of the commercial publisher. The work is clearly inspired by the art of the popular Keepsake volume, and participates in what was to become the highly lucrative business of producing images inspired by Shakespeare and his nineteenth-century interpreters, but it might also have been prompted by the popula-rity of Jameson's text, and the subsequent desire to replicate her structure in visual terms, as well as by the recent on-stage successes of Faucit and Kemble. It also works, however, as an attempt to re-assert both the primacy of the visual aesthetic for classifying women, and to bring to the fore a range of women whose relations with men were either relatively unproblematic, or subordinated. Unlike Jameson, Heath includes images of *Twelfth Night*'s Maria and Audrey from *Henry VI*, as well as Virgilia and the heroine of *The Taming of the Shrew*. Despite Heath's mindfully respectful preface, however, his publication scarcely seems intended as a serious interpretative response to the plays. Apart from a rather butch Lady Macbeth and a dishevelled Kate, the women of the plays are barely differentiated from each other, even those heroines who appear in breeches parts being depicted only from the waist up, and with nothing to distinguish them from the other heroines. Cleopatra is modestly attired in nineteenth-century dress, and the only passing reference to context is given in Desdemona's standing before Venice's lagoon. Juliet is perhaps the most radiant of the heroines, but all except Lady Macbeth share in her fundamentally flawless, unchallenging, unhistoricised type of prettiness.

Jameson, by contrast, is nothing if not historicised, pointing up the gaps between the nineteenth century and the Renaissance as part of an interpretative strategy which aims to free women from a form of aspiration based on the notionally timeless, idealised form of femininity which Heath's beauties represent, and which his commodification renders supremely vulnerable to the viewer's control. In this respect, Jameson works to effect a form of imaginative identification with the heroines which educates women not only about Shakespeare, but also about their own historical and historicised position as women of the nineteenth century. In this respect, her approach differs from that of writers such as Bowdler, Maxwell, Stickney Ellis and, later, Helen Faucit, whose reading of the heroines chimed rather with Heath's visual articulation of allegedly timeless ideals. Victorian women radicalise Shakespeare by making him speak explicitly to their own time, to their specific historical conditions, through which process he is himself realised as historically situated, rather than simply the purveyor of timelessness. Thus he is given a language in which to speak to nineteenth-century women.

We can see this counter-institutional radicalism even in the exercise books of Sarah Margaret Roberts, a girl at Cheltenham Ladies' College from 1896 to 1898. She appears to have been aged about fourteen to sixteen at this time, and the plays she covers in her English lessons are *The Merchant of Venice* and then *Hamlet*. There is evidence of some awareness of the political and literary contexts of the plays, some knowledge of Shakespeare's sources, and of metre. The work set for the girls included the compiling of glossaries of difficult terms in *Hamlet*, and the paraphrasing of extracts from the plays, but primarily the work carried out is in the form of short essays, which are concerned most often with the examination of character and motivation in each play. In *The Merchant of Venice*, the girls contemplate the character of Shylock's hatred, and tacitly implicate his social exclusion and Jewishness. His 'chief characteristics' are deemed to be 'Love of Nation & consequent hate of Christians; Avariciousness & Love of Gain; Desire for revenge'. The girls were also concerned with the racial otherness of the princes who came to win the hand of Portia, in writing on the topic 'Show the truth of Portia's words as applied to Morocco & the Prince of Arragon: "When they choose, they have the wisdom by their will to lose."' Roberts notes in response that 'the Eastern monarchs never knew what it was to exercise self-denial for they were always accustomed to have what they desired'. Thus Shylock is linked with the princes in an economy of Eastern excess which Portia and her entourage counter.

It is Portia, herself, however, who is the main focus of interest and enthusiasm on Roberts's part. She is certainly better thought of by the student than is Ophelia who, true to the lead apparently given by Miss Beale, is dismissed as disappointingly weak. In answer to the question 'What is your impression so far of the character of Ophelia?', Roberts writes that

Ophelia though pure and sweet was very weak and timid and although she had a loving nature yet she was too fragile [corrected to 'powerless' by her teacher] to help anybody in such trouble as Hamlet was. We see how weak she was in Act I Scene III where she was so influenced by what Laertes and Polonius told her that she began to distrust her lover and to take her father's part against him for they do not conceive that Hamlet may really be in love with Ophelia and they poison her mind against [him].

In Act II Scene I we have another proof of her weakness for when Hamlet was undecided what steps to take about his father's murder he naturally turned to Ophelia yet he thought in his inmost heart that she would not be strong enough to help him but he made a last attempt to disabuse himself of this impression but it was no good and he quitted her forever. Also she showed her weakness in the scene with Hamlet when she told the lie about her father, who she said was at home but who was behind the arras spying on Hamlet. Ophelia loved Hamlet but it was not a love that would help him in his troubles.

For this, Roberts achieved 6+. It's not a particularly perceptive essay, but does show a healthily pragmatic exasperation with Ophelia which belies the idealisation of the character ironised by Jameson who writes of Ophelia that she is

far too soft, too good, too fair, to be cast among the briers [*sic*] of this working-day world, and fall and bleed upon the thorns of life! What shall be said of her? For eloquence is mute before her! Like a strain of sad sweet music, which comes floating by us on the wings of the night and silence, and which we rather feel than hear like the exhalation of the violet dying even upon the sense it charms – like the snow-flake, dissolved in air before it has caught a stain of earth – like the light surf severed from the billow, which a breath disperses – such is the character of Ophelia; so exquisitely delicate, it seems as if a touch would profane it; so sanctified in our thoughts by the last and worst of human woes, that we scarcely dare to consider it too deeply. (Jameson, pp. 176–9)

The vehicle of Jameson's thought and language is profoundly literary: in references to the 'working-day world' and 'fall[ing] and bleed[ing] upon the thorns of life', she invokes Shakespeare (*As You Like It*, I.iii.12) and Shelley ('Ode to the West Wind'), and serves to stress Ophelia's ephemerality, her lack of situatedness.

By contrast, the character of Portia is assimilated much more readily into Roberts's sense of the contemporary and is much more enthusiastically received. An essay question entitled 'Do you think Portia's father justified in making the will or not?' equates her with the heroines of Victorian fiction, such as Rachel Verinder in Wilkie Collins's *The Moonstone* (1868), who need to be protected from mercenary adventurers such as Godfrey Ablewhite. Roberts writes that 'Portia's father therefore being taken from his child when she was still young did the best thing he could for her protection when he was no longer able personally to protect her'. But Portia is also more personally appealing as well as culturally familiar. When asked 'What special qualities are brought out in Portia's character' by the emergency of Antonio's predicament, Roberts writes enthusiastically that it is 'her love for Bassanio and her decisive intelligence which leads her to do the right thing at the critical moment'. She goes on in an attempt to blend womanliness with her own sense of exhilaration with Portia:

It is most probable that her womanly instincts are excited by the hope of an adventure and when she hears that a friend's life is at stake she forgets herself, and makes Bassanio leave her to go to his friend, while she also hurries to Venice firstly despatching her servant to her cousin Dr Belarius for robes and a letter of introduction to the Duke of Venice.

This slightly breathless prose relishes the adventure upon which Portia launches herself, and the opportunities it offers for cunning, intelligence and bravery. 'Righteous indignation' and 'clever insight' blend in the final outwitting of Shylock, and the essay ends with the judgement that '[t]hroughout this great emergency the keenness of Portia's judgement is only matched by the passion and purity of her love'. Thus for Roberts are the intellectual and domestic impulses of her education jointly figured in Shakespeare's most professionally able, and one of his most impulsive, heroines.

Roberts's preferences are anticipated in the information to be gleaned from the results of the essay competition on 'My Favourite Heroine from Shakespeare', which ran in 1887 in the *Girls' Own Paper*. Girls responded to Shakespeare, predictably perhaps, in a much greater variety of ways than the popular magazine expected. In their essays some of the girls (many of whom were in their thirties, and presumably mothers of younger readers), in an act of rebellion against the incredibly hectoring tone of the magazine's editorial voice, so far contravened the *Paper*'s expectations as to earn pretty severe reprimands from the judges. Admonitions were handed out to girls who didn't respond properly to the question set, and who rather wrote paraphrases of the plays, accounts of the life of Shakespeare, or descriptions of Shakespeare's influence on English literature. However, the greatest disapprobation is reserved for those girls who

wandered from the subject in a curious manner, and made their essays a vehicle for expressing their ideas on some social problem. The vexed question of 'women's rights' was answerable for four of these failures. For instance, one girl who commenced her essay in this way:- 'My favourite heroine from Shakespeare is the "Lady Lawyer, Portia." It is superfluous to describe her action and speeches in the *Merchant of Venice*. Far better will it be for me to transport her to the nineteenth century, and show how deeply she would have been interested in the great subject of women's rights … She is evidently Shakespeare's pet creation, and can we not deduct (sic) from this, that the great writer would give to women a more important position that they hitherto occupied?' Could anything be more inapropos than this, and yet three other girls wrote in a similar strain! Two girls wrote on the other side, and strongly deprecated 'a growing tendency of women to usurp the place of men. No wonder chivalry towards our sex is becoming a thing of the past.' These competitors also chose Portia, from the Merchant of Venice, as their heroine, 'and for the reason that, notwithstanding her vigorous mind, she is always gentle and womanly, and content to be dependent on her husband, although, I think, he must have been her inferior in many respects … My heroine would not support any of those fanciful opinions, advocated by some women of the present day – opinions which, if carried out, would result in our clever girls becoming second-rate men, instead of first-rate women.' How foolish girls are to become so exercised about one idea that they must fain 'drag it in,' when it has nothing to do with the subject they are writing about.[44]

It is interesting that, in an entry of nearly two hundred essays, these few should merit such attention. Interesting too that, as the *Paper* itself notes, Portia should be invoked to precisely such opposing ends.

Portia was the most popular heroine in these essays, and was the subject of more than a third of the essays submitted, a fact which goes some way to calling into question the *Paper*'s implication that 'women's rights' were the obsession of just a few girls, given Portia's widely acknowledged intelligence, and professional competence, and the centrality of her gender-challenging behaviour, implicitly recognised by Sarah Roberts, to the plot of the play. Indeed the *Paper* ingenuously quotes one girl who gives as reason for the grounds of Portia's popularity that 'she is one of those characters who combine so much that is excellent in man, with the gentle charm which is so essential in a woman' (p. 381), thereby highlighting a degree of gender reconfiguration which would reach its apogee in the next decade.

Also noteworthy in these essays is the extent to which the girls themselves repudiated the tragic heroines most often held up for their approval and edification. The *Paper* notes that 'The heroines who successfully overcome their troubles have been just six times more popular than those whose end is tragic' (p. 380). In particular Ophelia and Juliet have been neglected, which does not, however, stop the *Paper* from illustrating their report on the competition with engravings of these two heroines lying dead. The exemplariness of these tragic heroines for Victorian commentators is troubling, and it is highly instructive to see Victorian girls' own active rejection of such figures, and the aesthetically compelling and seductive response of the *Paper* to that act of rebellion.

The testimony of the *Girls' Own Paper* and accounts of girl readers themselves witness the ways in which those readers subverted the punitive aspects of Victorian readings of Shakespeare's plays, choosing instead those heroines who might provide a better adventure, or, alternatively, attempting sympathetically to re-write the tragic heroines' stories. In 1870, the year that her father's painting of a lustful Juliet and her Romeo was first exhibited, Lucy Madox Brown, then a relatively inexperienced artist aged twenty-seven, also showed her image from the play, *Romeo and Juliet in the Tomb* (illustration 3). This is one of a number of Shakespeare-inspired images produced by Lucy, and the one most obviously engaged in a dialogue with her father's work. Its structure and dynamics refuse its participation in the narrative of culpability which other contemporary artists invoked. Our foreknowledge means that we are aware that Juliet is only sleeping, so we are spared participation in a necrophiliac fantasy. Our response instead is filtered through an anticipation of frustration at what Romeo is about to do, at his unseeing eyes which will translate the pallor of a drugged sleep into the dullness of death. But lurking behind the dimensions of this particular image is the alternative story of 'Sleeping Beauty', which acts in this case as an example of the forestalling of the chaos of love until a more appropriate time, of the prince coming more knowingly upon the sleeping girl, whom it is in his power to awaken, and whose sexuality he can channel. There is almost a nostalgia in the configuration of this image which yearns for the fairytale which can counter both the Shakespearean model, and the punitive tale which the Victorians have attempted to extract from their Shakespearean source. In Perrault, the Prince trusts to the power of love and lives happily

3 Lucy Madox Brown, *Romeo and Juliet in the Tomb* (1870). Reproduced by kind permission of the National Trust. Photograph by permission of Cliff Guttridge and Angela Thirlwell.

ever after; the longing for transformation which Romeo and Juliet engender is satisfied; love works its magic in a sanctioned relationship, devoid of the chaos of the Victorians' use of Shakespeare. When read by a young woman a very different tale can emerge.

In her illuminating account of Portia in her study of *The Merchant of Venice* in late-Victorian culture, Linda Rozmovits aptly concludes that one can 'never anticipate every reading and every counter-appropriation of the cultural icons' (p. 58). As we have seen, that possibility of counter-appropriation has been implicit in the reading of Shakespeare's plays throughout the century, as readers negotiate the experience of responding to the promulgation of Shakespeare's timeless relevance. It is the extent to which readers recognise the oxymoronic qualities of this attribute that determines their responses to Shakespeare. As we have seen, for some commentators Shakespeare's women were most important when they were most redolent of a form of femininity which seemed to survive unscathed through the years between Shakespeare's time and their own. This form, 'idealised', 'timeless' as it was described, acted as the guarantor of sustained femininity whenever that category was under attack. For yet other readers, however, including Jameson and Eleanor Marx, Shakespeare's women were relevant and audible precisely because they were not timeless, because they were read as the products of another time and political context which could envisage and articulate a potential for women beyond the vision of the nineteenth century. For these women, the only possibility was to produce readings which ran counter to conservative gender ideologies, and which not only articulated their own freedom from the thrall of a prescriptive and limiting Victorian femininity but also freed Shakespeare from the trammels of institutionalised relevance.

CHAPTER 2

Elizabeth Barrett Browning and Shakespeare: translating the language of intimacy

The poet who famously bemoaned her lack of literary grandmothers was not lacking in gratefully acknowledged male forebears, particularly Shakespeare and Homer, whom she describes as the 'colossal borderers of the two intellectual departments of the world's age ... the antique and modern literatures'.[1] But EBB's[2] relationship with those figures, as she acknowledges in *Aurora Leigh*'s encounters with earlier poets has to be carefully managed, the possibility of her dependent and derivative status scrupulously recognised:

> My own best poets, am I one with you,
> That thus I love you, – or but one through love?
> Does all this smell of thyme about my feet
> Conclude my visit to your holy hill
> In personal presence, or but testify
> The rustling of your vesture through my dreams
> With influent odours?[3]

That such encounters are effected through her father's 'Books, books, books' (I.832) underlines the perils of the female poet's seeking to claim a part within a literary history told mainly through its published male poets. It also reflects the extent to which *Aurora Leigh*'s relationship with Shakespeare was one forged in the space of the family, like those of EBB herself and of some of the girls referred to in the previous chapter. In EBB's case, this was achieved through private tuition, an intimate shared family knowledge of the writer, and through her own reading.

This chapter examines diverse dimensions of the relationship between EBB and Shakespeare, and looks at her essays, poems and correspondence. As she tries to negotiate her own place with the literary world, I consider EBB's interest in the daughters in Shakespeare's plays and the ways in which EBB was herself lauded and constrained by the accolade of being a fit candidate to be Shakespeare's daughter. I will examine the strategic manipulations involved in according the accolade 'Shakespearean' to a woman writer, the ways in which EBB both recognises and resists the lure and the straitjacketing of such a term, and how instead she effects a 'dialectic of trust' in her reading and writing of Shakespeare which extends beyond the realm of the professional, and is indeed grounded in the personal.

The phrase is George Steiner's, and alludes to the mode of translation: it is a 'dialectic of trust, of reciprocal enhancement [which] is, in essence, both moral and linguistic … it is an instrument of relation' (Steiner, p. 396). In these terms, I would argue, we might also most aptly speak of EBB's relationship to Shakespeare. She is not a servile and circumscribed transcriber of his words, but rather one who makes his reputation anew by her attention to, and quotation from, his works. Her quotations from and allusions to Shakespeare, which are most notable and most frequent in her correspondence, are acts that can usefully balance and accommodate the recognition of historical difference and contemporary exigency, and that emphasise transmission and sympathetic interrelation. The model of translation suspends both parts in a delicate relationship of mutual recognition and co-existence, of cooperation and potential creativity. It signals the enriching of the source within a new set of resonances, rather than the wresting of power from the original source, and highlights the intellectual and creative activity which is accrued to the translator. From this intimate relationship, EBB achieves a language of intimacy in which to speak to her closest friends and her lover Robert Browning. It is a language which enables her, through role-playing, through the licence of shared knowledge and almost silent allusion, to find a means of articulation confined neither by Victorian conventions nor by expectations, and which allows for the exposure of private thoughts in a context which subtly protects and cherishes the speaker.

SHAKESPEARE IN BARRETT BROWNING'S POETRY

Shakespeare's presence in EBB's poetry is equivocal, and relatively infrequent. Though she wrote poems celebrating her contemporaries Byron, George Sand and Hugh Stuart Boyd, EBB did not write about Shakespeare, perhaps fearing that she might thus be bracketed with some of the more fulsome contemporary female poets, such as Caroline Norton who wrote in 'The Dream' (1840) of how, 'in his varied beauty dearer still, / Sweet Shakspeare changed the world around at will'.[4] In 'Reminiscences', Bessie Rayner Belloc's narrator claims that 'Shakespeare led me where the summer fays / Dance thro' the midnight hours beneath the moon'. In the same writer's 'Chiavenna on a September Evening', the narrator is reminded of an

> English home,
> And Shakespeare teaching us of what he learnt
> When his great spirit at midnight wandering went
> Far from the moonlit Avon, to discourse
> With the ghost of old Time Past.[5]

Eliza Cook celebrates Shakespeare in a 'Tercentenary Ode: Written for the Working Men's Shakspeare Celebration, April 23rd, 1864', and claims in another poem entitled simply 'Shakspeare' that

> If Man *can* be immortal here,
> if Soul *can* stay when life is done;
> If Dust *can* brave the levelling spear,
> *Thou*, Shakspeare, art that mighty one.[6]

In her celebration of 'Shakespeare's Birthday', Mary Colborne-Veel writes execrably of the boy Shakespeare that 'In learning he was still to seek. / He knew small Latin and less Greek.'[7]

There are, of course, some fine celebrations of Shakespeare by women poets, including series of poems by Fanny Kemble and Mathilde Blind, published respectively in 1883 and 1895. But the quoted examples of celebratory poems signal something of the risk which a writer associating her name too readily with that of Shakespeare might face. The establishment of a self-aggrandising proximity is clear in some, the preposterousness of such proximity in most. In 'Silly Novels by Lady Novelists' (1856), Marian Evans uses their appropriation of Shakespeare as one of the means by which she measures the vulgarity of the authors of the 'mind-and-millinery' school of fiction:

in the half-hour before dinner a young lady informs her next neighbour that the first day she read Shakspeare she 'stole away into the park, and beneath the shadow of the greenwood tree, devoured with rapture the inspired page of the great magician' … Commonplace people would say that a copy of Shakspeare lay on a drawing-room table; but the authoress of *The Enigma*, bent on edifying periphrasis, tells you that there lay on the table, 'that fund of human thought and feeling, which teaches the heart through the little name "Shakspeare".'[8]

In the face of Shakespeare's incorporation within such educationally and socially aspirational writing, it behoved the female writer to be cautious in espousing Shakespeare too openly, or at least in ways which simply acknowledge, rather than interpret, his greatness. Many of the poems quoted above simply seem to ventriloquise an understanding of greatness, effectively commenting unquestioningly on the phenomenon of Shakespeare, rather than engaging with his writing.

By contrast, Christina Rossetti uses tags from Shakespeare to prompt explorations of the psychological states of the speakers, but also to offer counter-readings of the world conjured by Shakespeare and his characters. One such poem is her 'Look on this picture and on this' (1856), inspired by *Hamlet*, III.iv.53, when Hamlet, having just killed Polonius, thrusts upon his mother contrasting images of his father and uncle. Rossetti's poem is written in the male first-person voice of one examining the relative merits of the worthy 'dove' and 'saint' to whom he is promised, and the lovelier 'peacock', the 'queen of devils', who is tempting him from the more virtuous course. The poem moves from a genuine vacillation between the two women, through a bitterly envenomed rejection of the virtuous woman, to the speaker's self-pitying recognition that he has killed the dove by his cruelty, and his plea that she pardon and love him still in death. Rossetti takes her emotional foundation from *Hamlet*, but transforms it through her adoption of a different speaker, and her recognition of the irresistible, though destructive, strength of the erotic, which necessitates sacrifice, and is a deathly force. Here, the speaker addresses the virtuous woman:

> I would that one of us were dead, were gone no more to meet,
> Or she and I were dead together stretched here at your feet,
> That she and I were strained together in one winding sheet.   (ll. 58–60)[9]

Rossetti's speaker comes nearer than Shakespeare to giving a voice to Gertrude's situation, to the ineluctability of her having to choose, and the necessary destructiveness involved in that choice. Her speaker recognises the terms of the choice in ways which are only articulated by Gertrude at the end of the play as she bewails her lack of independent power. Ultimately, however, the poem espouses Hamlet's anger at the degradation and suffering entailed in the choice of the erotic over the virtuous by showing that the speaker refuses to share that anger, indeed rather weakly hopes for forgiveness after death by the 'sister friend and dove' (l. 135; III, 259) whom he has killed. The poem, found 'embarrassing' by William Michael Rossetti,[10] articulates the grounds of Hamlet's anger, whispering of the elements of incestuous love for his mother, whilst recognising the helplessness of Gertrude's situation, and voicing the lure of the erotic for her in ways scarcely possible to her son.

Similarly in 'Books in the Running Brooks' (1852), Rossetti takes Duke Senior's transformative optimism in the Forest of Arden in II.i.16 of *As You Like It*, and ironises it through a female voice, not dissimilar in its distressed and disturbed tones to Ophelia's or Mariana's:

'It is enough, enough,' one said,
　At play among the flowers:
'I spy a rose upon the thorn,
　A rainbow in the showers'
....

'Enough?' she whispered to herself,
　As doubting: 'Is it so?
Enough to wear the roses fair,
　Oh sweetest flowers that blow?
....

'It is enough,' she says; but with
　A listless, weary moan:
'Enough,' if mixing with her friends;
'Enough,' if left alone.   (ll. 1–4, 21–4, 31–4; III, 57–8)

A change in speaker transforms the forest's isolation from a scene of uncorrupted potential and freedom from the court to one of desolation and a kind of synaesthesia which also marks her two poems inspired by Lady Macbeth's guilt: 'Will These Hands Ne'er be Clean?' (1846) and 'Cannot Sweeten' (1866). Rossetti's Shakespeare-inspired poems experiment with the effects of changes in gender and the emotional situation of the speaker, creating new imaginative worlds from the infinite suggestiveness of Shakespeare, but worlds which are centred more exclusively on the intimacy of the psychology of the speaker than on the political dimensions which frame Hamlet, Duke Senior and Lady Macbeth's words. Her poems move centripetally rather than centrifugally, embracing the inwardness of the diseased mind's state.

As such, these Shakespeare-inspired poems are absolutely distinct from EBB's *Aurora Leigh*, the work which, along with *Sonnets from the Portuguese* (1846; published 1850), is that in which Shakespeare's influence is most clearly evident. It rather self-consciously embraces Shakespeare as one of a range of inspirations and models including Homer, Milton, Tennyson, Dickens and Sand. As a letter from EBB to John Kenyon suggests, the outward movement in her poetry is particularly evident in this work. She describes it as 'An autobiography of a poetess – (not me) ... opposing the practical & the ideal lifes, & showing how the practical & real (so called) is but the external evolution of the ideal & spiritual – that it is from inner to outer, ... whether in life, morals, or art'.[11] *Aurora Leigh* is profoundly about that movement, about the social function of art and the artist, about poets' responsibility to 'represent the age' (V.201), to be

　　the only truth-tellers, now left to God, –
The only speakers of essential truth,

> Opposed to relative, comparative,
> And temporal truths.   (I.859–62)

    The poem itself is of its time, a social-problem novel in verse, dealing with poverty, the squalor of inner-city life, unemployment, illegitimacy, women's rights and Socialism. Yet it is also commensurately concerned with the relation of the contemporary poet to her predecessors, with the ways in which a tradition might be built upon. Alice Falk writes of the ways in which 'Barrett Browning's strength as a writer depends on revising, not abandoning her relationships' with poets from the past, and of how she can create ways of being 'grateful to her predecessors without being nostalgic',[12] how she can acknowledge them as great without conceding supremacy, without, as it were, surrendering the possibility of her own greatness. Amongst these predecessors, Shakespeare figures most prominently, being explicitly named, invoked, quoted, and more implicitly being allowed to inhabit the texture of EBB's writing in this poem. He is often invoked by speakers in the poem to negative effect. The three most easily recognisable citations from Shakespeare are put in the mouth of Lady Waldemar, the would-be lover of Romney Leigh and destroyer of Marian Erle. In the midst of her plea to Aurora for her help in dissuading Romney from marrying Marian, Lady Waldemar cites the all-encompassing nature of her love thus:

>   you eat of love,
> And do as vile a thing as if you ate
> Of garlic – which, whatever else you eat,
> Tastes uniformly acrid, till your peach
> Reminds you of your onion. Am I coarse?
> Well, love's coarse, nature's coarse – ah, there's the rub!   (III.450–5)

She invokes part of Hamlet's most famous 'To be or not to be' soliloquy, but in so doing, cheapens and reduces it by diminishing the scope of the words to which she refers to her own very limited plight. Shakespeare had written:

>   To die, to sleep;
> To sleep: perchance to dream: ay, there's the rub;
> For in that sleep of death what dreams may come
> When we have shuffled off this mortal coil,
> Must give us pause.   (*Hamlet*, III.i.64–8)

EBB cleverly and economically has Lady Waldemar damn herself by the suggestion in the reader's mind of all that goes unsaid by herself in comparison with Shakespeare's lines. Shakespeare's 'rub' concerns the admission of all that may be suggested in the dreams of the universe; Lady

Waldemar's, a little local complication of her scheming. A similar effect is produced in her later disingenuous description of herself as one who had, in an echo of Othello, 'done no better than to love, / And that not wisely' (IX.77–8). She goes on to vulgarise and traduce both Romney Leigh and Lady Macbeth in her suggestion that Romney is so abhorrently just that 'He'd wash his hands in blood, to keep them clean' (IX.119). The image is gross, filthy, coarsely insulting, and reveals her as incapable of making the imaginative effort of sympathy which Shakespeare, and indeed Romney Leigh, demanded. Her traducing the privilege of that learning in Shakespeare, which Marian Erle had achieved only piecemeal, from 'half a play of Shakespeare's torn across' (III.975) which a kindly pedlar threw down to her, goes some way to effecting the poem's radical critique of the class system by revealing Lady Waldemar as being less worthy than Marian.

In an extended conceit at the scene of Romney's intended marriage to Marian, the more sympathetic Lord Howe nonetheless also uses Shakespeare to mock the spectacle before him, by suggesting that Romney, like Hamlet, is staging a play 'To show what cruel uncles we have been' (IV.749), and goes on to suppose that, like Hamlet, Romney was mad too: 'What then? – he's mad, our Hamlet! clap his play, / And bind him' (IV.756–7). In fact Romney himself is allowed to echo some of Hamlet's thoughts on mortality to Marian; but whereas Hamlet reflects ironically on the equality to which all are subdued in the grave (V.i.81–120), Romney uses the same moment to argue that the living should enjoy that equality before death:

> Dear Marian, of one clay God made us all,
> And though men push and poke and paddle in't
> (As children play at fashioning dirt-pies)
> And call their fancies by the name of facts,
> Assuming difference, lordship, privilege,
> When all's plain dirt,– they come back to it at last;
> The first grave-digger proves it with a spade,
> And pats all even. Need we wait for this,
> You, Marian, and I, Romney? (V.109–17)

From Hamlet's sardonic reflections, EBB delicately wrests a political commitment and activity, which work by contrast with, and distinct from, their original source. She reads out from Shakespeare, inspired by his situations and words, but using those words for her own ends. Her source is left intact, its own dimensions informing the shape of EBB's use, but approaching no nearer than that. Both texts eventually stand discretely side by side.

The same insight informs Aurora's first description of Marian which begins 'No wise beautiful / Was Marian Erle. She was not white nor brown, / But could look either, like a mist that changed / According to being shone on more or less' (III.808–11). Its equivocation, and its invoking of available terms of conventional beauty in order to dispute them in Marian's case, are strongly reminiscent of Shakespeare's Sonnet 130 ('My mistress' eyes are nothing like the sun').[13] Once heard, the barely audible echo of Shakespeare, most clearly apparent in the tone of matter of fact appraisal employed by Aurora, works to dignify Marian, to accord her the heroic status which at this point in the poem is in doubt. But again, EBB's is no simple appropriation of Shakespeare. The worth afforded his mistress in the sonnet's closing lines, 'My mistress, when she walks, treads on the ground: / And yet, by heaven, I think my love as rare / As any she belied with false compare' (Sonnet 130, 12–14), works proleptically to signal Marian's value, but in no way anticipates that the grounds of her heroism will be other than her beauty. Whilst Shakespeare stops at an exploration of an unconventional beauty, EBB goes on to extend that lack of conventionality to other aspects of Marian's life, making her character rather a novelistic heroine and releasing her from the terms of the sonnet convention.

Shakespeare's Sonnets linger unavoidably in the mind as one reads EBB's own sonnet sequence, *Sonnets from the Portuguese*, written for Robert Browning shortly before their marriage in 1846, and published four years later. And yet, what precisely is the relationship between the two sequences? Dorothy Mermin argues that Shakespeare's Sonnets are one of the many contexts for EBB's poems, which also include the *Iliad* and Milton's sonnets.[14] Other recent critics have paused only briefly over the name of Shakespeare in writing of EBB's *Sonnets*, stressing rather the extent to which, as Angela Leighton points out, she is characteristically concerned with making over a tradition the better to articulate her female, nineteenth-century consciousness.[15] The challenges are only too obvious: she not only has to tackle formal issues, but the assumption at the heart of the sonnet tradition that the woman is traditionally placed as the beloved, and not the speaker. That she is speaking of another poet as the beloved also places her in the tricky position of having to write of one who can speak for himself, rather than as one occupying the traditionally mute subject-position of muse and inspiration. Shakespeare may seem to act primarily as a stimulus to a range of expectations which are not met in EBB's work.

Yet, her sonnets contain some distinct echoes of Shakespeare. For instance, as Dorothy Mermin notes (Mermin, p. 138), we hear sonnet 116

('Let me not to the marriage of true minds admit impediments') in EBB's sonnet 2:

> Men could not part us with their worldly jars,–
> Nor the seas, change us, nor the tempests, bend!
> Our hands would touch, for all the mountain bars;–
> And heaven being rolled between us, at the end,
> We should but vow the faster, for the stars.[16]

We can also hear *Romeo and Juliet* in the image of the beloved looking down at the 'poor, tired, wandering singer' of Sonnet 3, and Ophelia's doomed fate in the images of the poet's fearing to 'sink' in Sonnet 4, and in her retrieval of the flower-imagery associated with Ophelia in Sonnet 44:

> Beloved, thou hast brought me many flowers
> Plucked in the garden all the summer through,
> And winter, and it seemed as if they grew
> In this close room, nor missed the sun and showers.
> So, in the like name of that love of ours,
> Take back these thoughts, which here, unfolded, too,
> And which on warm and cold days I withdrew
> From my heart's ground. (Indeed, those beds and bowers
> Be overgrown with bitter weeds and rue,
> And wait thy weeding; yet here's eglantine,
> Here's ivy!) – take them, as I used to do
> Thy flowers, and keep them where they shall not pine!
> Instruct thine eyes to keep their colours true,
> And tell thy soul, their roots are left in mine.

But the images of powerless despair are transmuted by EBB into the signs of her love. The folkloric significations which are Ophelia's only means of telling her despair become EBB's means of reaching out to Browning, telling her love in ways which invite his participation too as the cultivator of her words.

She makes some of Shakespeare's most plangent symbols into the signs of her love, but transforms them in her speaking them as a woman, finally retrieving the silence of some of Shakespeare's heroines, and transforming the tradition by its immersion in the particularities of her female modernity. For instance, instead of the passion of earlier sonneteers, we read in Sonnet 38 of the intimacy of the individual kisses first given to EBB:

> First time he kissed me, he but only kissed
> The fingers of this hand wherewith I write,
> And ever since it grew more clean and white ...
> The second passed in height

> The first, and sought the forehead, and half missed,
> Half falling on the hair …
> The third, upon my lips, – was folded down
> In perfect, purple state!   (ll. 1–3, 7–9, 12–13)

Delicacy and specificity are the keynotes of the whole sonnet sequence's description of Victorian ardour, rather than the 'difficult and fumbling affair' that Erik Gray finds it.[17] EBB's sonnets also work within a different time frame. Shakespeare is convinced that his sonnets can confer immortality, on both his love, his lover and the poetry itself, whereas for EBB death is not an ending, but the beginning of love's afterlife in a specifically Christian heaven.

Though contemporary critics were relieved at the discipline which the sonnet form might force EBB into (see below), these sonnets are nonetheless, and particularly when compared with Shakespeare's beautifully complete conceits, straining and full of effort in their attempts to convey an experience of love which the sonnet had not yet encompassed, the love of a Victorian woman poet for a contemporary writer. EBB seems to find the consolations of the form as exploited by Shakespeare unsatisfactory for her own ends and rather transmutes them into efforts to realise the visceral effect of her passion, its roots in a familial love, and its straining to find a form of accommodation for her and for Browning's poetry.

In the case of both *Sonnets from the Portuguese* and *Aurora Leigh*, EBB takes a moment or an inspiration from Shakespeare, and transposes it into a new setting, translates it for another world, rather than appropriating it, or taking it over. Her words work best when read alongside, in full knowledge of, the original which inspires them. EBB is not aiming at what her character describes as 'lifeless imitations' (*Aurora Leigh*, I.974) of older poets, but rather at a poetics which is 'the witness of what Is / Behind this show' (VII.834–5). She goes on explicitly to repudiate imitation:

> If this world's show were all,
> Then imitation would be all in Art;
> There, Jove's hand grips us! – For we stand here, we,
> If genuine artists, witnessing for God's
> Complete, consummate, undivided work:
> – That not a natural flower can grow on earth,
> Without a flower upon the spiritual side,
> Substantial, archetypal, all a-glow
> With blossoming causes.   (VII.835–43)

I would suggest that EBB's use of Shakespeare involves a similar form of transference. Just as she Platonically translates God's work from the spiritual to the material world, writing of it so that it may be seen as being immanent in that material sphere, whilst the original persists unperturbed and discrete, so do Shakespeare's words inhabit EBB's poem. Shakespeare's works are both of the past and of the present within EBB's poetry. They live within, and give life to, her words, where her source is discernibly Shakespearean. In turn her words witness to Shakespeare's creative richness, but from another sphere, another century, which does not seek to supersede Shakespeare's own place and authority, but simply to make them available, in some sense to translate them, for EBB's contemporaries. This 'double articulation', to borrow Richard Halpern's phrase,[18] draws attention both to EBB's own innovations, and to the persistence of Shakespeare alongside her own voice.

The achievement of this relationship within *Aurora Leigh* takes place in parallel with a similar resolution with the figure of the eponymous poet's father who has haunted the poem since his death. Aurora's return to Italy is a necessary step in achieving her eventual acceptance of her orphaned state, and her decision no longer to seek for meaning primarily through the past. Indeed, the invoking of Shakespeare in some measure disputes the relative positions and connotations of past and present, specifically those which might site authority, judgement and superiority within the past. In book one of the poem, Shakespeare had been associated with the father figure. In Aurora's description of her father teaching her, we hear echoes of Prospero's instruction of Miranda:

> My father taught me what he had learnt the best
> Before he died and left me, – grief and love
> ....
> out of books,
> He taught me all the ignorance of men,
> And how God laughs in heaven when any man
> Says 'Here I'm learned.' (I.185–6, 189–92)

And later Aurora comes to believe 'I thought my father's land was worthy too / Of being my Shakespeare's' (I.1091–2), despite her initial incredulity on arriving from Italy that 'Shakespeare and his mates' were able to 'Absorb the light here' (I.266–7). Shakespeare initially carries the weight and resonance of that paternal authority, but as the poem progresses he comes to be more firmly associated with the person of Aurora, and with emotional, rather than pedagogic, possibilities: 'God has made me, – I've a heart / That's capable of worship, love, and loss; / We say the same of Shakespeare's' (VIII.734–46). The unmediated directness of the analogy with Shakespeare here is one more sign of Aurora's growing maturity and her emotional as well as literary deviation from the coercive influence of her father's memory.

BARRETT BROWNING, SHAKESPEARE
AND THE CRITICS

A crucial part of the narrative of *Aurora Leigh* is, then, the achievement of an enabling relationship with those literary predecessors who inform EBB's poetics. The poem is, in a sense, its own witness to the success of this project. However, the question of literary debts and precedents, and specifically her relationship with Shakespeare, was not so easily settled for EBB's critics, as the concentration on those questions in a range of obituaries and memorial articles on the poet demonstrates. They are concerned to reveal where responsibility for her achievements lies, be it with her husband, or the other writers whom she read. A year after her death, the *North American Review* was asserting that *Aurora Leigh* 'was written, not by Elizabeth Barrett, but by Browning's wife', and made of the epic tale simply a 'story of love, as it lay concealed in the heart of a woman, to rise in overmastering strength at the fulness of time'.[19] In the same year, the *Dublin University Magazine* asserts that 'she would never have reached so high a point if she had not married a great poet'.[20] The greater Barrett Browning's achievement, the greater her reliance on Browning; the broader her reading, the greater her indebtedness to a range of predecessors. These and similar articles are generous and admonitory in equal measure, seeking to evaluate EBB's standing for posterity, to analyse the terms of her acknowledged greatness, but also to use her achievements as a measure of how far women cannot go in rivalling the greatest male writers, and to suggest that even the success that Barrett Browning achieves may be misconceived, when 'The function of woman is – not to write, not to act, not to be famous – but to love', and when 'Perhaps, after all, the best poem she can offer us is a crowing child, with beautiful bright hair, pillowed upon her loving breast' (*Dublin University Magazine*, p. 162). How far that final image may be inspired by the moving pictures of Marian Erle's son in *Aurora Leigh* is not dwelt on, nor perhaps can it be, by this particular critic.

The evaluation of EBB's 'genius' inevitably involves extended comparisons with Shakespeare, both in general terms, but also more specifically on the grounds of their respective sonnet sequences. EBB's *Sonnets* were regarded by some critics, including William T. Arnold and Edmund Gosse, as her best works. For Mary Russell Mitford, and the *North American Review* respectively, the *Sonnets* were 'glowing with passion, melting with tenderness. True love was never more fitly sung' than in them, making them 'the finest love poems in our language'.[21] As Tricia Lootens notes in her enlightening study of the critical reception of the *Sonnets from the Portuguese*, however, they are far from typical poems about love, revealing psychological peculiarities in EBB's position which would have been shared by few readers.[22] Indeed, for G. B. Smith, in the *Cornhill Magazine*, the *Sonnets* 'are more explanatory [of] her own very distinct individuality ... than any other of her writings'.[23] Yet for most critics the *Sonnets* offered an opportunity for comparing EBB with other poets which the rest of her determinedly more experimental oeuvre precludes. The sonnet form offers a measure. The rigorousness of the form was felt by Arnold, Gosse and G. B. Smith to discipline both EBB's more accustomed exuberance of imagery and the 'loose, wild form' of her lyrics which were 'fit to receive her chains of adverbial caprices and her tempestuous assonances'.[24] More specifically, Gosse adds that 'her love of Shakespeare and Wordsworth drove her to emulation' (p. 6), while for W. H. Smith, she equalled or exceeded those figures:

we will venture to say – if we may reduce our general praise to a numerical specification – that from no English writer, with the exception perhaps of Wordsworth, shall you select half-a-dozen sonnets so excellent as you might with ease extract from these volumes of Elizabeth Barrett Browning. In saying this we do not forget that Shakespeare wrote sonnets.[25]

Shakespeare's Sonnets could be, as Smith goes on to suggest, problematic for the Victorians, in terms of attribution and subject matter. As Gosse writes in the more self-conscious 1890s, EBB's are 'more wholesome' in treating of 'a mood that [by comparison with Shakespeare's] is not rare and almost sickly, not foreign to the common experience of mankind, but eminently normal, direct, and obvious' (Gosse, p. 10). As Lootens notes, 'If Gosse terms Barrett Browning's "wholesome" Sonnets more "intelligible", it is clearly because ... they express a love that dares to speak its name' (Lootens, p. 143).

Long before the 1890s, however, Shakespeare's was a name which could readily be invoked both to praise and to delimit a woman writer's achievements. The *North British Review* critic begins his assessment of EBB's works by asserting that woman 'has not yet produced her Shakspeare, her Newton, her Bacon, her Handel; and most likely never will' (p. 514). Of EBB in particular, he writes that she is 'so much in earnest, that she cannot hide her efforts to grasp reality', whereas with Shakespeare, 'All is', in that most fundamentally loaded term, 'natural, and like the working of natural forces without personal effort. He is so perfectly *en rapport* with his work, that his mastery over it seems as natural as play' (pp. 530–1). For the *North American Review*, she 'was not, indeed, another Shakespeare, but she came nearest to being Shakespeare's counterpart' (p. 353). The precise nature of that relationship remains to be specified here, but was given a name in the following

decade by the American critic E. C. Stedman. His account of EBB works on
two axes which he somehow needs to bring together into fruitful relationship: she is both the best-educated of women poets who spent 'her novitiate
in the academic groves and at the fountain-heads of poetry and thought' and
the woman in whose life 'the chief event ... was her marriage'.[26] Within his
description of her as 'Shakespeare's daughter', that resolution, between
academic and literary learning and domestic inspiration, is achieved in a
neat synthesis of appropriate femininity. He writes:

> The English love to call her Shakespeare's Daughter, and in truth she bears to their
> great poet the relation of Miranda to Prospero. Her delicate genius was purely
> feminine and subjective, attributes that are made to go together. (p. 147)

This suggestion was taken up in the *Cornhill* by G. B. Smith, who, after
having rejected a number of comparisons between EBB and her contemporaries as unsatisfactory, expanded on the conceit thus:

> That was a happy observation passed upon her by one critic, who described her as
> Shakspeare's daughter. The same large-heartedness which pertained to the great
> dramatist is shown by the later-poet. The benevolent eye looks out on men and
> nature with the same imperishable love. If the world has at any time possessed its
> ideal poets, she is worthy to be counted one of them. (p. 475)

But a sting lies hidden in this particular compliment: 'we can feel that her
genius stands in the same relation to that of the transcendent poet of the
world as does a daughter to her parent. The lesser is the true miniature
representation of the greater' (p. 480).

SHAKESPEARE'S VICTORIAN DAUGHTERS

In some respects of course, these critics are simply taking up the suggestion
made by EBB herself in *Aurora Leigh* about the conjunction between
Shakespeare and the poet's father, but they ignore the concomitant development in the poem which shows the poet explicitly, and necessarily, out-
growing the familial dimension – specifically the obedience of a daughter – to
evolve her own aesthetic. The apparent accolade traps her within a dynamic of
emulation, imitation, and the preordained limits which her own poetry was
constantly seeking to override. As would have been readily appreciated in
the 1870s, by which time the story of EBB's upbringing was well known, the
family metaphor also operates with a particularly coercive resonance in the
case of EBB.

Stedman's explicit reference to the relationship of Prospero and Miranda
is worth investigating further. The peculiarities of that relationship are

extreme, though echoed in other of Shakespeare's plays, where the daughter's function is often crucial,[27] but revealing about what was currently believed about EBB. For twelve of Miranda's fifteen years, she had lived alone with her father, save for the presence of Caliban and Ariel. She depended on him for all language, learning, and practically all her company. Through his authority as a father, and his skill as a magician, he controls her environment, her knowledge, and her interactions with others. That both fathers are also implicated in slavery, in the mistreatment of Caliban and in the ownership of slaves on the Barretts' Jamaican plantations, solidifies the authoritarian nature of their relationship with their daughters. Prospero goes on to attempt to orchestrate Miranda's relationship with Ferdinand, but finds the limit of his powers when he is forced to realise the autonomy generated in her by Miranda's love for another man:

FERDINAND: What is your name?
MIRANDA: Miranda. – O my father!
I have broke your hest to say so.

(*Tempest*, III.i.36–7)

Amongst the gallery of disobedient daughters created by Shakespeare, this is a relatively minor offence, and, as Charles and Mary Lamb note, in some ways simply furthers Prospero's plans: 'Prospero only smiled at this first instance of his daughter's disobedience, for having by his magic art caused his daughter to fall in love so suddenly, he was not angry that she showed her love by forgetting to obey his commands' (Lamb and Lamb, pp. 9–10). To insert EBB into this narrative is to suggest that, like Miranda, she was effectively at the behest of her father until Robert Browning came along, albeit without Mr Barrett's connivance, to tempt her to speak out of turn. So EBB gains not only a determining father figure in Stedman's allusion, but also a husband to usurp the father's place in the normal course of things.

Anna Jameson's account of Miranda highlights the ways in which she shares in EBB's early isolation from society and the wiles it expects of women, and the extent to which the poet had been known to be emotionally declarative. Jameson writes of Miranda that 'she has never caught from society one imitated or artificial grace', and celebrates her apparently naive giving of herself to Ferdinand by suggesting that Miranda was 'Only conscious of her own weakness as a woman, and ignorant of those usages of society which teach us to dissemble the real passion, and assume (and sometimes abuse) an unreal and transient power' (Jameson, pp. 190, 192). The same moment from *The Tempest* is the basis of an important scene in William Black's novel, *Judith Shakespeare*, which first appeared in *Harper's*

New Monthly Magazine, and was published in volume form in England in
1884. The plot of what is a pretty tedious romance is based around the figure
of the beautiful and slightly rebellious younger daughter of the playwright,
who has, during the course of the play, to be tamed by true love, and to
recognise her failings as a daughter. During the course of the novel, Judith is
persuaded by a handsome, but scurrilous, young stranger, working for a
rival of her father, to steal the manuscript of his latest play, which happens
to be *The Tempest*, in order that the young man, Leofric Hope, might read
and admire it for himself. The father–daughter relationship in the novel
echoes that of Prospero and Miranda, not least because Shakespeare has
determined that Judith be illiterate, and thus controls the information to
which she has access. Her illiteracy also facilitates some set piece moments
in the novel where Judith's friend Prudence is persuaded to read her father's
latest works aloud to her. During one meeting, she reads the scene of
Miranda's declaration:

> 'Nay, is she not fair and modest?' Judith exclaimed, when Miranda had timidly
> avowed her admiration for this new friend; and, as the reading proceeded, she
> began to think of how Master Leofric Hope would regard such a maiden. Would he
> not judge her to be right gentle, womanly withal, and frank in her confiding? And
> he – supposing that he were the young Prince – what would he think of such an
> one? Was it too submissive that she should offer to carry the logs? Ought she to so
> openly confess that she would fain have him to be her companion? And then at last,
> when the two lovers had declared their love, Judith clapped her hands and laughed –
> in delight and triumph.[28]

As we have seen, Miranda's apparent freedoms are actually manifestations of
duty, whereas Judith has to be tamed back into appropriate obedience. In
true Victorian fashion, her indiscretion in stealing the manuscript, as well
as in borrowing it for her own enjoyment, is punished by illness, which she
comes through a better and more virtuous girl, and one finally resigned to
marrying the local man, Tom Quiney, who has long courted her. Educational
ambition is equated with sexual indiscretion, and both are subsequently
contained and corrected within Judith's return to being the dutiful daughter
she had been at the opening of the novel, where we first saw her longing for
her adored father's return from London.

   In EBB's case, the iconic status of Miranda works to naturalise and
smooth out an intractability by which earlier critics had been troubled,
and to rewrite EBB's canon as a de-politicised one of love poems and *Aurora
Leigh*, which, though self-described as 'unscrupulously epic' (V.213), is
mollified into a more tractable and tamer autobiographical shape. The
ultimate irony is that, via this analogy with Miranda, EBB could ultimately

be rewritten, recuperated, as a Judith Shakespeare, the dutiful daughter which she had notoriously not been.

The image of Shakespeare's daughters could also work in reverse, however, making of the playwright's creations more dutiful daughters within a Victorian economy of the family. Such a result might plausibly seem to accrue from Mary Cowden Clarke's accounts of the girlhood of a number of Shakespeare's heroines. Her narrativised versions of the pre-life of fifteen of Shakespeare's women are particularly interesting in the ways in which they seek to anticipate the details of the lives to be revealed in Shakespeare's plays, to such an extent that they remove any possibility of agency from the women themselves. A small example of this is the way in which the double death of Romeo and Juliet is anticipated in Lady Capulet's witnessing a distraught young man's committing suicide on the bier of his secretly wed wife. The young heroines of Cowden Clarke's text become blameless because they are so clearly the sums of their upbringing, and particularly of the shortcomings of their parents, one of whom is usually dotingly, neglectfully benevolent, whilst the other is equally dangerously coercive and strong-willed. The failure of parenting which results produces women who cannot help but live out the dynamics of the place assigned to them. Lady Macbeth's determined bloodthirstiness and ambition is the result of her mother's thwarted ambition and her father's easygoing neglect of the opportunity to correct his daughter's political scheming by attaching her more firmly to him by ties of emotion and duty. Desdemona's deceit in secretly marrying Othello is engendered in her by her father's own clandestine marrying of her mother, and by that mother's various acts of subterfuge in seeking not to antagonise her choleric husband: 'the courage of transparent truth ... that would have proved her best protection against the diabolical malignity by which she was one day to be assailed, and borne her scathless through the treachery which wrought her fate', was not taught her.[29] That a daughter can be blamelessly bad and/or disobedient seems to be the cumulative message of Cowden Clarke's work. Those daughters who dared to disobey were only fulfilling their fate, and were being in fact perversely dutiful.

Trained in how to read Shakespeare at school, encouraged by Mary Cowden Clarke to speculate on her stories, which would 'afford scope for pleasant fancy, and be productive of entertainment' (I, xi), and encouraged to emulate aspects of Shakespeare's heroines, Victorian women might, it is possible to argue, all be seen as, in some sense, Shakespeare's daughters. Such, as we will see in the next chapter, was clearly the determination of Helen Faucit, who chooses to be parented by Shakespeare in her narrative of

her early years. And such would certainly seem to be the implication
of Ruskin's *Sesame and Lilies*, in which he famously invokes the 'perfect
woman' of almost every Shakespeare play. His is, however, as we have seen
already, a highly selective list, and a highly selective vision, and one which
excuses the sins of daughters such as Desdemona and Imogen in the light of
their virtues as wives. It is also a list which notably excludes Ophelia, on
whom, and on whose failing Hamlet 'at the critical moment', 'the bitter
catastrophe of *Hamlet* is said to rest (¤58). Ophelia arguably allows herself to
be guided by her father, rather than her love and her lover, and pays the
price, not only in the action of the play, but in Ruskin's later denunciation.
She also emerges more distressingly in Ruskin's so-called 'Brantwood
Diaries', which chart the troubles of his mental illness in later life.
Quoting from the diaries in *After Shakespeare*, John Gross suggests that
the echoes of *Hamlet* and images of Ophelia which precede his breakdown
in 1878 signal his dwelling on thoughts of Rose La Touche, the much
younger woman loved by Ruskin, whose father would not permit their
marrying.[30] Like Ophelia, Rose obeyed her father's injunctions. In an
elision of himself and Hamlet, Ruskin's invocations of Ophelia also
suggest his own sense of damage as a result of Rose's misplaced daughterly
obedience. But it is also possible that Ophelia acts as an analogue for
Ruskin himself, as a virginal figure distressed by longing and a sexual
knowledge which outruns the capacity to deal with it.

Within Shakespeare's orbit, these examples of Victorian readings seem to
suggest, a daughter's disobedience is not necessarily a bad thing, insofar as it
is seen to recognise a higher form of authority. However, such dangerous
actions must ultimately recognise some form of authority, and the most
readily invoked is that of Shakespeare. The suggestion that EBB is most
appropriately fathered by Shakespeare is both an admission of her disobedience, emotional, familial, and generic, and of the need to place that
disobedience within a carefully policed regime which can absorb acts of
disobedience within an ultimately sanctioned framework. Such a framework was permitted to Shakespeare who is thus made to act as both emotional and literary guarantor and jailer to EBB's love and creativity.

SHAKESPEARE: A MAN OF LETTERS

Within EBB's own writing, however, as we have seen, an entirely different
kind of dialogue is being established between the two writers. As her letters
show even more acutely than her poems, that dialogue emanates from
within the familial setting, whilst eluding its conventional power structures.

Elizabeth Barrett's first recorded encounter with Shakespeare appears in a letter to her aunt Arabella Graham-Clarke, when, at the age of eleven, she makes a joke about being an idle correspondent, then writes, 'tho' perhaps "rude am I in speech", yet I can justify myself by repeating I do not love you less', quoting *Othello*, I.iii.81.[31] The identification with the spell-binding Othello, whose very rudeness, which he is defending before the Duke of Venice, is the source of the witchcraft which has seduced Desdemona away from her father, is an intriguing and proleptic instance of self-aggrandisement, in which EBB is both captivated by, and (through her act of quotation) the source of, a language of fascination. *Othello* continues to haunt her letters. It is one of the plays from which she quotes most frequently (the one most frequently referred to being *Hamlet*), in part perhaps because it enables her imaginative identification with a world absolutely beyond her own, the world of the 'pomp and circumstance of glorious war' (*Othello*, III.iii.354), and with the battles she enthusiastically discussed in letters with Uvedale Price as a young woman (*Correspondence*, I, 280; 30 December 1826, and II, 4; 11 January 1827). It is, however, important to note that in the letters which quote Othello's despairing speech, in which he turns away from his vocation, and claims he would have been happy for the 'general camp' to have 'tasted' Desdemona's body, 'So I had nothing known' (III.iii.346–8), EBB is applying Othello's words to her dog. Flush 'does not seem to understand the glory of fighting – whether through philosophy or good temper, "the pomp and circumstance of glorious war" never move his ambition' (*Correspondence*, V, 53; 11 June 1841), and Flush 'turned his back on the "pride, pomp and circumstance of glorious war"' (*Correspondence*, VII, 202; 23 June 1843). The usage acutely debunks Othello's self-pity and the grossness of his denial of Desdemona's dignity, whilst also, in a manoeuvre typical of EBB, domesticating Shakespeare within her own world.

Shakespeare is a crucial part of the intimate language EBB and her family use to address each other, in birthday poems and in letters where he provides a means of approaching the most delicate of subjects with tact and humour. On 30 December 1825, her mother writes to EBB: 'the mind cannot retain its powers, if the casket which contains it, be injured or weakened, and you cannot encrease your hours of study, without sacrificing your health. You may think this "stale and unprofitable" [*Hamlet*, I.ii.133] but it is the anxiety of our hearts dearest BA!' (*Correspondence*, I, 229). The letter risks turning Barrett's cherished literature against her, but its gentle and self-effacing humour, the very homeliness of her mother's concern, and the recuperation of Hamlet's despair within a family dynamic manage in fact simply to acknowledge that literature as being of a piece with the family's own love of EBB. The letter also parallels the variety of voices which are extracted from *Hamlet* in EBB's correspondence. She ironises the play's words, in describing her own aching head as a 'distracted globe' (*Correspondence*, V, 162; 4 November 1841) from *Hamlet*, I.v.97, but also uses it to write lovingly to numerous correspondents, including Mary Russell Mitford, to whom she writes that it is '"Stale and flat," to take more from Shakespeare' [*Hamlet*, I.ii.33] to talk by pen and ink rather than in person (*Correspondence*, VIII, 37; 8 November 1844). She is also fond of providing new and lighter contexts for Hamlet's 'though by your smiling you seem to say so', for instance in challenging Richard Hengist Horne's ironic amusement at the news that EBB was having a portrait of herself painted (*Correspondence*, V, 56; 13 June 1841).

The affection and domesticity of these letters are echoed later by EBB as she seeks to distinguish between the competing dignities of love and familiarity and of title and position in a letter to Mary Russell Mitford, in which she uses her love of Shakespeare as an exemplar of the former: 'Which of us wdnt. like to know how Shakespeare came down stairs one Wednesday morning with his hose ungartered? Wdnt. you climb your ladder ten times, to catch the colour of the garters?' (*Correspondence*, V, 75; 15 July 1841). The ease and familiarity of her relationship with Mitford is both enabled by, and an extension of, her relations with Shakespeare. Her first letter to Mitford thanks her for '[naming] me as a "household word" [*Henry V*, IV.iii.52] to your father' (*Correspondence*, III, 175; 8 June 1836), and later that summer she writes: 'For all the kindness, the far far too much kindness of your words to me, how can I thank you enough? Let me be silent, & love you' (*Correspondence*, III, 192; 29 September 1836). The letter alludes to Cordelia's words to her father in *King Lear*, I.i.64,[32] and is the first of Barrett's references in her letters to the vexed question of women's voices, speaking, and silence in *King Lear*. The allusion silently acknowledges Barrett's affection, and also enacts a necessarily unspoken acknowledgement of the two women's shared experiences of living with demanding fathers. Furthermore, the allusion itself is silent, being without quotation marks, and thereby all the more delicately enacting its thanks. The omission of quotation marks enables a greater intimacy with Shakespeare as he seamlessly moves into the texture of EBB's own language, but it can also promote the intimacy between correspondents, as the recipient recognises and responds to the Shakespearean offering placed before her, and the writer's trust that it would be recognised.

That Shakespeare in particular, amongst the many writers from whom EBB quotes, was a vehicle of intimacy is shown in the pattern of references to, and quotations from, him in EBB's correspondence. These references tend to cluster around the person with whom she was most intimate at any one time. From 1836 to 1845 this was Mitford, before she was succeeded by Robert Browning.[33] The first correspondent with whom she was intimately Shakespearean, however, was the blind Classical scholar Hugh Stuart Boyd, with whom she studied, and who lived near the Barretts at Hope End. The relationship is both based in and conveyed through texts. Her visits to Boyd seem to have been rather an obsession with EBB. Relatively early in their relationship, she writes anticipating an imminent visit to the Boyd household, and continues: 'You have made me very curious, & have induced me to think of many things in Heaven & Earth never dream't of in any PHILOSOPHY, since Cornelius Agrippa's!' (*Correspondence*, II, 147; 6–7 June 1828). The quotation from *Hamlet*, I.v.166–7[34] inverts the intellectual relationship between the speaker and auditor of the original to flatter the older man, even to set up a form of intellectual flirtation with her tutor. As is the case elsewhere, EBB uses Shakespeare to play, to act, to extend the range of roles and voices available to her.

As for many women later in the century, Shakespeare was for EBB a means of escape from the limitations and dimensions of her social, and even her literary, roles. She enjoys that freedom here whilst remaining confident and secure in her intellectual status, for her compliment only works if the knowledge in which it is based is acknowledged as being shared; and she is confident too that the freedoms permitted by the quotation are balanced by the distance also implicit in the use of someone else's words. Indeed the frisson of the letter, which would of course have been read to Boyd by his daughter or wife, rests in the fine judgement EBB expends in seeing how far she can go within boundaries which still acknowledge Shakespeare's mediating authority. The lack of quotation marks seems to signal the intimacy of the relationship with both Boyd and with Shakespeare that she is setting up here, rather than to seek to elide Shakespeare's part in the letter. Margaret Forster's biography of EBB suggests that the young woman's relationship with Boyd was one which moved between public displays of scholarship and friendliness, and private confessions to her journal of her obsession with the older, married man. She suggests: 'If there were only Elizabeth's letters to him upon which to depend, then the degree of attachment she felt for him would remain obscure: he would remain a scholarly friend who probably aroused no deeper feelings than admiration and interest.'[35] In fact, as this letter and others from the period demonstrate, EBB was equally demonstrative in her letters.

The relationship in play here is a three-way one, resting on a joint ownership of the language of the letter. Shakespeare retains ultimate authority and ownership of the words, his continuing presence investing EBB's quotations with distance and timelessness, or at least a temporal otherness, which is itself a crucial part of the freedom which Shakespeare gives to the nineteenth-century woman; EBB and Boyd actively meet in recognising and interpreting the quotation; and EBB herself exercises her learning and autonomy in using Shakespeare, in re-making his words for her own ends, but in never entirely subduing the poet and the original context of his writing. As is so often the case in EBB's quoting from Shakespeare, her use of the quotation from *Hamlet* rests here upon a tacitly intended recognition of the force of the original context of the quotation, and of the way in which she is adopting it here; the success of her allusion rests upon a mutual acknowledgement of the persistent otherness of Shakespeare's words. Furthermore, the shared intellectual activity of using and recognising the allusion works as part of the force of her letters' meaning, as well as acting as the vehicle for developing her epistolary relationships through the mixture of intellectual and emotional interaction that seems for EBB to be peculiarly the essence of Shakespeare.

When reading EBB's correspondence, one is struck by two interrelated factors: first, how very intimate is the relationship between EBB and Shakespeare, the way it almost seems to inhabit her emotional being, as Shakespeare inhabits her written language; and secondly, how profoundly her Shakespeare is of the page rather than the stage. Their relationship is one that can only be brought into being in intimacy. EBB writes sceptically of the more public forms in which the playwright was made available to Victorian audiences, whether in the undue speculation of publicly available criticism,[36] or in the theatre. For her, the latter can only involve the 'translation [of poetry] into a grosser form' (to Hengist Horne, 3 June 1840; IV, 273). As she writes later to the same correspondent, himself a fervent believer that contemporary theatre could be redeemed by Shakespeare, even that playwright bowed 'his starry head' to 'write down his pure genius into the dirt of the groundlings' (9 January 1841; V, 5). The following year, she writes to Mitford, herself a successful playwright, again invoking the mechanism of interpretation:

In regard to the drama, I have been to the theatre – I have seen Shakespeare in London – but it was when I was a young child: and I admit to you willingly that in reading & taking pleasure from the written Drama, my ideas of it never enter the theatre from first to last. I have a notion, – that the theatre interprets between the dramatic poet and the unpoetic multitudes, – & always where the poetry is high, desecrates it in translation. (4 July 1842; VI, 26)

We cannot, of course, be sure that what EBB was taken to see was Shakespeare, rather than one of the many adaptations which were more usually seen in the early nineteenth century before William Macready began to retrieve Shakespeare for the stage, but what comes most clearly through her letter is her profound distrust of theatrical space, and of the unruly multitudes. She is agitated by this distrust of the theatrical process, by the metamorphosis of the mob into an audience, and fails to envisage that the multitude could be trusted to be one part of the mutually consenting dyad upon which the mechanism of translation rests.

It is in EBB's correspondence with Browning that we see the culmination of this mode of translation (seen previously in her writing to Boyd) in their shared intimacy with Shakespeare, and her expression of what Shakespeare means to her. She writes to Browning of her isolated childhood in a letter of 20 March 1845:

You seem to have drunken of the cup of life full, with the sun shining on it. I have lived only inwardly, – or with sorrow, for a strong emotion. Before this seclusion of my illness, I was secluded still – & there are few of the youngest women in the world who have not seen more, heard more, known more of society, than I, who am scarcely to be called young now. I grew up in the country .. had no social opportunities, … had my heart in books & poetry, … & my experience, in reveries […] It was a lovely life – growing green like the grass around it. Books & dreams were what I lived in – & domestic life only seemed to buzz gently around, like the bees about the grass. And so time passed, and passed – and afterwards, when my illness came & I seemed to stand at the edge of the world with all done, & no prospect (as appeared at one time) of ever passing the threshold of one room again, – why then, I turned to thinking with some bitterness […] that I had stood blind in this temple I was about to leave … that I had seen no Human nature, that my brothers & sisters of the earth were names to me, … that I had beheld no great mountain or river – nothing in fact. I was as a man dying who had not read Shakespeare … & it was too late!'[37] (X, 133)

EBB sets herself up here as potentially Mariana-like in her description of a life entrapped, and sinking ever deeper in its seclusion. This account invokes Daniel Karlin's 'scepticism in the light of her *Diary* (1830–1), in which "social opportunities" are not so much absent as spurned when available'.[38] He is equally scathing about the letter's final analogy, in which EBB seeks to convey the full horror of her fear of an early death which would rob her of the potential of experiencing all that she had so far missed: Karlin comments: 'How revealing that last analogy is of the very bookishness it laments! The perverse aptness of it is almost suspect' (p. 68). And yet it need not be: Shakespeare does not operate here as simply an analogy for life, in a curiously gender-inverted model, but as life itself. In his case, the art–life split collapses as EBB invokes the experience of living in Shakespeare, not as a substitute for a more active life, but as an image of what that more active life might be. We get our sense of the potential of life through its proximity to Shakespeare, rather than vice versa.

Browning enters into EBB's letters through a Shakespeare quotation which she uses in explaining her enthusiasm for *Paracelsus* to Mitford:

I ... would wish for more harmony & rather more clearness & compression – concentration – besides: but I do think & feel that the pulse of poetry is full & warm & strong in it, & that, – without being likely perhaps to be a popular poem, – it 'bears a charmed life' [*Macbeth*, V.viii.12]. There is a palpable power! a height & depth of thought, – & sudden repressed gushings of tenderness which suggest to us a depth beyond in the affections. (*Correspondence*, III, 186; 10 August 1836)

She later uses the same play to rebuke a by now determinedly sceptical Mitford for her severity to Browning: 'Ah – you speak more severely of Mr. Browning, than I can say' "Amen" to. Amen wd. stick in my throat [*Macbeth*, II.ii.29–30] – even suppose it to rise so high' (*Correspondence*, VI, 111; 19 October 1842). The quotations convey a self-deprecatory humour about the extent of EBB's enthusiasm for the other poet, a humour which continues in EBB's first letter to Browning, in which she asks 'only for a sentence or two of general observation – and I do not ask even for that, so as to tease you – but in the humble, low voice, which is so excellent a thing in women – particularly when they go a-begging!' (*Correspondence*, X, 19; 11 January 1845). As Daniel Karlin notes, EBB adds 'humble' to Lear's memory of the dead Cordelia's voice as 'ever soft, / Gentle and low, an excellent thing in woman' (*King Lear*, V.iii.273–5), and also interpolates the notion of begging, which, as Karlin also notes, is not something that Cordelia ever does (Karlin, p. 57). It is possible that EBB hears an echo in the word 'humble' of the slightly brutal use which Hamlet, ever to the forefront of her writing mind, makes of it to describe his perception of the proper state of his mother's blood at a period when she ought not to be falling in love at all, and least of all with his uncle: 'You cannot call it love, for at your age / The heyday in the blood is tame, it's humble, / And waits upon the judgement' (IV.iii.69). Her letter comes to seem both emotionally timorous and freighted with a sense of the potential enormity of the relationship about to be commenced here. EBB feints behind Shakespeare's language, using him as an emissary to sound out a potential romance.

EBB had used the *King Lear* quotation from V.iii twice before in letters to Mitford: once to express her own liking for a 'soft, low voice' (*Correspondence*, VII, 278; 12 August 1843), and once to describe the state of her own voice, as 'still too low for Lear' after a cold (*Correspondence*, IX, 282; 16 December 1844). Within a month, the quotation is transformed in her letter to Browning with a self-deprecating humour which flatters the younger poet, and tentatively acknowledges her own eagerness for the correspondence to last, but which also draws attention to the changes she has made to her source. She thus engages Browning from the start in a written relationship which foregrounds Shakespeare but in which EBB is unafraid to take liberties with her source. She is confident in her literary status, but diffident emotionally. As she humbles herself to Browning, she plays in humbling Shakespeare to her own ends, and presumably expects Browning to recognise her doing so.

If this seems overly ingenious, or to demand too much of her correspondent, the challenge is ably met by Browning, who writes to EBB on 31 July 1845 of his equally demanding expectations of her: 'In all I say to you, write to you, I know very well that I trust to your understanding me almost beyond the warrant of any human capacity – but as I began, so I shall end' (*Correspondence*, XI, 8). This letter itself carries a muted reference to *Julius Caesar*, V.iii.24, in its last words, and again the context of the original, once recognised, carries an even greater freight of meaning. The words are Cassius's: 'This day I breathed first; time is come round, / And where I did begin, there shall I end.' Browning adopts these words to suggest that in EBB he has found a form of new birth, and were she to leave him, she would effect a kind of death. Through Shakespeare, Browning picks up and adopts the metaphor of death which had previously been the fearful EBB's domain in their correspondence. So resonant are these lines of Browning that EBB repeats them in her next letter to him (*Correspondence*, XI, 10; 31 July 1845). Browning's first use of the lines picks up on his punning conclusion to his previous letter, in which he quotes IV.iii.218–19 of the same play when he writes that 'If I venture to weary you again with all this, is there not the cause of causes, and did not the prophet write that "there was a tide in the affairs of men, which taken at the E.B.B. led on to the fortune" of your RB' (*Correspondence*, XI, 3; 25 July 1845). Though both were entirely capable of using Shakespeare humorously, Browning's letter of 31 July to EBB insists here on the gravity of their situation; it is not a question of 'fortune' but, as for Cassius, of life and death.

One of EBB and Browning's most intimate exchanges involves an absolutely silent quotation from Shakespeare, which neither needs to quote on the page because they are each sufficiently sure of the reference being clear to the other without further prompting. Browning writes of a word of Juliet's which rises to his lips, and EBB assures him in her next letter that she 'guessed at once' what his meaning was (27 January, 3 February 1845; X, 44, 53). Under the guise of an exchange about their friendship, the two poets seem to be referring to Juliet's 'It is an honour that I dream not of' (*Romeo and Juliet*, I.iii.66), words which are applied in the play to the young lovers' marriage. Shakespeare is not simply the language in which EBB and Browning speak to each other, the way in which they acknowledge their shared status and knowledge as poets; he is of the very essence of their relationship, and it can come as no surprise when EBB uses a reference to Shakespeare to describe her response to Browning's proposal: 'How would any woman have felt ... who could feel at all ... hearing such words said (though "in a dream" [*Tempest*, I.ii.487] indeed) by such a speaker?' (*Correspondence*, XI, 100; 26 September 1845). Such immersion in Shakespeare is rare, even in the bardolatrous nineteenth century, and to find it shared to this extent is, I think, unprecedented.

TRANSLATING SHAKESPEARE

In the courtship correspondence, we see the evolution of a number of relationships. Most notable, of course, is that between EBB and Browning, but we also see her trust in Shakespeare increase too, as she uses him as a medium, a bridge, through which she can reach Browning. She uses his words to translate herself to Browning, but also perhaps to present her emotions to herself as well, to give them form. Yopie Prins writes of translation as a 'Contractual agreement [that] depends on an awareness of difference that does not reduce the other to identity, but allows for a mediation between "my tongue" and "the other's"'.[39] In this transaction, there is 'a necessary displacement of meaning' (p. 436) which also occurs in EBB's use of Shakespeare. Prins is primarily concerned with the use by EBB and Browning in their courtship correspondence of *Prometheus Bound*, by means of which 'they perceive their language as interchangeable, secondary, and not subject to ownership. Instead, each translates and is translated by the other' (p. 436). Precisely the same might, however, be argued of their use of Shakespeare in their letters, and of EBB's use of Shakespeare in her poetry.

In her preface to her translation of *Prometheus Bound*, EBB specifically distinguishes between the two modes of imitation and translation. Defending her decision to attempt a translation of an ancient writer against claims that an age ought more properly to aim to be 'original', she writes that the act of translation does not mean that an age is in 'servilely imitative' thrall to its predecessors. Rather, she goes on: 'Surely [an age] may think its own thoughts and speak its own words, yet not turn away from those who *have* thought and spoken well.'[40] Translation then is defined in opposition to imitation in EBB's early aesthetic, and is an act which, crucially for this writer, is simultaneously a form of conveying information and an opportunity for self-expression:

It is the nature of the human mind to communicate its own character to whatever substance it conveys, whether it convey metaphysical impressions from itself to another mind, or literary compositions from one to another language. ('Preface', p. 81)

Indeed, it comes to seem that translation is of the essence of the creative act for EBB, an act which necessarily involves an imaginative translation of something already in existence. She writes, for instance, of images of natural beauty that they do not demand slavish imitation: rather we should make them

subjects of contemplation, in order to abstract from them those ideas of beauty, afterwards embodied in our own production; and, above all, in order to consider their and our Creator under every manifestation of His goodness and His power … All beauties … are multiplied reflections … of one archetypal beauty. (p. 83)

The works of the poet and artist thus translate divine power and splendour for the world. G. B. Smith wrote in 1874 of EBB's *Prometheus Bound*: 'In this, as in her other translations, she desired it to be understood that her one great idea was to catch the spirit of the original' (p. 478). However, one might as easily apply that judgement to the rest of her work, whilst bearing in mind her comment in 'The Book of the Poets' that 'Art lives by nature, not by the bare mimetic life generally attributed to Art: she does not imitate, she expounds. *Interpres naturae* – is the poet-artist' (p. 153). We should remember too that EBB's most famous work is ostensibly a translation. The *Sonnets from the Portuguese* are advisedly so called, and elaborately and transparently feign transmission of an original source which simultaneously gives voice to the contemporary woman poet. The manoeuvre exactly mirrors EBB's use of Shakespeare, as she employs his words to voice her emotions, and gives to those words a powerful nineteenth-century resonance whilst insisting on the persistent presence of the earlier writer.

CHAPTER 3

'She had made him, as it were, the air she lived in': Shakespeare, Helen Faucit and Fanny Kemble

The theatre, as we have seen, is not a space that occurs in accounts or theories of girls' education, and yet the rhetoric of pedagogy substantially informs the working lives, writings and subsequent reputations of Helen Faucit and Fanny Kemble, the two most notable actresses of Shakespeare in the legitimate theatre in the first half of the nineteenth century. Both in the eyes of reviewers and in their own prolific accounts of their relationship with Shakespeare, the desire to educate their audiences is paramount and urgent. And yet what each sought to teach, as well as the motivations, methods, work and reputations of Helen Faucit and Fanny Kemble, was absolutely distinct. From the same plays and parts they could extract entirely distinct methodologies and careers based upon their differing conceptions of themselves as teachers, their understanding of the theatre, and the genealogy of their relationship to Shakespeare.

Faucit's explicit endeavour was to 'present a living picture of womanhood as divined by Shakespeare, and held up by him as an ideal for woman to aspire to, and for men to revere'.[1] In her published account of Beatrice, which took the form of an open letter addressed to John Ruskin, Faucit makes explicit, through commenting on Ruskin's own writings on Shakespeare's heroines in *Sesame and Lilies*, what impact Shakespeare's heroines can have upon the lives of contemporary Victorians:

how thorough has been your study of Shakespeare's heroines, and with what loving insight you have used them to illustrate the part women have played, and are meant to play, in bringing sweetness and comfort, and help and moral strength, into man's troubled and perplexing life. (Faucit, p. 291)

As an actress and writer, Faucit's vehicle for teaching such lofty aspirations was herself, as her widower points out in his hagiographic biography of her, published shortly after her death:

how great an influence for good her so potent art had been to thousands who, but for her, would never have known the impulses of elevating thought and feeling, which a woman of a lofty nature can arouse, by the living commentary of voice and look and movement, in the impersonation of ideal characters upon the stage. (Martin, p. 231)

That effect was itself the result of a life-long effort to 'educate and elevate' herself up to the level of her most 'purifying and ennobling' art, as she writes to the Bishop of Manchester in 1878 (quoted in Martin, p. 350). In her work she sought to elevate that stage, both as a site for the promulgation of a particular Shakespeare-inspired form of ideal Victorian womanhood, and also necessarily as a space where she would herself effectively enact that ideal nature, bringing upon herself the adoration of playgoers who saw in her the embodiment of feminine virtue, if not indeed of 'woman' herself. As a critic wrote of her first appearance in Manchester in 1845: 'Miss Faucit's nature is not so much that of a woman, as that of WOMAN. She infuses, so to speak, the *personality* of the feminine character into every delineation' (quoted in Martin, p. 161). The carefully constructed synonymity of Faucit and Shakespeare's heroines, which her own writings would subsequently do so much to enforce during a period of gender instability, was both justified by, and enabled, Faucit's presentation as one unselfconsciously teaching women to aspire to emulate 'the types of noble womanly nature as they had been revealed by our best dramatic poets, and especially by Shakespeare' (Martin, p. 166). Faucit's justification for occupying the stage is based on a recognition of her opportunity to teach from the stage, to use its publicity as a suitable medium for her Shakespeare-inspired message to Victorian men and women, and of Shakespeare's ultimate authority. This was teaching which worked within clearly established parameters of extant power, and worked to maintain that power structure by invoking Shakespeare's eternal relevance and wisdom as fundamental to it. It was a primarily conservative ethic and aesthetic which found its fulfilment in Faucit's favoured position within the royal court, effected through her husband's role as biographer of Prince Albert, and cemented through her own acting, specifically her work in Shakespeare.[2] Faucit was of course in her early career in the 1830s and 1840s credited with creating a number of stage heroines, most notably Pauline in Bulwer's *Lady of Lyons* (1838) and Clara Douglas in the same writer's *Money* (1840) and with collaborating extensively with Robert Browning in his career as a playwright, as well as in reviving heroines of Classical tragedy such as Iphigenia and Antigone. However, it is through her roles as a Shakespeare actress that Faucit tried to influence the terms of her subsequent reputation.

Fanny Kemble's pedagogic intent was quite other, but equally bound up with her sense of responsibility and indebtedness to Shakespeare. A much more reluctant occupant of the stage than Faucit, as she professed herself to be, she adopted the medium of public readings of Shakespeare's works when she retired from acting. Waiting until her father, the actor Charles Kemble, gave up his Shakespearean readings in 1848 lest she seem to be in competition with him, Kemble embarked upon her readings with the dual motivation of having to support herself, which she did successfully for twenty-five years, and of wanting, as she writes:

in undertaking my readings from Shakespeare … to make, as far as possible, of each play a thorough study in its entireness; such as a stage representation cannot, for obvious reasons, be. The dramatic effect, which of course suffers in the mere delivery from a reading-desk, would I hoped be in some measure compensated for by the possibility of retaining the whole beauty of the plays as poetical compositions. I very soon, however, found my project in making my readings 'studies of Shakespeare' for the public quite illusory.

To do so would have required that I should take two, and sometimes three, evenings for the delivery of one play; a circumstance which would have rendered it necessary for the same audience to attend two or three consecutive readings; and in many other respects I found the plan quite incompatible with the demand of the public, which was for a dramatic entertainment and not for a course of literary instruction. I was grievously disappointed, but could not help myself.

I was determined not to limit my repertory to the few most theatrically popular of Shakespeare's dramas, but to include in my course all his plays that it was possible to read with any hope of attracting or interesting an audience. My father had limited his range to a few of the most frequently acted plays: I delivered twenty-four. I invariably read them through in rotation, without repeating any of them: partly to make such of them as are seldom or never acted familiar to the public, and partly to avoid becoming mechanical or hackneyed myself in their delivery by perpetual repetition of the same pieces. I persisted in this system to the very considerable detriment of my gains.[3]

The plays she and her father both read were the highly popular *Hamlet, As You Like It, The Merchant of Venice, Much Ado About Nothing, Julius Caesar, King John, Romeo and Juliet, Othello, Henry IV 1* and *2, Henry V, Macbeth, Coriolanus, Richard III*, and *Henry VIII*, to which she added *King Lear, Richard II, Antony and Cleopatra, The Winter's Tale, Measure for Measure, A Midsummer Night's Dream, The Merry Wives of Windsor, Twelfth Night* and *The Tempest.*[4]

Kemble's account of her work could scarcely be more distinct from Faucit's, devoid as it is of any sense of Shakespeare's being employed in a morally utilitarian way for his Victorian auditors, or of any mention of herself as the necessary transmitter of Shakespeare's greatness. Indeed, Henry James notes in his obituary of Kemble: 'What would have been precisely insupportable to her was that people should come not for Shakespeare but for Fanny Kemble.'⁵ Rather, Shakespeare was simply something that everyone ought to be exposed to, educative in the broadest sense possible. James recalls how he was taken as a boy to hear her read precisely 'for education's sake' (p. 96). James's superbly sensitive account of Kemble accords with her own blunt record of her readings and their rationale, and with the way in which she sacrificed financial gain to her intransigent loyalty to her repertory and 'to her master. If on a given evening the play didn't fit the occasion, so much the worse for the occasion: she had spoken for her poet, and if he had more variety than the "public taste," this was only to his honour' (p. 106). James highlights, as her own modesty and unselfconsciousness would preclude her from doing, the extent to which

The only thing that, during these busy years, she had been 'thinking of' was the genius of the poet it was her privilege to interpret, in whom she found all greatness and beauty and with whom for so long she had the great happiness … of living in daily intimacy. (p. 107)

James might perhaps protest too much: Kemble had to think of supporting herself during the years of her estrangement, and finally divorce, from her American husband Pierce Butler, and undoubtedly many of the audiences who crowded to see her during her first American readings in New York in 1848–9 were attracted to the spectacle of the woman who was then involved in a highly acrimonious and very public divorce hearing. Indeed, her friend Philip Hone records:

The fashionable world is agog again upon a new impulse. Mrs Butler, the veritable Fanny Kemble, has taken the city by storm. She reads Shakespeare's plays three evenings in the week, and at noon on Mondays in the Stuyvesant Institute in Broadway, a room which will hold six or seven hundred persons, and which is filled when she reads by the elite of the world of fashion; delicate women, grave gentlemen, belles, beaus and critics flock to the doors of the entrance, and rush in to such places as they can find, two or three hours before the lady's appearance. They are compensated for the tedious sitting on hard seats, squeezed by the crowds, by an hour's reading, and very fine certainly, for Fanny knows how to do it – of the favourite plays of the Immortal Bard, she makes $2,000 or $3,000 a week and never was money so easily earned.⁶

Nonetheless, the essence of James's interpretation of Kemble as one primarily concerned with Shakespeare, and only with her artistry as a means of making him better known, holds good, especially to the extent that it strengthens the fundamental differences between her and Faucit.

Radically uninterested in newspapers in the age of celebrity, and distrustful of the theatrical, as opposed to the dramatic, Kemble refused to obtrude her self in the relationship she hoped to create between audiences and Shakespeare; whereas for Faucit and her admirers, her own physical self, and later her writing personality, was a compulsory part, the substance, even the very essence of her 'message', so embroiled was that message within the co-ordinates of contemporary femininity. As we will see, these differences determine the women's relationship and work with Shakespeare, and inform their self-writings and reviewers' responses, as well as the terms of their memorials. Superficially, the two women share remarkable similarities. Near contemporaries born respectively in 1809 and 1814, Kemble and Faucit were actresses from theatrical dynasties, were both domestic performers, and prolific writers on Shakespeare. Yet though both were definitively Shakespearean, their fortunes and reputations diverged dramatically. This chapter will be concerned to assess the resonance of that term as it was applied to both women, and to argue that the forms of their difference set the parameters for two key strands evident in women's responses to Shakespeare throughout the century, strands which rest fundamentally on opposing ideas of history.

Of the two theatrical families, Faucit's was the less distinguished, but her mother did appear on the London stage, where, according to Carol Jones Carlisle, she was well established, often playing opposite Charles Kemble at Covent Garden.[7] Faucit's own subsequent re-telling of her life is not forthcoming about her family, perhaps because her mother created something of a sensation in 1820 by leaving her husband to live with the then married actor William Farren, with whom she remained for the rest of her life, and who became the acknowledged step-father of Helen and her elder sister Harriet. In her autobiographical writings, compiled after she had left the professional stage, Faucit elects to give herself an alternative parentage, far removed from the life of the jobbing actor and the scandal of her mother's relationship. *On Some of Shakespeare's Female Characters* was first published in book form in 1885, and was a collection of semi-public letters which had appeared in *Blackwood's Magazine* in the early 1880s. Faucit uses her recollections of certain roles to comment on her professional life, and on theatre history, but also uses those roles to construct her autobiography. She does this in the first instance by suggesting that she is most appropriately conceived of as being parented by Shakespeare. The process of her construction as a Shakespearean heroine begins while she is still at school. During what appears to have been at times a lonely childhood, Faucit writes: '[my books] filled my young heart and mind with what fascinated me most – the gorgeous, the wonderful, the grand, the heroic, the self-denying, the self-devoting'.[8] Within her reading, which included *The

Arabian Nights, Pilgrim's Progress and *Paradise Lost,* Shakespeare was the greatest influence. Faucit's own account suggests that she is in some measure parented by Shakespeare, his visions of femininity shaping her own from an early age. She makes no mention of her actual parents in her writings, though Theodore Martin would later explain, in his biography, that they were professional actors who had separated when Faucit was young (Martin, pp. 1–3). Faucit replaces a genealogy of the professional theatre, common to actresses at the time, with one which has a far more exalted literary basis. The strategy of claiming a childhood blessed by the shade of Shakespeare was not of course unique to Faucit. Ellen Terry would make a similar gesture in her 1908 autobiography *The Story of My Life*, where she makes a virtue of being born in Coventry by reminding her readers that it is in Shakespeare's county of Warwickshire. However, this works alongside her parallel assertion of her acting parentage, and the early education and opportunities which her father Ben Terry gave her in acting Shakespeare. At no point does she try to effect the substitution mechanism that Faucit employs.

Kemble's account of her upbringing is much more diffuse, being spread across numerous autobiographical volumes which appeared in her later life. Like Faucit's account, it too is found in letters, in this case originally private letters written to her friend Harriet St Leger which were subsequently returned to her and which make up *Records of a Girlhood* (1878), the three volumes of *Records of Later Life* (1882) and the two volumes of *Further Records, 1848–1883* (1890), as well as in the journal entries of her first visit to America in 1832–3 which she subsequently edited as the *Journal of a Young Actress* in 1835, and in her slight volume of *Notes Upon Some of Shakespeare's Plays* (1882). In 1863, she also published *Journal of a Residence on a Georgian Plantation, 1838–1839*, which recorded the early days of her marriage to Butler, and her horror at the life he expected her to live on his plantation. The timing of its publication in the midst of the American Civil War was highly controversial. In this corpus of writings, 'copious and delightful', and 'which form[s] one of the most animated autobiographies in the language', according to Henry James (*Essays*, p. 113), she gives a full and slightly star-struck account of her theatrical dynasty, of her celebrated aunt and uncle (Sarah Siddons and John Philip Kemble), and her French mother – an actress who brought her skills as 'a dancer, a mime, a singer and a low comedienne' to her august in-laws.[9] After her marriage, Marie-Therese de Camp was tried out in Shakespeare, as Ophelia and as Dorinda in *The Tempest* (Jenkins, p. 70), but was found lacking and the experiment was not repeated. Fanny, however, writes back to the official Kemble tradition in *Records of a Girlhood*, in claiming that:

The great actors of my family have received their due of recorded admiration; my mother has always seemed to me to have been overshadowed by their celebrity; my sister and myself, whose fate it has been to bear in public the name they have made distinguished, owe in great measure to her, I think, whatever ability has enabled us to do not unworthily.[10]

This is both a girl's spirited defence of her mother, and also a veiled critique and acknowledgement of the fact that the Kemble tradition was a creation, skilfully manipulated by their own writing, by favourable portraits (Siddons and John Philip Kemble were variously painted by George Henry Harlow, Joshua Reynolds, Sir Thomas Lawrence and Sir Thomas Beech), and sympathetic critics. According to Rebecca Jenkins, the great tragedians in fact played more melodrama than Shakespeare (Jenkins, p. 46), but that has been written out of their history.

Fanny's own subsequent interventions mediate those early celebrities through a prism far more concerned with family than with public renown, and with the kind of careful attention to Shakespeare's words that could not be fostered by the early nineteenth-century stage. As such, the leading figure in her family saga is her father Charles whom she frequently invokes as both a pseudo-lover and as profoundly Shakespearean. Apparently anxious to wrest him from the minor, supplementary role he usually occupies in accounts of the Kemble family history, Fanny celebrates him, tellingly I would argue, as one somewhat out of his true context:

[T]hough his workmanship may be far finer than that of any other artist I ever saw, yet its very minute accuracy and refinement renders it unfit for the frame in which it is exhibited. Whoever should paint a scene calculated for so large a space as a theatre ... would commit a great error of judgement. The great beauty of all my father's performances, but particularly of Hamlet, is a wonderful accuracy in the detail of the character he represents. But the result is not such as he expects, as the reward of so much labour ... The amazing study of it requires a study in those who are to appreciate it, and this is far from being what the majority of spectators are either capable of or desirous of doing. I think that acting is best which skilfully husbands the actor's and spectator's powers. ... Polished and refined tastes, an acute sense of the beauty of harmonious proportions, and a native grace, gentleness and refinement of mind and manners, have been his prompters. But they cannot inspire those startling and tremendous bursts of passion which belong to the highest walks of tragedy, and to which he never gave their fullest expression. I fancy my aunt Siddons united the excellencies of both these styles.[11]

As, she might have added, did Edmund Kean, another example of all that her father was not. Shakespeare is both the measure of her father's relative lack of success, and also the compensation for that, and the marker of something greater, more significant and more enduring.

As a space for sympathetic interpretative expression, the stage was as profoundly inimical a place to Fanny Kemble as it would become to Henry James just after she died. In December 1893, the year of Kemble's death, he wrote to his brother William of the difference between theatre and drama in terms which clearly have their roots in Kemble's own theatrical analysis. He writes:

The whole odiousness of the thing lies in the connection between the drama and the theatre. The one is admirable in its interest and difficulty, the other loathsome in its conditions. If the drama could only be theoretically or hypothetically acted, the fascination resident in its all but unconquerable (*circumspice!*) form would be unimpaired, and one would be able to have the exquisite exercise without the horrid sacrifice.[12]

The terms might have come straight out of Kemble's *Notes upon some of Shakespeare's Plays*, which opens with an elaboration of her basic belief that drama and theatre represent respectively the real and the false, that contemporary stage conditions militated against the dramatic, and that even Shakespeare was not immune to its taint.[13]

This text plays its part in constructing Fanny's self-identification as a writer rather than as a performer, and yet she was persuaded to go on the stage in 1829, as the result of a series of events which compellingly combine the imperatives of financial disaster for her family, and the enabling allure of Shakespearean language. When John Philip Kemble retired in 1817, the management of Covent Garden fell to Charles, but at that stage it was a rather dubious legacy. Charles lacked the aptitude for business needed to turn the theatre's finances around, and in 1829, after a number of near collapses, the family finally faced bankruptcy. Fanny's first response to this crisis, in a letter to her father, echoed one that would be required of generations of suddenly impoverished young Victorian women – to become a governess. Crucially, this was something she invited. Unlike George Eliot's Gwendolen Harleth in *Daniel Deronda* (1876), in another of the many instances in the nineteenth century when the choices of governess and actress almost coincide, Kemble's first choice of role is that of governess. Her mother, however, would have none of it, and asked her instead whether she had any talent for the stage. Fanny was persuaded to learn the role of Portia, at the time her favourite heroine, and as a result she found herself subsequently auditioning as Juliet in front of her father. The shift in parts is redolent of the urgent need that this production succeed financially, and reveals Charles Kemble's understanding of the tastes of his audience. It also speaks to the commercial aspects of young beauty, as well perhaps as the darker side of its allure.

The choice of part is crucial and obvious. Juliet was the ingénue part in the nineteenth century, and was that in which Faucit not only premiered, but was literally discovered. Lacking the family duty and financial imperatives which forced Fanny Kemble unwillingly onto the stage, Faucit creates another narrative belying her voluntary entry into the theatre. Their two accounts of finding themselves on stage for the first time are revealing. Kemble writes in the second volume of *Records of a Girlhood* of how

[s]et down in the midst of twilight ... with only my father's voice coming to me from where he stood hardly distinguishable in the gloom ... I was seized with the spirit of the thing; my voice resounded through the great vault above and before me, and, completely carried away by the inspiration of the wonderful play, I acted Juliet as I do not believe I ever acted it again, for I had no visible Romeo, and no audience to thwart my imagination. (II, 7)

With her ideal audience of one, Fanny is able to effect her own form of acting, a bodying forth of her imaginative response to the play, which has no basis in theatrical dynamics, either in the sense of her interaction with other actors, or the mood of the period. Her acting is the sounding out of the inspiration that the play has achieved in her imagination, a bodying forth which is visceral only as the voice is: there is no sense in the account of the effect of Kemble's physical appearance or acting; it is as private and interiorised a form of acting as can be imagined. Her audience helps to perfect this experience for Kemble, potentially removing the impulse to achieve a sexual impact, and allowing Kemble to perform with the unselfconsciousness of a child.[14] The challenge of managing her first public appearance would be to find a way of transposing that familial privacy into the glaring publicity of a debut performance on which the theatre's future rested.

A few weeks later, on 5 October 1829, surrounded by her family, Fanny Kemble came out theatrically. With her mother playing Lady Capulet and her father Mercutio,[15] Fanny achieved an extraordinary success which did indeed rescue the ailing Covent Garden, and save her family from bankruptcy. Her account of that first performance of Juliet, whose 'every line ... was familiar to my mind',[16] is an exercise in attempting to convey the achievement, the experience, of that kind of intense familiarity on stage, a familiarity which speaks of an unthinking assumption of, and identification with, the part. The writing of such an identification is bound by paradoxes and contradiction: how can one write credibly of the loss of self-awareness? The dilemma goes to the heart of the paradox of acting identified by Diderot, and yet even if we can only convincingly say that Kemble chooses to assume the guise of unselfconsciousness, her account is nonetheless telling in the particularities of its assumption of that possibility. Fanny began the play in a trembling state of fear, clinging to her mother for support, but in the ballroom scene she writes:

I began to forget myself; in the following one, the balcony scene, I had done so, and, for aught I knew I was Juliet; the passion I was uttering sending hot waves of blushes all over my neck and shoulders, while the poetry sounded like music to me as I spoke it, with no consciousness of anything before me, utterly transported into the imaginary existence of the play. (*Records of a Girlhood*, II, 59)

Paradoxically, Kemble's acting is at its best for her a means of returning to the realm of the imagination, ideally finding in the stage a sufficiently strong impulse to send her back into those private realms which are only incidentally made public. A few pages later in *Records of a Girlhood*, she records that she never went 'before an audience without a shrinking feeling of reluctance, or [had] withdrawn from their presence without thinking the excitement [she] had undergone unhealthy, and the personal exhibition odious' (II, 61). Shakespeare is for her a fundamentally private pleasure, and one whose exposure is almost necessarily demeaning. The extreme, antitheatrical privacy of her art is evinced by Kemble's response to those who have 'accused [her] of studying [her] attitudes'. She writes that 'the truth is that most things that are presented to my imagination, instead of being mere abstractions immediately assume form and colour, and become pictures; these I constantly execute on the stage as I had previously seen them in my imagination.'[17] Fanny's rebuttal is subtle and crucial – she works out from her mental pictures, rather than seeking in the actress's 'attitudes' the articulation and embodiment of her inspirations. Kemble is only incidentally spectacular in a theatre which was increasingly known for its visual dimension.

   In *Notes Upon Some of Shakespeare's Plays*, Fanny again asserts the primacy of the pictorial – rather than the merely visual – in giving an account of her 'first possession in the kingdom of delight which [Shakespeare] has since bestowed' upon her (p. 128). Her story is fascinating in asserting the dimensions of a passion which is effectively pre-verbal, in the sense that it pre-dates the age at which she could read and understand Shakespeare for herself. She had grown up hearing Shakespeare spoken all around her, and thus it was experienced first as a form of semiotic discourse, redolent of its being embedded in, indeed synonymous with, her earliest experiences of her family. But in this account, what is stressed is the extent to which her grounding in Shakespeare rests in the invoking of an intuitive sympathy provoked by a painting and based in her love of her father, and in the intimate enchantment of the voicing of that picture. Shakespeare's impact is aural, pictorial, familial, even before Kemble has knowingly heard one of his lines. The whole episode is framed by the mature Fanny within an evocation of the house in which it occurred as having surely long since fallen victim to the 'encroaching tide' of London, the 'hideous process' whereby outlying suburbs such as the Blackheath of which she writes are assimilated into 'more London' (p. 123), making Shakespeare akin already to something pre-lapsarian, and certainly pre-Victorian. She finds herself in a drawing-room in the company of a woman who was descended from one of Venice's noblest ducal families. Her face 'was like one of Giorgione's pictures' (p. 125). In a voice 'low, distinct, full, and soft', she describes to Fanny the story of the one large picture in the room:

a helmless, mastless, sailless bark lay weltering giddily, and in it sat a man in the full flower of vigorous manhood. His attitude was one of miserable dejection. [One hand covered his eyes.] His other hand rested on the fair curls of a girl-baby of three years old, who clung to his knee, and, with wide, wondering blue eyes, and laughing lips, looked up into the half-hidden face of her father. (p. 127)

It is a painting of Prospero and Miranda in the years before *The Tempest* begins. Kemble goes on:

There was something about the face and figure of the Prospero that suggested to me those of my father; and this, perhaps, added to the poignancy with which the representation of his distress affected my childish imagination. But the impression made by the picture, the story, and the place where I heard the one and saw the other, is among the most vivid that my memory retains. And never, even now do I turn the majestic page that holds that marvellous history, without seeing again the lovely lady, the picture full of sad dismay, and my own six-year-old self listening to that earliest Shakespearian love that my mind and heart ever received. I suppose this is partly the secret of my love for this, above all other of the poet's plays:— it was my first possession in the kingdom of unbounded delight which he has since bestowed upon me. (pp. 128–9)

In some ways, the scene is vividly theatrical, with the large drawing-room, the beautiful hostess, the dramatic painting, and the awe-struck six-year-old spectator who finds in the painting an echo of her beloved father. It also affords the adult narrator a proleptic instance of her desire to nurture her father through the difficulties which would come upon him as they had Prospero. However, the moment is more than simply dramatic. It rests on narratives and histories beyond the moment, on delayed knowledge, and the subtle interweaving of those histories across decades. It is a scene essentially about forms of revelation: about the history of the beautiful Italian who was one of Queen Caroline's retinue, and thereby involved in matters which could only become clear to the child many years later; revelations about her own father's position and powers, which sadly fell short of those of Prospero; and the revelation of the importance of Shakespeare to Fanny which could only be known subsequently. The scene operates like a temporal Russian doll as it gradually accrues layers of meaning across time. The moment exceeds theatricality, appealing rather to the writer and historian in Kemble, who can employ, but will not be immersed in, the moment of drama.

If we turn now to Helen Faucit, and to her first public engagement with Shakespeare, we can begin to uncover the grounds of the differences between the two women's responses to Shakespeare and the contemporary theatre. Faucit was discovered accidentally, so her account goes, whilst living in Richmond in 1833. On a hot summer's day, Faucit and her sister Harriet stopped for a rest in the empty, cool theatre en route for the river. Having spotted a flight of steps and a balcony on the stage, and believing themselves to be alone in the theatre, Harriet cried out: 'Why this might do for Romeo and Juliet's balcony! Go up, birdie, and I will be your Romeo' (Faucit, p. 89). They acted the balcony scene, but, as they subsequently discovered, they had been overheard by the theatre's manager. As Faucit goes on:

When our friends arrived some days later, the lessee told them that, having occasion to go from the dwelling-house to his private box, he had heard voices, listened, and remained during the time of our merry rehearsal. He spoke in such warm terms of the Juliet's voice, its adaptability to the character, her figure, I was tall for my age, and so forth, that in the end he prevailed upon my friends to let me make a trial on his stage … Thus did a little frolic prove to be the turning-point of my life. (p. 90)

The anecdote cannot help but sound contrived. It is not impossible that events happened just as she suggests, but even Carol Jones Carlisle, Faucit's biographer, only recommends that we accept 'some version' of it (Jones Carlisle, p. 25). She implicitly raises questions about the accidental nature of Faucit's discovery, by suggesting instead that 'the sisters cleverly arranged an "audition" in the guise of a lark' (p. 25) in order to precipitate Faucit's entry on to the stage for which her family feared she might not yet be quite ready. There is then an eagerness here which was not part of Kemble's narrated experience, but one which is readily dissimulated beneath an assumption of naive playfulness, guaranteed by the instigating presence of her older sister. The dissembling of self-aggrandisement through Shakespeare is arguably one which we see perpetuated throughout Faucit's connection with the role of Juliet, and her Shakespearean roles more generally. The assumption of a reluctance to go on stage perhaps speaks to the assumption of a more delicate late-Victorian audience for whom she had achieved an iconic Shakespearean function.

In her letters on Juliet in *Shakespeare's Female Characters*, Faucit is at pains to emphasise both her own reluctance to recount her own story – doing so only at the behest of the 'dear friend' who, along with 'many other friends', had, she said, 'so strongly urged me to tell you of my past in relation to the work I did' (p. 104) – and her lack of self-consciousness on stage. This, of course, echoes Kemble, and is part of a rhetoric of passive enablement for creative women throughout the century, but her use of that rhetoric belies its credibility as she describes the 'lovely vision' who is 'unconscious of admiring eyes upon her, herself delighting only in the simple enjoyment of the dance' (p. 113). The described dimensions of this moment are changed ineluctably by Faucit's uttering them herself, as are her professions of gratitude to Shakespeare 'for all the lovely and noble things he has put into his women's hearts and minds' (p. 113). Of Juliet in particular she writes:

Only one who knew of what a true woman is capable, in frankness, in courage, and self-surrender when her heart is possessed by a noble love, could have touched with such delicacy, such infinite charm of mingled reserve and artless frankness, the avowal of so fervent yet so modest a love, the secret of which had been so strangely stolen from her. (p. 119)

Such a gesturing towards ideality is a trope repeated throughout Faucit's career, both by herself and by her admirers, two of whom wrote in 1885 that she 'opened a world of poetry undreamed by [her audiences] – filled their eyes with visions of beauty and grace and dignity, living yet ideal'.[18] This notion of the ideal is Faucit's key justification as a performer, but is not one articulated in the same terms by Kemble who refuses to espouse the social functionality of the performer which Faucit relies upon. In the introduction to her book, Faucit positions herself as a mediating agent placed between the 'sister-women' of her time and Shakespeare, and suggests that her primary interest in doing so lies in enhancing the love and understanding of the former for the playwright. She writes:

My best reward would be, that my sister-women should give me, in return, the happiness of thinking that I have helped them, if ever so little, to appreciate more deeply, and to love with a love akin to my own, these sweet and noble representatives of our sex, and have led them to acknowledge with myself the infinite debt we owe to the poet who could portray, as no other poet has so fully done, under the most varied forms, all that gives to woman her brightest charm, her most beneficent influence. (Faucit, pp. viii–ix)

In the letters which follow, Faucit's primary means of achieving this end is to position herself as one essentially formed, as we have seen, by Shakespeare, and thus as exemplifying the benefits he can confer on Victorian women. Faucit creates herself, and is seen, despite and because of her professional identity, as a Shakespearean heroine, but one who is also thus a most exemplary Victorian woman. In the carefully constructed narratives of her life, the terms 'Victorian' and 'Shakespearean' are synonymous; they translate each other in Faucit's lexicon of idealized femininity.

Faucit's relationship with Shakespeare is facilitated through her imagination, and through as close an identification as possible with Shakespeare's women. As she writes at the end of her letter on Ophelia, 'I tried to give not only [Shakespeare's] words, but, by a sympathetic interpretation, his deeper meaning – a meaning to be apprehended only by that sympathy which arises in, and is the imagination of, the heart' (p. 20). Faucit does not share the fascination of Anna Jameson – a friend and admirer of Kemble – with the sheer variety of Shakespeare's heroines – indeed her examples are carefully selected – but is attracted rather by the ways in which they seem to her to be able to articulate either her own predicament, or her youthful sense of a feminine ideal. In Faucit's usage, and in that of her critics and reviewers, the term 'imagination' would be used to signal not an intellectual effort of affiliation with the unfamiliar, but rather a form of instinctive identification with what is already either known or desired.

There is something in this, of course, of Kemble's description of losing herself in the part of Juliet, a similar surrender of the self to the part, but in Faucit's case, that self is strategically surrendered for a specific end, and is notionally lost only to be found again in the part. Kemble loses herself to Shakespeare, and to the flights of imagination which take her out of herself. Faucit rather finds her self and her age in Shakespeare, rendering him fundamentally Victorian in her efforts to use his women to 'put in living form before her audiences the types of noble womanly nature as they had been revealed by our best dramatic poets, and especially by Shakespeare' (Martin, p. 166). Faucit was, as Martin writes, 'in herself a "Shakespeare-lady" to many in her social life, as well as upon the stage' (p. 105). There is something essential in this relationship, something mutually life-conferring which is based on, and facilitated by, both the reverence in which Shakespeare and his female characters were held and by the particular form of theatrical aesthetic that Faucit was adopting. Her very choice of the characters about whom she wrote is significant in signalling the approach she took to Shakespeare, and the ways in which she set about writing her own story alongside her tribute to the playwright. Ophelia, Portia, Desdemona, Juliet, Imogen, Rosalind and Beatrice are, without exception, in Faucit's hands, rendered exemplary women who are capable of rousing an audience to that height of moral appreciation which was the end of Faucit's art. Her art was to be a potent influence for good in her audience, and Shakespeare provided the best means of achieving that end: but for her, as Martin observed, audiences 'would never have known the impulses of elevating thought and feeling, which a woman of lofty nature can arouse, by the living commentary of voice and look and movement, in the impersonation of ideal characters upon the stage' (p. 231). Faucit is thus elevated by enabling newly idealised versions of Shakespeare's women to be staged.

Faucit's own conception of her function is indicated in a characteristically fulsome tribute to the recipient of her letter on Beatrice, John Ruskin. In the opening comments of her letter on Beatrice, she writes of how Ruskin had used Shakespeare's heroines 'to illustrate the part women have played, and are meant to play, in bringing sweetness and comfort, and help and moral strength, into man's troubled and perplexing life' (Faucit, p. 291). These words are of course far more appropriate to Ruskin's project in texts such as *Sesame and Lilies* than they could possibly be to Beatrice, whose function is, Anna Jameson notes, that of a 'character of the intellect' rather than of the emotions. Faucit goes on to compare Beatrice unfavourably with Rosalind: '[Beatrice's] character is not to me so engaging. We might hope to meet in life something to remind us of Beatrice; but in our dreams of fair women Rosalind stands out alone' (p. 292). Most transparently, she writes of Rosalind that 'in impersonating [her], I was able to give full expression to what was best in myself as well as in my art' (p. 238). In the intensity of this process of identification, Faucit thus makes of Shakespeare's women Victorian heroines, and renders his timeless ideal real in the Victorian arena.

There might seem initially to be a potential contradiction in Faucit's own espousing of a self-professed ideal status in her extensive writings on Shakespeare's women, and in her own approximation to their outstanding virtues, of which modesty is an important component. However, Faucit avoids this problem by insisting on the 'naturalness' of what she is doing, the lack of an artificial layer of consciousness between herself and her characters. Faucit reports the advice of an older actor, a Mr Elton, that she must stop thinking of herself and her shortcomings, lest she 'should spoil [her] style, the charm of which was [her] self-forgetfulness and power of identifying [herself] with the character [she] was acting' (p. 51). This self-forgetful identification is the keynote of Faucit's performances, and that which enables her to be found most natural when she is identifying most successfully with those characters who were especially favoured by her Victorian audiences.

The rhetoric of the natural is inevitably an ideologically significant one, telling more perhaps of expectations satisfied than of what is actually to be seen in a performance, and it dominates those critical responses to Faucit which are painstakingly recorded by her biographer and husband. Martin often invoked his wife's 'natural' acting in order to counter the popularity, and what he saw as the highly trained acting style and moral improprieties, of the French stage. He describes how the 'natural' actor will first approach a part with the two elements of patience and conscience which enable interpretation, and ensure that 'no personal considerations' can interfere with the actor's interpretation of 'the author's purpose'. He goes on: 'It is only when so prepared, that the actor will be free .... without losing his hold of nature, [to] surround with a halo of ideality what will otherwise not rise above the level of the commonplace. Truth to nature is the basis of all good acting' (Martin, p. 337).

The location of the natural, the means of its discrimination, is often seen to reside in the wisdom and authority of Shakespeare. Martin describes Faucit as being 'true both to Shakespeare and nature' (p. 276), in such a way as to collapse the gap between the two. Faucit herself writes in her diary, 'How ever fresh and new, like nature herself, are these exquisite women of Shakespeare!' (5 October 1869; quoted in Martin, p. 302), and in her study notes of Portia that she seemed to the actress to be a 'perfect piece of Nature's handiwork' (pp. 25–6). This conjunction, then, of the specially favoured actress, the playwright and nature seems to have been almost impervious to criticism. Indeed, criticism seems scarcely to have been allowed space within the Faucit–Martin ambit. As Carol Jones Carlisle records, the drama critic G. H. Lewes gave a slightly mixed review to Faucit's revival of Rosalind in March 1865, noting that her performance was 'freckled occasionally' by over elaboration in detail and occasional slowing of the tempo, but tempering his response by suggesting that overall her performance was like 'a diamond with many facets, remarkable for the variety and delicacy of its effects'.[19] After this muted response, Lewes and George Eliot experienced a cooling in their otherwise friendly relations with the Martins: 'The Martins, as I feared, are disgusted with my notice of Rosalind. She is so accustomed to be smeared with fulsome undiscriminating praise that criticism is an offence.'[20] The couples were subsequently reconciled, but the incident shows not only how precious and protective the Martins were about Faucit's renown, but also how universally favourable were the usual responses to her work.

The benefits to Faucit of her part in the relationship with Shakespeare are evident and indisputable. Despite appearing in the works of other highly reputable and popular playwrights, it was as a Shakespearean actress that she was principally known for the entirety of her career, which stretched from 1836 to her benefit performance of Rosalind in Manchester in 1879. The benefits to Shakespeare and to his plays of this relationship are evident in critics' recognition of the ways in which Faucit bases her interpretation of her parts on her direct study of Shakespeare's texts, rather than on her understanding of a corrupted stage tradition. Martin writes that Faucit 'took her inspiration direct from the text of the poet' (Martin, p. 40), and that in the case of Rosalind, her depiction was 'of the Rosalind whom Shakespeare drew', rather than the character of 'hoydenish vivacity' (p. 65) to whom audiences were more accustomed. In contrast to Hazlitt, the Victorian critic George Fletcher maintained that it was only on the stage that 'current misconceptions regarding Shakespeare' could be rectified, and only by such an artist as Faucit.[21] To this end, he hopes that Helen Faucit may find 'in our metropolis, a stage and a manager equally capable and willing with herself, to return to Shakespeare, to nature, and to everlasting truth' (Fletcher, p. 198).

Faucit had of course previously enjoyed such a relationship with William Macready, with whom she worked at Covent Garden and Drury Lane in the 1830s and 1840s, and made an important tour to Paris in 1844–5. Macready was responsible for popularising the effort to restore Shakespearean acting texts to the Victorian stage, editing Shakespeare rather than relying solely on the bastardised versions of the plays by Cibber and Davenent which had long dominated the theatre. In 1838, he enabled the 'return to the stage of a wholly Shakespearian *Lear* – if not of the whole of Shakespeare's Lear', as Stanley Wells puts it.[22] Macready and Faucit's relationship was intense and increasingly difficult for both of them, as the young Faucit developed a serious infatuation for her married and much older co-star. He handled her ardour with tact and gentle forbearance, but was less forgiving of her growing popularity on stage. Initially unimpressed when he saw her as Julia in Sheridan Knowles's *The Hunchback* in 1836 – he thought she had 'force and some intelligence, but no elegance, little real abandonment, and little true pathos – occasionally violent, flurried, larmoyante, and almost always stagey'[23] – Macready nonetheless took her on as his leading lady, but, as his journals reluctantly record, he gradually saw her reputation and popularity increase, to the extent that they threatened to eclipse his own.

His exasperation pours out most vituperatively when he hears of Faucit's desiring to become known professionally by the far more Shakespearean name of Helena. On being asked for an autograph, he found:

The leaf marked for me contained Miss H. Faucit's name, with the signature of Helena Faucit. A feather shows the direction of the wind. The conceit and affectation attributed to her is put beyond doubt in my mind by this little instance. I am greatly mistaken in my reasoning (which very likely I am) if real talent of any very high grade can co-exist with such want of truth and genuineness. (Macready, pp. 240–1)

He had effectively been outmanoeuvred by someone who was nothing if not a supreme strategist, but most infuriatingly, she had taken some of Macready's own less self-aggrandising strategies and turned them to even greater effect in her own hands. Specifically, the possibilities of 'authenticity' and respect for the text that Macready initiated in the nineteenth-century theatre had always to be mediated through the possibilities acceptable to a Victorian audience. And Shakespeare was most congenial to the extent that he seemed to enamour audiences of Faucit's palpable version of femininity. Macready's textual restoration laid the grounds for Faucit's success, but it was she who fully realised the strategic importance of the authenticity that Macready sought, and who capitalised upon it to best effect, both for her and for Shakespeare.

It is perhaps no surprise that Faucit's two most popular parts were Rosalind and Juliet. Of the former she writes that 'in impersonating [her] I was able to give full expression to what was best in myself as well as in my art' (Faucit, p. 238), but she reserves her closest identification for the part of Juliet, which, she writes, 'seems inwoven with my life' (p. 85). The aesthetic of sympathetic femininity, though it served Faucit well, is of course replete with limitations for the Shakespearean stage and its audiences, as becomes clear when we consider Faucit's responses to her two most frequently acted Shakespearean roles, Rosalind and Lady Macbeth. In many respects these roles are diametrically opposed: Rosalind is, as Faucit notes, 'evermore tatt-ling', whereas Lady Macbeth is 'ominously terse' (quoted in Martin, pp. 319, 161); the former, in Faucit's hands, became an idealized heroine, in her words, 'dear and fascinating', full of 'grace and dignity' (Faucit, pp. 238, 239), whom she always delighted in acting, whereas of the latter she writes: 'To the last time of my performing the character I retained my dread of it' (p. 223).

Faucit gave a private reading in 1879, when the planned rendition of parts of *Romeo and Juliet* and *As You Like It* was supplemented at the audience's request by the sleepwalking scene from Macbeth. We have accounts of that evening given in two letters to Faucit, from Dorothea Baird Smith and Jane Lushington. Baird Smith writes that she and her sister had never 'seen anything so overwhelming in its terrific majesty and pathos as the Lady Macbeth. The Rosalind and Juliet were all of the perfect loveliness we remembered them, but her Lady Macbeth leaves me without words to express the deep sense of awful grandeur, pity, and terror with which it impressed me' (Martin, pp. 357–8). In similar vein Lushington writes to thank Faucit for 'one of the greatest pleasures I have ever had. The graceful sweetness of Rosalind – dear Rosalind – made me really love her so … and Lady Macbeth has left me awed and trembling with an almost painful pleasure that I can not put into words' (p. 358). In some respects, the two parts seem almost to produce each other in the minds of her audiences, and indeed in Faucit's own writings. She does not give a whole letter over to Lady Macbeth, but the fullest account of that role appears as a preliminary to her letter on Rosalind.[24] The connection between the two characters seems to be closer than a simple opposition would suggest.

The more one reads of responses to both her Rosalind and her Lady Macbeth, the more one notices the extent to which there is a continuity in critical language and in the paradigms extracted from Faucit's appearances. Her readings might have stirred her listeners to a sense of Faucit's range on a single evening, but accounts of her theatrical rendering of the two parts suggest rather that her performances risked collapsing her parts into the homogenising aesthetic of her exemplary femininity. In some measure, the lasting success of Faucit's influence on perceptions of *As You Like It* seems to be that she had gone some way to erasing from critics' and audiences' minds the earlier tradition of playing Rosalind as a boisterous, hoydenish figure. As Charles H. Shattuck suggests, it was Faucit who definitively effected Rosalind's transition from a merrily comic breeches part to a type of exemplary femininity.[25] The opportunities in the role which made it attractive to the popular burlesque actress Madam Vestris were explicitly repudiated by Faucit who, when playing Imogen, had quarrelled with Macready over his expectation that she would wear revealing tights when she had to appear as a young boy (Faucit, p. 162). In her hands, according to Martin, Rosalind became a new part, as her audiences realised: 'she showed them a Rosalind – Shakespeare's very own – which all their reading had never led them even to surmise … she *discovered* Rosalind' (p. 16). The Rosalind who was 'so dear to [Faucit's] imagination' becomes, in a female friend's words, 'so pure, so innocent, so earnest, so noble!' (Martin, p. 248).

Such responses are generated by Faucit's reading of the role as one in which Rosalind's femininity is inescapably present to the audience, even when she is dressed as Ganymede. She held it to be necessary that she should 'preserve a refinement of tone and manner suitable to a woman of Rosalind's high station and cultured intellect' (p. 264). The woman is never forgotten in the guise of the boy, and that not in order that greater comic effects might be enjoyed, but rather that the essence of her femininity might be seen to permeate even the rustic boy's disguise. In many ways this makes for a rather serious reading of the play, and one which emphasises the differences of masculinity and femininity rather than their liminality. Juliet Dusinberre suggests that, in Arden, 'Theatrical disguise robs courtship of the artificial exaggeration of masculine and feminine difference sustained in the skirmishes between Phoebus and Silvius',[26] but such a reading was not available to the spectators of Faucit's Rosalind. Her 'exuberance of sportive raillery' is not celebrated for its own sake, but for the emotion 'palpitating at the speaker's heart' (Faucit, p. 273) which is strong enough to shine even through Ganymede's boyish zest. Recent critics have seen, in the metatheatricality of a disguised Rosalind performing Rosalind, a demonstration of the 'constructed nature' of the feminine rather than its innateness.[27] Faucit's performance insists rather upon the ineluctability of her femininity.[28]

The same function is performed by Faucit's Lady Macbeth in whom critics seemed relieved to find an essential femininity which went some way to explaining, if not quite to justifying, her part in her husband's crimes. In Faucit, audiences felt again that they had found 'the true Lady Macbeth', a 'natural character, a generous woman, depraved by her very self-devotion to the ambitious purpose of a merely selfish man', a character who had been produced by Faucit's 'own womanly instinct thoughtfully working upon the lucid indications of the poet' (George Fletcher, quoted in Martin, p. 228). Womanliness is the key-note of Faucit's appearance, and it is especially felt in the banquet and sleepwalking scenes, where her displays of wifely tenderness, and of chilling remorse and despair, may be seen to best effect. Fletcher suggests that recent critical readings of the part accord with Faucit's understanding of it, but that it takes a woman of her kind to exemplify, and definitively to establish, a new reading, unhampered by the 'traditional perversions' of the stage. A later critic compared Faucit's rendering of the role with that of 'Mrs Siddons's massive and sculptured genius', and finds in comparison that Faucit's was an 'essentially human, and even womanly representation of Lady Macbeth' (quoted in Martin, p. 312). The complexities of Shakespeare's part are scarcely discernible in the satisfaction with which the critics welcome Faucit's simply feminine, even rather pitiable, Lady Macbeth.

The Victorian critics, as so many critics both before and since, are
concerned to emphasise that they have found the true Shakespeare, that
something of the dramatist's essence has been uniquely revealed to their
enlightened perceptions. Helen Faucit was crucial in effecting this privileged relationship with Shakespeare, the primary vehicle of which was her
femininity. It is this aspect of her work and reputation which forges the
link between Victorian audiences and Shakespeare. Again, it is this femininity which becomes the medium which enables Shakespeare's translation
into an important Victorian playwright, and contributes considerably to
Shakespeare's official confirmation at the end of the century as England's
national poet, complete with his own Memorial Theatre in Stratford. Faucit
played the leading role in the production of *Much Ado About Nothing* with
which the theatre opened in 1879. Thus, far from always being the vehicle of
an actress's memory and repute, the playwright may sometimes be beholden
to his female translators for his own standing, even for his survival in the
theatre. The acceptability and desirability of his female performers helped
enable Shakespeare's transition from the Romantic page to the Victorian
stage.

The transaction between Faucit and Shakespeare ensured, for her, financial security, a professional life which appears to have been genuinely
sustaining and fulfilling, the adoration of generations of theatregoers, and
an entrance into spheres of society not usually visited by theatre professionals. More importantly perhaps, Shakespeare's plays, as employed by her
and her reviewers, enabled the synonymity, in her and in responses to her,
of the artist and the woman. As Martin, ever her greatest champion, writes,
'The artist reacted on the woman and the woman on the artist' (Martin,
p. 405). Only in Shakespeare could such a symbiosis be envisaged at that
time, and arguably only in the Shakespeare of Helen Faucit.

There is then both in Faucit's acting and in her later writings, produced
after she had left the professional theatre, a profound symbiosis between
herself and Shakespeare, a symbiosis which takes effect not only theatrically,
but also culturally and socially, as we have seen. In her writings, she draws
on that unimpeachable authority which she herself had done so much to
confer, and uses it to enable the telling of her career, her private life and
social standing, to claim for herself a considerable authority as a commentator on the stage, and to give readings of her own performances. She makes
claims for her autonomy, independence and critical self-awareness as an
artist, which might otherwise have been overlooked. Whilst adopting the
rhetoric of the day in noting her capacity for losing herself in her part, for
achieving a complete identification with her role and thus seeming to

relinquish agency to the playwright, in fact Faucit finds not only herself in Shakespeare, but also the means of claiming textual and cultural authority which finally suggests that her writing is a measure of her own success rather than Shakespeare's. In that writing, she makes both herself and Shakespeare celebrities for a modern age.

Her private readings too, at least in the account she gives of them in her book, and specifically her quotations of the more laudatory members of her audiences, also work to promote her own celebrity specifically by further eliding the possibility of a gap between Faucit and the heroines who had become her own during the century. The readings' location – in her and her friends' homes – in spaces which were both domestic and semi-public, serve only to highlight the mutual identification of the actress, the Victorian wife and Shakespeare. The specific interpretation of the readings that I've been outlining is further confirmed for me by comparing them with those given by Fanny Kemble in her celebrated career as a reader of Shakespeare from the late 1840s onwards. One might have expected that Kemble and Faucit would have spent the nineteenth century in a state of rivalry, and indeed their performances were compared – inevitably – by some critics. However, that their status as rival queens was not more pronounced was because in 1834 Kemble departed from the professional stage in order to marry Pierce Butler, a wealthy landed Southerner whom she had met during her first tour of the States. As is fairly well known, the marriage was profoundly unhappy, as Fanny discovered the incompatibilities inherent in being married to a slave owner. Inevitably, perhaps, Kemble's life on the Butler plantation, memorably recorded in her *Georgian Plantation* journal, invokes critical attention to *The Tempest* again, for instance in Alison Booth's description of Kemble's new life as 'a sort of negative pastoral or disenchanted Prospero's island, in which the workers are brutalised, the country house is a worn cabin, the master is a licentious monster, and the mistress herself a gothic captive'.[29] The attention to the play is authorised in part by Kemble herself, who writes of her attempts to induce the slaves to pay more attention to personal hygiene by rewarding them to do so: 'I have ingeniously contrived to introduce bribery, corruption, and pauperism, all in a breath, upon this island, which, until my advent, was as innocent of these pollutions, I suppose, as Prospero's isle of refuge' (*Georgian Plantation* journal, p. 77; quoted in Booth, p. 239). Kemble seems hesitantly, ironically, to liken herself to Prospero, though in fact her financial and political powerlessness must have echoed rather the dilemma of Miranda, or even of the Caliban-like slaves themselves, with whose position of entering into a forced relation with work some critics have likened Kemble's experience of being chained to the stage.

However, Kemble's life on the plantation was relatively short-lived as she spent increasing amounts of time in Britain throughout the 1840s, finally leaving Butler – and her daughters – in 1847. She returned briefly to the stage in that decade; however, it is in her subsequent career as a reader that she was most financially successful, and it is that in which I am most interested. Known since her divorce as Mrs Fanny Kemble, the erstwhile actress is now in a position poised between being her father's chosen successor and a kind of wife to the man who arguably, Prospero-like, had dominated her imagination. While Faucit left the theatre to read and write about strategically chosen Shakespearean heroines, Kemble was reading all the roles from an unprecedentedly broad repertoire of plays. Fanny's practice as a reader is absolutely at odds with the self-glorification that Faucit achieves through her strategic manipulation of Shakespeare. Still profoundly anti-theatrical, Kemble's staging of her readings speaks to a desire to proselytise rather than straightforwardly advertise or promote – the marketing implications of these terms are of course telling. She took up her father's repertoire of sixteen of Shakespeare's most widely performed plays (minus *Cymbeline*), and added to them nine more to give her the broadest repertoire of any reader at the time.

However, the public taste for 'dramatic entertainment', and her own need for financial success, clashed with her desire to concentrate on 'literary instruction'. She maintained her integrity as far as possible by insisting, to her manager's despair, on performing her broad repertory, despite audiences' marked preferences for certain plays – most notably, *Macbeth*, *Hamlet*, *Romeo and Juliet*, *The Merchant of Venice* and *A Midsummer Night's Dream*. To extend her readings was necessary, she suggested, for her not to become hackneyed, but also 'for my own "soul's sake" and not to debase my work more than was inevitable, to the very considerable detriment of my gains' (pp. 632–4). She concludes this account of balancing the variety of her needs thus: 'My great reward has been, passing a large portion of my life in familiar intercourse with that greatest and best English mind and heart, and living almost daily in that world above the world, into which he lifted me' (pp. 632–4).

The language might almost be Faucit's, but only almost. Kemble does not go beyond that mode of exaltation to suggest that she is herself in any way responsible for exalting her audience except insofar as she is a medium for Shakespeare. The means of self-exaltation open to Faucit are of course denied to Kemble, as she reads all the plays' parts and not just those of the heroines. Her virtuosity stunned her audiences, who reacted particularly enthusiastically to her Hamlet, which Longfellow described as having been 'sublimely read; with the only true comprehension and expression of the melancholy Dane I have ever had the good fortune to hear' (quoted in Kahan, p. 87). He would later commemorate his evenings spent listening to Kemble, those 'precious evenings all too swiftly sped', in a sonnet which concludes with an address to Shakespeare: 'O happy Poet! by no critic vext! / How must thy listening spirit now rejoice / To be interpreted by such a voice!' As Anne Thackeray Ritchie would later recall, it was not so much Kemble that one recalled, but the transformative impact she engendered:

Suddenly, as if by a miracle, the little room seemed transformed; there were the actors, no, not even actors; there stood Rosalind and Celia themselves, there stood Jacques, there was Orlando. One spoke and then another, Rosalind pleading, the stern Duke unrelenting; then somehow we were carried to the forest with its depths and its delightful company. It all lasted but a few moments, and there was Mrs Kemble sitting in her chair in her usual corner; and yet I cannot to this day realise that the whole beautiful mirage did not sweep through the room, with colour and light and emotion, and the rustling of the trees, and the glittering of embroidered draperies.[30]

Ritchie records her father's wonder at Kemble's so completely forgetting herself in her reading – 'how she flings herself into it all' (p. 78) – before concluding that 'Mrs Kemble possessed to a rare degree the gift of ennobling that to which she turned her mind … that touch which makes others feel akin to qualities greater than any they are conscious of in themselves, was, I think, the virtue by which she brought us all into subjection' (p. 92).

When Kemble retired from reading, it was to return to her first love of writing, as she put together her volumes of autobiography, and wrote poetry and fiction, producing her first novel at the age of eighty. Lacking the marital and financial security of Faucit, Kemble was perhaps compelled to try new fields of work, but that level of activity also speaks to James's sense that 'The great thing was that from the first she had abundantly lived' (James, *Essays*, p. 90). That abundance belies the lapidariness of Faucit's memory, and rather spills over profusely into the adulatory poems on Shakespeare which Kemble published in 1883, and pours through her volumes of autobiography. There is a dissipation of self perhaps in these texts, rather than the concentration that Faucit achieved, but Kemble's tribute to Shakespeare is all the more eloquent in its testament to a life lived through the variety of Shakespeare. In one of her poems, she writes almost blasphemously of the needs he can fulfil:

> Shelter and succour such as common men
> Afford the weaker partners of their fate,
> Have I derived from thee – from thee, most great
> And powerful genius! whose sublime control,

Still from thy grave governs each human soul,
That reads the wondrous records of thy pen.
From sordid sorrows thou hast set me free,
And turned from want's grim ways my tottering feet,
And to sad empty hours, given royally,
A labour, than all leisure far more sweet:
The daily bread, for which we humbly pray,
Thou gavest me as if I were thy child,
And still with converse noble, wise, and mild,
Charmed from despair my sinking soul away.[31]

It is a life which rejects the theatrical which had been forced on her, and which returns at last to the pages she had longed to write as a child. In death, she also effects a return to that family with which her love of Shakespeare was intimately entwined, as she was buried in Kensal Green cemetery next to her father, the person through whom she found Shakespeare.

Helen Faucit was buried in Brompton Cemetery in 1898. On the tombstone commemorating his wife, Sir Theodore Martin had inscribed Leontes' description of Hermione: 'The sweet'st companion, that e'er man / Bred his hopes out of' (*The Winter's Tale*, V.i.11–12). In their new setting, the lines are peculiarly poignant: unlike Leontes, Sir Theodore will witness no miraculous rebirth, except possibly in a Christian sense, and will experience no forgiveness for the failures and shortcomings which Leontes' words tacitly acknowledge. Whilst speaking of a present loss, the lines also work to recollect the past of a woman whose life was bound up in Shakespeare's words, an actress known pre-eminently for her work in Shakespearean roles, and whose husband, appropriately enough, fell in love with her as Rosalind in Edinburgh in 1844. But her relationship with Shakespeare pre-dates her entry onto the professional stage and her relationship with the gallery of spectators who would celebrate her Shakespearean interpretations. She recollects of her childhood that 'I had lived again and again through the whole childhood and lives of many of Shakespeare's heroines long before it was my happy privilege to impersonate them and make them, in my fashion, my own' (Faucit, p. 6). If Sir Theodore bred his hopes out of Faucit, she bred her hopes – and herself – out of Shakespeare.

In 1893, Henry James paid his tribute to the recently dead Fanny Kemble, writing of her:

She was so saturated with Shakespeare that she had made him, as it were, the air she lived in, an air that stirred with his words whenever she herself was moved, whenever she was agitated or impressed, reminded or challenged. He was indeed her utterance, the language she spoke when she spoke most from herself. He had said the things that she would have wished most to say, and it was her greatest happiness, I think, that she could always make him her obeisance by the same borrowed words that expressed her emotion. (p. 98)

It's instructive to compare this tribute with the one on Faucit's tombstone. They are of course different in mode, the one a funerary monument, the other a long, considered obituary, but their emphases are different too: the one speaks of silence, the other of utterance; one of the woman as inspiration, the other of the inspired woman; one of a poignant recollection which subsumes Shakespeare within its elegiac mode, the other of a vitality which is perpetual and mutual. As such they appropriately articulate not just memories and the terms of future recollection, but two distinct and exclusive ways in which Shakespeare might be experienced by Victorian women.

These discrete experiences are determined, for Faucit and Kemble, as for other Victorian girls of whom we have read, by the circumstances of their first connections with the playwright. Kemble's relationship with Shakespeare first took shape, as we have seen, through a non-verbal image, the painting of Prospero and Miranda. It operates within the field of the semiotic order, experienced before Shakespeare was known to her linguistically. It originates in a space of pre-social structures, in a pre-utilitarian space, beyond the structured history of which the occasion would later become redolent. Within this scene of course is the figure of the father, traditionally signifier and representative of the symbolic order, but in this instance, and in Kemble's later accounts of her father, he occupies a realm distinct from that range of traditionally patriarchal systems, residing instead in a space which, defensively perhaps, Fanny tries to construct for him and which is explicitly beyond historically progressing time, in a realm ordered through altogether other precepts. There is in Kemble's account of their relationship a lack of competition and liberating antagonism, which arguably leads her to a lifetime of remaining Fanny Kemble, never quite leaving behind the space of the child, and of finding the connective tissue which keeps her in that space, and in close communion with her father, through Shakespeare. This triangular relationship is ideally removed from the world of the symbolic, of ideological apparatuses, in which Shakespeare and the theatre might be employed as regulating structures. Rather Shakespeare is simply fundamental – as James suggests, the air she breathes. Ironically, this total immersion in Shakespeare might make Kemble seem rather dated: Henry Irving would mock the ageing actress's 'fierce and sectional enunciation' to Ellen Terry in terms which effectively consigned her to a bygone era.[32] But in fact, Shakespeare was for

Kemble timeless, as her poem suggests, by simply being out of time, before a symbolic time erupts into her consciousness. It is a form of timelessness which, in her account, perpetually reiterates its first moment, and which constantly alludes to the significance of Shakespeare as reiterative of the terms of its first being known. Kemble's Shakespeare career, closely enmeshed with that of her father, re-lives the terms of her childhood introduction to the playwright.

Helen Faucit rather comes to Shakespeare, in her own account, through reading, when Shakespeare has necessarily already taken a place within a signifying system based in and guaranteed by the language of the symbolic, here manifested in the explicitly literary frame of reference which inspires Faucit's developing persona. Shakespeare is consciously invoked to found a family unit for Faucit, to guarantee her place within a signifying system which she explicitly bases in Shakespeare's ideological function. He is for her then necessarily of her historical moment, bound within, even as he shores up, its ideological apparatuses. Faucit invokes Shakespeare in ways entirely distinct from Kemble's: her application of Shakespeare's timelessness in fact enacts a translation of Shakespeare's voice for the Victorian period which interprets and shapes his writing by filtering it through modern concepts. By using herself as both the medium and the meaning of the translation, Faucit updates Shakespeare and the latter is enabled to address contemporary concerns. By contrast, Kemble's perception of the timeless exempts Shakespeare from the conditioning climate of the nineteenth century, and instead subjects the times to him.

CHAPTER 4

George Eliot and Shakespeare: defamiliarising 'second nature'

Like Barrett Browning's, George Eliot's relationship with Shakespeare was an enduring one, which was manifested throughout both her correspondence and her professional works, and which informed and helped to shape her relationship with G. H. Lewes. It was also one repeatedly articulated by others. The coupling of the names of George Eliot and Shakespeare became a familiar critical trope which was initiated in 1859, when Theodore Martin described the 'views of life and character' in *Adam Bede*, whose authorship was at that time unknown to him, as being 'Shakespearian in their breadth of sympathy'.[1] It was a practice which continued in later reviews which saw in Eliot's last hero, Daniel Deronda, significant echoes of Hamlet.[2] Henry James's review of the novel acknowledges the extent of this tendency by parodying it:

THEODORA: [The Meyricks] are a delicious family; I wish they lived in Boston. I consider Herr Klesmer almost Shakespearean, and his wife is almost as good. ... if they say nothing to your own imagination the fault is yours, not theirs.

PULCHERIA: Pray don't say they are Shakespearean again. Shakespeare went to work another way.[3]

In 1873, John Fiske wrote to his wife: 'I call [George Eliot and George Henry Lewes] a wonderful couple. Spencer thinks she is the greatest woman that has ever lived on the earth – the female Shakespeare, so to speak; and I imagine he is not *far* from right'.[4] It is unclear from this letter whether it was Fiske or Herbert Spencer who took responsibility for the translation of Eliot into 'the female Shakespeare', but it is notable that she is not, like Barrett Browning, a daughter of the dramatist, but his Victorian equivalent.

In later criticism and obituaries of the novelist, which strive to produce the sage-like figure that was part of Eliot's initial posthumous reputation (and was designed to lay the scandal of her past to rest), Shakespeare figures almost inevitably as part of that canonisation process. Alexander Main claimed in his preface to *Wise, Witty and Tender Sayings in Prose and Verse, selected from the Works of George Eliot* (1872) that 'what Shakespeare did for the Drama, George Eliot has been, and still is, doing for the Novel',[5] and in such moments the novel comes of age as a form of art, as not only Eliot herself but her genre too benefit from the stature and legitimacy jointly conferred by the reference to Shakespeare. Oscar Browning mentions in answer to a silently understood question, that '"Middlemarch" gives George Eliot the chiefest claim to stand by the side of Shakespeare'.[6] The grounds of this judgement are not specified as Shakespeare is invoked as a matter of course, with no comment or justification needed. The parallel was not, however, always propitious. In an 1881 memorial article, 'The Moral Influence of George Eliot', Julia Wedgwood invokes Shakespeare to position and define an understanding of moral or didactic fiction, despite her admission that such labels are inappropriate to Shakespeare, since 'To speak of the moral element in Shakespeare would be like speaking of the moral element in life itself', and to look for signs of disapprobation in the writer would be to 'quit the right point of view for judging of Shakespeare'.[7] Nonetheless, the comparison has to be made before Wedgwood can go on to consider the 'large part of [Eliot's] immense popularity which is traceable to the didactic element in her works' (p. 176). The fit attempted here is crude and awkward but seems necessary to Wedgwood's celebratory strategy.

In a way it is a more appropriate memorial and invocation of the links between Eliot and Shakespeare than Wedgwood might have supposed, for Eliot's relationship with Shakespeare is far from the thoroughly symbiotic relationship generated between Barrett Browning and Shakespeare, and appears at times to be fundamentally cautious, even suspicious and rebarbative. She is certainly suspicious of the usefulness of seeing Shakespeare acted on stage, and indeed of theatricality generally, despite the influence of G. H. Lewes, one of the most important theatre critics of his day. Lewes's journal records that 'Polly came home in a fever of excitement' after seeing one of Tommaso Salvini's appearances as Othello in April 1875 (quoted in 3 April 1859; *GE Letters*, VI, 142), but this is a rare moment. More typical is her response to Helen Faucit's 1865 performance of *As You Like It*, which was referred to in the previous chapter. Lewes wrote in his review of 'A great writer, who sat near me during the performance [who] asked with something of triumph, whether this did not satisfy me that it was a great mistake ever to see one of SHAKSPEARE'S plays acted' (*GE Letters*, IV, 186, n. 5). Many more recent critics have responded to the awkwardness of Eliot's take on Shakespeare: John Lyon writes that 'George Eliot's creativity is in large part hostile and negative', and that 'such hostility extends into her

relationship with Shakespeare'.[8] Marianne Novy finds that 'Eliot simultaneously claims and critically transforms Shakespeare' (*Engaging with
Shakespeare*, p. 65), while Adrian Poole is surely right in arguing that Eliot
is 'divided between admiration and suspicion' when she 'calls attention to
the points at which her own plot-lines, story patterns, dramatic figures and
predicaments converge with [Shakespeare's], then asks her reader to reflect
on the likeness and difference between them'.[9] In a variety of ways, these
critics are responding to an influence reluctantly felt, a hierarchy fearfully
encountered though neither perhaps actively recognised nor conceded.
This chapter will be concerned to map the genealogy of Eliot's apparent
difficulties with Shakespeare, and will traverse both public and private
spaces in attempting to define further, to find the root of, her anxieties
about Shakespeare, and, more importantly, about his strategic appropriation in the nineteenth century. For Eliot's own allusions to and quotations
from Shakespeare are very often comments on her contemporaries' burgeoning bardolatry.

The earliest part of the relationship between George Eliot and
Shakespeare was far from sympathetic. As Eliot's letters, essays, poems
and novels indicate, Shakespeare had been a constant presence throughout
her reading life, though her early letters to Maria Lewis, written in the
days of her fervent Evangelicalism, manifest an uneasy consciousness of
the dangers of reading Shakespeare: 'we have need of as nice a power of
distillation as the bee to suck nothing but honey from his pages' (16 March
1839; *GE Letters*, I, 22). A letter written the previous month had tried to
effect an assimilation between the evangelical God and Shakespeare:

I set so high a value on 'the sweet uses of adversity' that I am in danger of failing in
sympathy for those who are experiencing it, and yet the word of God is not more
express on any point than on the inevitable endurance of suffering to the Christian
more peculiarly than to the worldling and on the special blessings derived from that
endurance. (27 February 1839; *GE Letters*, I, 15–16)

The eager over-insistence on the good of suffering belies the gentle cajoling
and sympathy of the Duke's speech in *As You Like It*, I.ii, where he tries to
reconcile his men to their exiled lot, and it demonstrates a form of unde-
veloped reading practice which extracts support for the writer's own religious convictions. A later use of the same phrase from *As You Like It*,
which Marianne Novy and Adrian Poole note is the play most often quoted
by Mary Ann Evans in her early correspondence,[10] shows a much more
sympathetic reading, both of Shakespeare and of suffering, and no longer
feels the need to assert, with the ease of immature conviction, the 'special

blessings' of that state. In the later letter, indeed, the Shakespearean phrase operates as a starting-point for a more expansive sympathy:

I have found already some of the 'sweet uses' that belong only to what is called trouble, which is after all only a deepened gaze into life, like the sight of the darker blue and the thickening of stars when the hazy effect of twilight is gone. (to Sara Hennell, 26 April 1848; *GE Letters*, I, 259)

Rather than ending in an invocation to an Old Testament God, the Shakespearean phrase now sounds out into a poignantly infinite and beautiful universe, and gives the first intimation of the dimensions of what would become a central creed of Eliot's fiction, and especially of *Middlemarch* (1871–2):

That element of tragedy which lies in the very fact of frequency, has not yet wrought itself into the coarse emotion of mankind; and perhaps our frames could hardly bear much of it. If we had a keen vision and feeling of all ordinary human life, it would be like hearing the grass grow and the squirrel's heart beat, and we should die of that roar which lies on the other side of silence.[11]

Through the Shakespearean lines, Eliot begins to recognise the ineluctability of suffering in the 'working day world', another 'favourite little epithet' from *As You Like It*,[12] and rather than allow it to exist as a selfish Evangelical good, makes it instead part of the foundation of the community.

It is perhaps not surprising then, in the light of this favourite phrase, that it is for his more colloquial qualities that Eliot seems most particularly to value Shakespeare. She writes to her friend and French translator Francois D'Albert Durade in 1861 of this literary characteristic:

Balzac, I think, dares to be thoroughly colloquial, in spite of French strait-lacing. Even in English this daring is far from being general. The writers who dare to be thoroughly familiar are Shakspeare, Fielding, Scott (where he is expressing the popular life with which he is familiar), and indeed every other writer of fiction of the first class. Even in his loftiest tragedies – in Hamlet, for example – Shakspeare is intensely colloquial. (29 January 1861; *GE Letters*, III, 374)

In her letters, Shakespeare does indeed become part of her colloquial vocabulary: usually less emotionally intense than EBB's can be, Eliot's use of Shakespeare is less quotation than a seamless, spontaneous conjuring of his words, as in this letter to Cara Bray: 'We are under the care of Dr Andrew Clarke who ministers to all minds diseased by telling them to diminish their allowances of puddings and draughts of tea'.[13]

One of the components in effecting the shift of Shakespeare from morally dubious force to embedded part of Eliot's life was her relationship with the scientist, novelist, playwright and theatre critic G. H. Lewes. One of her earliest meetings with Lewes was at the theatre, when they shared a box at an 1851 production of *The Merry Wives of Windsor*. She records in a letter to Cara Bray that Lewes 'helped to carry off the dolorousness of the play' by his witty remarks.[14] Shakespeare was a conspicuous part of their early life together, and is particularly evident after they had effectively eloped to Germany in July 1854. Once settled in Berlin, they began the practice which would persist throughout their life together of reading to each other in the evening. During those months of early intimacy, Shakespeare was an almost constant presence. Between mid-November 1854 and early February 1855, Lewes and Evans read together, usually with Lewes reading aloud, *Julius Caesar*, *Antony and Cleopatra*, *Henry IV* parts *1* and *2*, *As You Like It*, *Hamlet*, *King Lear*, *The Taming of the Shrew*, *Coriolanus*, *Twelfth Night*, *Measure for Measure*, *A Midsummer Night's Dream*, *The Winter's Tale*, *Richard III* and *The Merchant of Venice*. They also went to see a number of professional Shakespeare productions, which were supplemented by Lewes's acting for their domestic circle as well as by discussions of contemporary criticism of Shakespeare, and a general immersion in the Germans' enthusiasm for the playwright.

In Eliot's 'Recollections of Berlin, 1854–55', written whilst alone in Dover immediately after the couple's return to England, she recalls 'the delightful, long evenings in which we read Shakspeare, Goethe, Heine and Macaulay, with German Pfefferkuchen and Semmels at the end, to complete the "Noctes coeneque deum"'.[15] In that brief stay in Dover, whilst Eliot anxiously awaited the end of Lewes's search for accommodation and the more complex negotiation of the family life which awaited his return, her reading of Shakespeare was even more intensive. In one month, she read *Venus and Adonis*, *Two Gentlemen of Verona*, some of the Sonnets, *The Tempest*, *Macbeth* (twice), *Romeo and Juliet*, *Henry V*, *Henry VIII* and *Henry VI*, *1*, *2* and *3*, and began *Richard II*. Part invocation of the absent Lewes's voice, part continuation of their German reading programme, these Shakespearean evenings helped to initiate an intimate domestic and professional relationship which would persist until Lewes's death in 1878. In her journal for 1 January 1879, Eliot writes, 'Here I and sorrow sit', quoting from *King John*, III.i.73 (*GE Journals*, p. 154). A relationship cemented in a joint love of Shakespeare finds its most appropriate voice of loss in him too.[16]

Their joint relationship with Shakespeare is mapped in most detail through the couple's heavily annotated copy of Nicholas Rowe's 1832 edition of *The Dramatic Works of William Shakespeare*. This shows the couple's lively engagement with former editors and commentators, with each other, and with Shakespeare. The Rowe volume[17] contains a mass of annotations by Lewes and Eliot which sees them comparing textual variants from earlier editors, and considering the views of Coleridge, with whom both find considerable sympathy. They also suggest their own variants and quarrel over the likeliest solutions. Questions are asked, emendations suggested and answers sought, such as in this exchange over Hamlet's final speech in II.ii, where Lewes, writing in ink as he does throughout, has crossed through 'oppression' in 'To make oppression bitter' (II.ii.614), and has suggested 'transgression' in the margin. At the bottom of the page, Eliot has noted, in the pencil that she uses, 'oppression seems just as good as transgression'. It has to be said that in these exchanges she usually has the last word, as she does in the margins of *The Winter's Tale*, IV.ii, when Lewes ventures upon what seems to be a joke at the expense of Eliot's pug dog in a note to Autolycus's song which opens the scene. In his note to 'pugging teeth' (IV.ii.7), Lewes has written 'pugging teeth, i.e. grinding teeth, there is a machine called a pugging or pug which [is] used for crushing hard substances'. Eliot has responded by crossing through the entire note. The text is then a record of their relationship, as much as it is an account of their ongoing engagement with Shakespeare, and is one which was maintained for most of their relationship.

Their interventions are quite distinct. Lewes writes extended notes which draw together editorial comments and literary parallels, while Eliot most often sidelines passages which interest her, and underlines and/or ticks words, usually archaic or colloquial, which are particularly apposite. In a rare headnote, Eliot writes at the top of *Troilus and Cressida* that it is 'Full of antique words and phrases'. She is not, however, above poking fun at the anachronisms and mistakes of the plays, being, for instance, quick to point out the absurdity of the mention of a palm-tree in the Forest of Arden in *As You Like It*, III.ii.187. She also notes and provides cross-references for key terms which recur throughout the plays, such as 'tender', 'remorse', 'ecstasy' and 'secure'.[18] The last provoked a characteristic exchange, begun by Lewes's suggesting that Gloucester's line in IV.i.20 of *King Lear* should read 'Our means secure us' instead of 'Our mean secures us; and our mere defects / Prove our commodities', as Rowe has it. Beneath Lewes's suggestion, Eliot notes 'but perhaps secure means to make careless by leading us to suppose we are secure', and she cites a number of parallels to support her case.[19] This state, made precarious, and characterised, by its oxymoronic qualities, represents a species of psychological tension which she frequently notes in Shakespeare, and which has a variety of aspects and significances: whether conjured by the dreams and magic of *A Midsummer Night's Dream*, where Oberon speaks of 'the fierce vexation of a dream' (IV.i.75), or the evil of which Antonio speaks in *The Merchant of Venice* ('An evil soul producing holy witness, / Is like a villain with a smiling cheek' (I.iii.100–1), or residing inevitably contrarily in human experience, as King Henry suggests in *Henry V*: 'There is some soul of goodness in things evil / Thus we may gather honey from the weed, / And make a moral of the devil himself' (IV.i.4–6; the emphasis is George Eliot's). All these lines are highlighted (by means of marginal sidelines) by Eliot in her text, as are many besides which similarly speak to the complexities which belie an easy categorisation and articulation of experience, and which would increasingly become a trademark of Eliot's own work, and indeed of her uses of Shakespeare in that work. She is responding particularly to what we might now term aspects of defamiliarisation in Shakespeare, to his interest in psychological complexity, and to his skill in harnessing language so adeptly as to produce a new form of knowledge in his readers and audiences.

It is this quality of newness and challenge to which Eliot responds most vibrantly in Shakespeare's work, and it is this too that necessitates her resistance to the easy appropriation of Shakespeare by her contemporaries. This can be demonstrated if we compare Eliot's use of *Coriolanus* in *Felix Holt* (1866) with that of Charlotte Brontë in chapter six of *Shirley* (1849). Infrequently performed in the nineteenth century, the play, or its classical hero, nonetheless had considerable cultural resonance for the Victorians, as witnessed by the number of ships and racehorses named after the Roman hero, and by the way in which, as Marianne Novy demonstrates, he became a figure susceptible of adoption by a variety of politicians of radically differing standpoints (*Engaging with Shakespeare*, p. 70). The tension of the play rests in the even-handedness with which it represents both Coriolanus's pride and his inflammatory disdain of the Roman citizens, his greatness and ardour alongside his democratic blindness. As such it was a play of which Hazlitt wrote that 'Any one who studies it may save himself the trouble of reading Burke's Reflections, or Paine's Rights of Man, or the Debates in both Houses of Parliament since the French Revolution or our own',[20] so profoundly did he see it as articulating some of the fundamental political conditions of the late eighteenth and early nineteenth centuries, a period in which the rise of the mob or multitude was ever more apparent in the agitation for universal suffrage. In I.i, Caius Marcius specifically declaims against the mechanisms of burgeoning democracy in Rome in his assessment of the function of the tribunes:

> Five tribunes to defend their vulgar wisdoms,
> Of their own choice: one's Junius Brutus,
> Sicinius Veletus, and I know not – 'sdeath!
> The rabble should have first unroof'd the city,
> Ere so prevail'd with me; it will in time
> Win upon power, and throw forth greater themes
> For insurrection's arguing.   (I.i.221–7)

He anticipates the terms of the struggle for democracy in Britain, but also unwittingly articulates the more fundamental distrust between classes which generated the generic conflicts underlying the developments of modern society.

Brontë's Caroline Helstone uses the play to attempt to instruct her Coriolanian cousin Robert Moore about his responsibilities to his workers, his own pride, and a form of Englishness which, as Novy suggests, his upbringing in Belgium may not have equipped him to recognise (*Engaging with Shakespeare*, p. 34). In a sleight of hand which would be repeated throughout the century, Shakespeare's Roman hero becomes archetypally English in Brontë's context of a clash between a despairing mob or multitude and the figure of a charismatic and disdainful leader. As we see in Caroline and Robert's conversations, each clearly finds support for their own ideological position in Shakespeare's play, and they thus act out the terms of the play's dilemma. Robert finds a self-justificatory power in Coriolanus's speeches, whereas Caroline seeks to impress upon him the personal dangers of inflexibility and austerity:

Coriolanus in glory; Coriolanus in disaster; Coriolanus banished, followed like giant-shades one after the other. Before the vision of the banished man, Moore's spirit seemed to pause. He stood on the hearth of Aufidius's hall, facing the image of greatness fallen, but greater than ever in that low estate. He saw 'the grim appearance,' the dark face 'bearing command in it,' 'the noble vessel with its tackle torn.' With the revenge of Caius Marcius, Moore perfectly sympathised; he was not scandalised by it; and again Caroline whispered, 'There I see another glimpse of brotherhood in error'.[21]

As Margaret Arnold notes, Brontë takes *Coriolanus* and places it within a familiar Victorian setting: 'She has placed the poverty and class struggle of *Coriolanus* in the industrial world she and her readers understand and has invited them to note the parallels between a young, militant business "hero" and the isolated, proud soldier of Shakespeare's tragedy.'[22] Though Arnold claims that Brontë transforms her source material through investing in the figures of Caroline Helstone and Shirley Keeldar, who 'build mental alternatives to nineteenth-century patriarchal structures' (p. 87), nonetheless, the terms of their dissent are implicit in Shakespeare's own dissection of his flawed hero, that is, the authority of their insight comes from Shakespeare. Brontë's use of her Shakespearean source represents less of a transformation than a simple transference of his dynamics into a modern setting, an allegorisation of the play which acts to naturalise its structural dynamics.

On the face of it, Eliot's use of Coriolanus as one of the inspirations behind her 'radical' Felix Holt, as evidenced in the epigraphs to chapters 27 and 30, is much more curious. Eliot's hero is an artisan demagogue who rejects the possibility of affiliating himself with a higher and more aspirational class, determined as he is to achieve political representation for the working classes. However, Felix shares certain fundamental qualities with Coriolanus. He too is proud and independent, and disdains those whom he would help, fearing the implications of their too ready assimilation into a political process for which they are insufficiently prepared. However, Felix is subject, as Coriolanus is not, to an educative process which takes the motivation of pride and seeks to re-shape its aggressive potency for more socially ameliorative and less exclusive ends. Coriolanus's pride and his exceptional status are the foundations of a fundamental isolation which is his greatest vulnerability, and Eliot's greatest abhorrence, working as it does against the possibility of achieved community. Unlike Coriolanus, Felix can be assimilated back into the social structure he has previously shunned, through the agency of Esther Lyon, an agency which again contrasts markedly with that of Virgilia, her nearest counterpart in *Coriolanus*. Esther acts decisively, not to try to change Felix's mind at a crucial public moment as Virgilia and Volumnia do Coriolanus's, but rather to translate him to his contemporaries, using her sympathy and love in the novel's courtroom scene as cross-class conduits of what she interprets as Felix's misunderstood heroism. In a moment which is theatrical and pictorial, but also profoundly literary, Esther takes the witness stand at Felix's trial and inserts into an event of grave political and criminal considerations her feminine sympathies, which are manifested in an ardour which 'breaks through formulas too rigorously urged on men by daily practical needs ... she is the added impulse that shatters the stiffening crust of cautious experience'.[23]

Esther takes a stance against the formulaic application of legal and capitalist interests, and also, arguably, against her Shakespearean source: Virgilia, who is practically mute, both as wife and mother, is easily cowed by her mother-in-law, and who finds her greatest eloquence in silence. By contrast, Esther is moved to misery by 'the sense that all had not been said which might have been said on behalf of Felix', and is subsequently impelled to speak, thus displaying that feminine 'ardour which has flashed out and illuminated all poetry and history [and which] was burning today in the bosom of sweet Esther Lyon' (p. 447). Esther may have her literary forebears, may indeed have found those forebears in the reading which Felix had earlier denigrated, but they are not to be found in *Coriolanus*. Eliot has taken a skeletal emotional plot from *Coriolanus*, and rewritten it. She has reconceived it for a new fictional form, for a new industrial, capitalist audience, and for an audience of women readers being educated, possibly reluctantly, by Ruskin to find Virgilia 'perhaps [the] loveliest' of Shakespeare's heroines, 'conceived in the highest heroic type of humanity'ᵈ56. *Felix Holt* shows Eliot to be impatient with such a form of over-determination, and indeed with Shakespearean forms of tragic heroism. Her heroes must survive, and must return to the working-day world which John Lyon argues is Eliot's refuge and riposte against Shakespeare's aristocratic settings (Lyon, p. 114). It is within the 'home epic' celebrated by the Finale of *Middlemarch* that heroism is to be resituated; that is, within the domestic, familial and communal. It is a form of heroism that is also profoundly available to, and may indeed be exemplified by, women. The aversion to the exceptional that Gillian Beer noted in Eliot's works[24] is clearly in evidence here, and is activated in the emotional, rather than political, radicalism of Esther which is determined to foster sympathy wherever possible and at whatever cost to herself in terms of her lost inheritance.

Eliot is then both borrowing from, and arguing with, Shakespeare. She disputes the power relations, and gender assumptions, of *Coriolanus*, just as she is inspired by the image of an independent, radical leader of unparalleled integrity. But what she is also doing here, and I believe elsewhere in her references to Shakespeare, is disputing the ways in which Shakespeare was being appropriated by her contemporaries, the ways in which Shakespeare was becoming part of an accustomed vocabulary within a too glib translation. Charlotte Brontë's characters and contemporary politicians might dispute ownership of the play's meanings, but their right to claim that ownership was not at issue. Shakespeare was comfortably being appropriated into Victorian usage, and in that appropriation his historical integrity was being elided. George Eliot is responding as a fellow author to this implicit false idealisation of an earlier colleague, but she is also reacting viscerally to what 'Susan Buck-Morss, paraphrasing Adorno, calls second nature', that is, 'a negating, critical concept which referred to the false mythical appearance of given reality as ahistorical and absolute'.[25] This is to suggest that, as Martin Harries goes on to elaborate, 'Shakespeare may be part of a nearly impermeable second nature' (Harries, p. 4) adopted unthinkingly, automatically, and specifically as part of a constructed form of Englishness whose political resonance rests precisely on its being recognised as a form of 'second nature'. However, as Harries also goes on to suggest, 'Once in a while … that easy order of things goes awry, and Shakespearean language that at other times might fertilize second nature becomes a symptom of faults in its carapace', and may act to 'defamiliarise the supposedly solid structure of second nature' (p. 4). It is this capacity for defamiliarisation that Eliot builds on in her relationship with and adaptation of Shakespeare, a relationship that might seem hostile towards the playwright but which, as I will argue, is more properly seen as disputing his too easy appropriation by her contemporaries. In the rest of this chapter I will show how Eliot effects this through *Middlemarch*, the novel in which we may see her most deliberately engaging in a generic dispute with Shakespeare, and by means of which her version of realism is most fully realised; and through her resistance to a biographical critical approach to the playwright.

Eliot refused to prioritise attempts to read Shakespeare through his biography. She was herself subject to just such impulses, as we can see in Julia Wedgwood's article which is signed by 'One Who Knew Her', and which attests to the personal impact of Eliot herself as being indivisible from that of her works. As Wedgwood writes, 'This attempt at an appreciation of her influence is made by one in whom, to the influence felt by many, was added the enlightening power of such an acquaintance as any of them might have gained, had chance thrown it in their way' (p. 177). In making a point about the lack of exclusivity of Eliot's influence, both personal and fictional, 'the wonderful degree to which she has lighted up the life of commonplace, unheroic humanity' (p. 177), Wedgwood uses the social and personal figure of the novelist as a valid interpretative key to her work, a tendency from which Eliot herself would have demurred, particularly in light of the prurient attention which her figure attracted throughout her working life and in the years immediately following her death. As she wrote in 1879 to Mrs Thomas Trollope, on being asked whether there was a biography of G. H. Lewes:

The best history of a writer is contained in his writings – these are his chief actions. If he happens to have left an autobiography telling (what nobody else can tell) how his mind grew, how it was determined by the joys, sorrows and other influences of childhood and youth – that is a precious contribution to knowledge. But Biographies generally are a disease of English literature. (19 December 1879; *GE Letters*, VII, 230).

She does not suggest that the biographical speculations of others can in any way add to an understanding of the author's work, because for Eliot the only lasting and appropriate memorial for the writer was the work that was left behind.

In contrast with this view is the huge body of Victorian criticism of Shakespeare's works, and in particular his Sonnets, which was little more than a pretext for speculating about the few facts that were known about his life. Hannah Lawrance's review of Gerald Massey's 1866 edition of the Sonnets, *Shakespeare's Sonnets, never before Interpreted; His Private Friends Identified: together with a recovered Likeness of Himself,* is entitled 'Shakespeare in Domestic Life', and trawls both the Sonnets and Massey's work for the answers to question such as 'John Shakespeare – Was he a Roman Catholic?' and 'Was Anne an Unloved Wife?'.[26] The *Westminster Review* believed that

in these sonnets, we see him face to face. We see how the man who portrayed the loves of Romeo and Juliet really loved, – how he, who drew the scepticism of Hamlet, himself also doubted, – how he, who could paint the trials of friend deserted by friend, of Helena forgotten by Hermia, and Lear cast off by his daughters, felt when also deserted and forgotten … The dramas are as it were his monument which we gaze at from afar: these sonnets the miniature which we can hang around our necks, and wear close to our bosom.[27]

The young Helen Taylor's sophisticated recognition in her commonplace book that the Sonnets might be fundamentally dramatic productions was an opinion largely unshared by her contemporaries.[28]

In 1877, Eliot had been invited by Alexander Macmillan to write the life of Shakespeare in John Morley's prestigious series English Men of Letters. She declined (*GE Letters*, VI, 416), perhaps because a large part of Shakespeare's attraction and significance for Eliot was his very impersonality,[29] the extent to which his name could stand metonymically both for the writer and for the body of his work, the way in which that name had itself increasingly become a thing apart from the private man. Constantly and resentfully aware of the biographical speculation which her own work attracted, Eliot was offered in Shakespeare the inspiration of a writer who had undoubtedly achieved literary renown, even a form of literary immortality, despite, or perhaps because of, the paucity of information available about his actual life, and the ways in which he managed to elude biographers.[30] As well as presumably feeling that such a biography would have been fundamentally superfluous, the constructed writerly persona that was 'George Eliot' might have found it hypocritical to seek to disperse an elusiveness in another which she cultivated for herself.

Part of the Sonnets' fascination for putative biographers, and perhaps the licence for their intrusions, is the extent to which the poems are themselves concerned with the ways in which writing both commemorates and confronts the limitations of life, and the way in which writing can be itself immortal, and can confer immortality. Eliot was struck by the poems' preoccupation with, as she put it in a heading from her notebooks, Shakespeare's 'Confidence in his poetic immortality'.[31] In quotations from Sonnets 18, 19, 55, 32 and 81 she traces the efforts of the poet to create monuments in verse to his beloved which also guarantee the perpetuity of his writing:

Confidence in his poetic immortality

18.   'So long as men can breathe or eyes can see,
       So long lives this, and this gives life to thee.'
19   Yet do thy worst, old Time: despite thy wrong,
       My love shall in my verse ever live young.
55   Not marble, nor the gilded monuments
       Of princes, shall outlive this powerful rhyme
       . . . .
       So till this judgment, that yourself arise
       You live in this, & dwell in lovers' eyes.

On the other hand, in S. 31 [32] he depreciates his own verse,

       'These poor rude lines of thy decease'd lover,
       Compare them with the bettering of the time,
       And though they be outstripped by every pen,
       Reserve them for my love, not for their rhyme,
       Exceeded by the height of happier men.'

But in Sonnet 80 [81] the confidence sings more vigorously than before.

       'Your monument shall be my gentle verse
       Which eyes not yet created shall o'wer-read,
       And tongues to your being shall rehearse
       When all the breathers of this world are dead:
           You still shall live – such virtue hath my pen
           Where breath most breathes, even in the mouths of men.

                                             (*Notebooks*, pp. 209–10)

Eliot's reading of the Sonnets, and her notebooks' often quite technical interest in them, are in part accounted for by the sonnet sequence which she herself wrote in 1869, the 'Brother and Sister' sonnets, which she described to John Blackwood as being 'after the Shakspeare type, on the childhood of a brother and sister' (19 April 1874; *GE Letters*, V, 402). Eliot's poems are inspired by her early life, and speak of a time which can best be remembered, revisited, revised in writing, lacking as Eliot did the opportunity to reminisce about it in conversation with her own estranged brother. For Eliot, literary immortality becomes a resource when other forms of commemoration are denied. Eliot's sonnet sequence carries within it the implicit knowledge of a future which failed to fulfil the promise of 'the time / When our two lives grew like two buds that kiss / At lightest thrill from the bee's swinging chime, / Because the one so near the other is' ('Brother and Sister' 1, ll. 1–4). In these poems, written after the passage of 'Long years [that] have left their writing on my brow' ('Brother and Sister' 2, l. 1), the poignancy of the lost childhood is at its greatest, as the lost love of Shakespeare's Sonnets is in the disappointment of the beloved's subsequent disdain. In each case, the passage of time brings personal disappointments made all the greater by their failing to fulfil familiar expectations of affection and generic convention.

Eliot was writing the sonnets against a background which more immediately brought the connections between remembering, childhood, immortality and the sonnet form to a further sharper and more poignant focus. George Eliot and Lewes spent the summer of 1869 in nursing Thornie Lewes on his return from Natal in May. Thornie died from tuberculosis of the spine in October aged 25. In her Journal for 1 August 1869, Eliot records: 'Since last Sunday I have had an uncomfortable week from mental and bodily disturbance. I have finished eleven Sonnets on "Brother and Sister" … Yesterday, sitting in Thornie's room I read through all Shakspeare's Sonnets. *Poor Thornie has had a miserably unsatisfactory week, making no progress*' (*GE Journals*, p. 137. The emphasis is Eliot's own). Eliot's reading of Shakespeare's Sonnets, in the room that was to see Thornie's death in the next few months, gives a more personally conflicted edge to the concerns of the Sonnets with mortality and writing. Thus, as well as acknowledging the questions of professional immortality that the editors of Eliot's *Middlemarch Notebooks* discern in her reading at this period, we need also to be alert to Eliot's situation both as an affectionate and grieving stepmother, and as one who, herself childless, was nursing the child of Agnes and George Henry Lewes. The promises of literary and professional immortality are surely tested almost unbearably in the face of such an untimely and lingering death.

The summer of 1869 also saw the start of *Middlemarch*, which Eliot began to write on 2 August, just two days after immersing herself in the Sonnets. It is a novel concerned throughout with the search for immortality, be it through Casaubon's scholarship, Lydgate's research, Ladislaw's political faith, Dorothea's tributaries of influence, Caleb Garth's desire to put a bit of land in order, or Peter Featherstone's more mischievous plans to ensure his being remembered and his name perpetuated. And fittingly, it is also a novel curiously preoccupied by the sonnet form itself. Eliot's notebooks from this period show her to be ambivalent about Shakespeare's Sonnets in particular. She lists a number as containing fine lines, but notes:

Here are only 24, & some of these one lingers over rather for the music of a few verses in them than for their value as wholes. I am convinced that the greater number of the sonnets are artificial products, governed by the fashion of sentiment which had probably grown out of the imitation of the Italian poets. These 'sugared sonnets among private friends' have owed much of their mysteriousness to the imaginations of writers who set out with the notion that Shakespeare was in all things exceptional, & so never think of comparison with contemporaries even when the occasion is thrust upon them.

She went on to add later: '1872. Nevertheless I love the Sonnets better & better whenever I return to them. They are tunes that for some undefinable reason suit my frame.'[32] Her condemnation of the Sonnets as derivative, artificial, conventional, suggests that, as Otice C. Sircy claims, they are 'not a product of an aesthetic she trusts'.[33] And indeed some of the use that Eliot makes of Shakespeare's Sonnets and the sonnet form more generally in *Middlemarch* confirms that understanding.

Following Casaubon's speech announcing his pleasure at Dorothea's acceptance of him, a speech which tacitly adverts to *King John* in its assertion of woman's 'fitness to round and complete the existence of our own',[34] Eliot writes of its frigid sincerity, but asks, 'Would it not be rash to conclude that there was no passion behind these Sonnets to Delia [by Samuel Daniel, published in 1592] which strike us as the thin music of the mandolin?' (*Middlemarch*, p. 50, ch. 5) There is, she implies, no way of easily translating the conventions of the sixteenth century to the nineteenth; they want a discriminating ear now hard to find. She goes on to write of Casaubon in terms which show him struggling with the sonneteers' legacy as a form of textual authority which he has in his scholarly naivety to respect, but which is fundamentally outdated. In marriage:

he should receive family pleasures and leave behind him that copy of himself which seemed so urgently required of a man – to the sonneteers of the sixteenth century. Times had altered since then, and no sonneteer had insisted on Mr Casaubon's leaving a copy of himself. (p. 278, ch. 29)

With such comments Eliot enters into a direct conversation with the sonnet tradition, challenging it as a model both of expression and emotion, and also tacitly criticising Casaubon's reliance upon the set of assumptions believed to be embodied in the Renaissance sonnet, and his inability to generate a more appropriate language of his own. In Casaubon's case, the baffled resort to the sonnet is part of his blind adherence to a textual tradition rather than a lived experience of emotion.

Different forms of expression are needed for a man like Sir James Chettam, who, disappointed in Dorothea's love, 'had no sonnets to write, and it could not strike him agreeably that he was not an object of preference to the woman whom he had preferred' (p. 61, ch. 6). The blunt commonsense and emotional generosity behind Sir James's denial of the sonnets' tradition of commemorating rejection require a different register, and it is one of the many markers of the difference between Dorothea's first two suitors that they respond so differently to the promises of the sonnet sequence.

The affection of Will Ladislaw for Dorothea, an affection whose evolution is minutely traced from its early over-hasty antipathy to its fruition in a devotion much misunderstood by its witnesses, similarly engages with the sonnet sequence. On one occasion, while Casaubon is still alive:

Will wanted to talk to Dorothea, and was impatient of slow circumstances. However slight the terrestrial intercourse between Dante and Beatrice or Petrarch and Laura, time changes the proportion of things, and in later days it is preferable to have fewer sonnets and more conversation. (p. 361, ch. 37)

In his comments on this passage, Adrian Poole notes that 'Shakespeare does in fact write a sonnet that is a conversation. It is the one he gives to Romeo and Juliet when they first meet, which they seem miraculously to make up together' (Poole, p. 139):

ROMEO: If I profane with my unworthiest hand
          This holy shrine, the gentle sin is this;
          My lips, two blushing pilgrims, ready stand
          To smooth that rough touch with a tender kiss.
JULIET: Good pilgrim, you do wrong your hand too much,
          Which mannerly devotion shows in this;
          For saints have hands that pilgrims' hands do touch,
          And palm to palm is holy palmers' kiss.
ROMEO: Have not saints lips, and holy palmers too?
JULIET: Ay, pilgrim, lips that they must use in prayer.
ROMEO: O! then, dear saint, let lips do what hands do;
          They pray, grant thou, lest faith turn to despair.
JULIET: Saints do not move, though grant for prayers' sake.
ROMEO: Then move not, while my prayers' effect I take.
                                    (*Romeo and Juliet*, I.v.93–106)

Such is not the lot of Will and Dorothea. Eliot explicitly suggests that the sonnet sequence is no longer an appropriate language for lovers, nor for those who would write of love. Her own sequence deals with another form of love, and much of its impact derives from its differing from its Shakespearean prototype. Prompted by the inadequacy of the sonnet, Eliot instead takes the novel in all its potential expansiveness and variety, its ability to suspend different views in delicate, tremulous relationship, to represent and engage in conversation, and substitutes that instead for the sonneteers' outmoded tradition. In particular, the narratorial voice, with its multiple sympathies, its movement in and out of individual characters' registers, allows a play of sympathy which Theodore Martin had described as Shakespearean, but which had surely come by 1870 to be distinctively recognisable as Eliot's own. Rather than being concerned to find their voices within existing forms, Eliot's lovers are being written anew in the realist tradition, and some, perhaps most especially Casaubon, are perplexed to find themselves in such uncharted territory.

'Nevertheless', the final two sentences interpolated above in Eliot's *Middlemarch* notebooks, accord a deeper emotional resonance to Shakespeare's Sonnets than such scepticism about their derivative character would seem to allow, and as *Middlemarch* goes on, we see Eliot using the alien aesthetic of the Sonnets to inform her own realism, and specifically her emotional vocabulary. Specifically, we see her rejecting the artificialities of the sonnet sequence, but engaging with particularities in Shakespeare's Sonnets. Within Eliot's vocabulary of affection and sensibility, Shakespeare has an important contribution to make, as Eliot revises his legacy, expanding and elaborating on his conceits for a Victorian audience and a new genre. One line from the Sonnets which particularly struck Eliot was that concluding Sonnet 23: 'To hear with eyes belongs to love's fine wit'. Eliot quotes it in the *Middlemarch Notebooks* as an example of a 'fine ending' (p. 212), and uses a version of it as the epigraph to chapter 27 of *Felix Holt*, where it prefaces Esther's growing apprehension of her love for Felix and her misery at being misunderstood by him.[35] Eliot uses a form of the quotation again in *Middlemarch* of Mrs Vincy's love for Fred as he lies recovering from typhoid: 'No word passed his lips [of his wanting to hear of Mary], but "to hear with eyes belongs to love's rare wit", and the mother in the fulness of her heart not only divined Fred's longing, but felt ready for any sacrifice in order to satisfy him' (p. 266, ch. 27). Typically of the Middlemarchers, this finer impulse does not last long.

The line as used by Shakespeare explicitly refers to the act of reading the lover's words which might please more eloquently than speech, and to being positioned as the beloved of the Sonnet sequence. They are part of an injunction to be a good reader, one who can appreciate the nuances of the Sonnet addressed to them:

> O learn to read what silent love hath writ,
> To hear with eyes belongs to love's rare wit. (Sonnet 23, ll. 13–14)

Eliot, however, as the practitioner of a different medium, and one who is sceptical of the formulaic element of the Sonnets' promises and demands, takes the notion of hearing with the eyes and extends it beyond the immediate reference to poetry, thinking about how love's language can be apprehended in more ways than through the ears and the reading eye. In the novel, the eyes become a channel that can both hear and speak, that can even surpass the limitations of language, and certainly the formal limits of the sonnet. By invoking the hearing eye, Eliot creates silence as a powerful medium through which love can be transmitted, and its full sensuality admitted, a silence which would have been largely beyond the resources of the Victorian or Renaissance stage, but which the novelist can fully realise. In 1872, Matilda Benham Edwards wrote to George Eliot of a line in 'The Spanish Gypsy': '"Speech," is as you have said, in that wonderful Shakespearian line, "but broken light, upon the depth of the unspoken"' (30 April 1872; *GE Letters*, IX, 55). The invocation of the synaesthetic hearing eye is an investment in the effort to navigate, and to plumb, those depths. It contains a recognition, not only of the emotional complexities that Shakespeare can articulate, but also of the extent to which such depths can often not be spoken, but can be shown by the novelist, and 'seen' by readers and characters alike.

The hearing eye is most evident in *Middlemarch* in the relationship between Will and Dorothea, the course of which may be plotted more accurately through their looks than through their words. Every meeting contains an account of their looks as well as their speech, something true of no other characters. In the Casaubons' apartment in Rome, Will smiles and Dorothea is unable to resist smiling back, despite her recent tears. His smile is 'a gush of inward light' (p. 205, ch. 21), and seeing him is, for Dorothea, 'a glimpse of the sunny air' (p. 361, ch. 37). Such images remind us of Sonnet 18, 'Shall I compare thee to a Summers Day? / Thou art more lovely and more temperate' (ll. 1–2), but in Eliot, of course, the perceiving eye is a woman's. These images contrast with Casaubon's weak eyes, and the feeble taper with which he is imagined stumbling through the dark labyrinths of his studies, but there is also a mutual childlike trust in such openness, and the dawning of an innocent, irresistible eroticism in their looks: 'Each looked at the other as if they had been two flowers which had opened then and there' (*Middlemarch*, p. 363, ch. 37). When Dorothea longs for Will, she longs to *see* him (p. 539, ch. 54), a colloquialism newly invested with the burden of all that their looks convey. In a rather clumsy image, Eliot goes on to liken Dorothea to a princess, exiled from a gaze once known:

If a princess in the days of enchantment had seen a four-footed creature from among those which live in herds come to her once and again with a human gaze which rested upon her with choice and beseeching, what would she think of in her journeying, what would she look for when the herds passed her? Surely for the gaze which had found her, and which she would know again. (p. 539, ch. 54)

Their conversations are choreographed looks, glances, gazes, ending in Dorothea's 'tear-filled eyes looking at his very simply' while she declares her love for him 'in a sobbing childlike way' (p. 812, ch. 83).

That lovers should exchange significant looks is not noteworthy, but that Eliot should so consistently use that medium to articulate the growing attraction between Dorothea and Will is striking. Their looks, supported by her explanatory prose, delicately map the progress of an affection which lies beyond the categories familiar to Middlemarchers, and which thus demands another language in which it can be made intelligible. Their love is one of the principal ways in which Eliot challenges the complacent expectations of Middlemarch, its confidence in being able to swallow and assimilate its newcomers 'very comfortably' (p. 154, ch. 15). In order to do so, she invests in new means of articulation, and a new form of heroic femininity which owes something to her reading of Shakespeare.

Dorothea's antithetical positioning in the Vatican, as the Quakerish 'consciousness of Christian centuries' (p. 189, ch. 19), next to the Ariadne or Cleopatra, embodies more complexities than even Naumann's deliberately anachronistic conception of her as a 'Christian Antigone' (p. 190) can begin to recognise. Dorothea eludes familiar forms of categorisation, but Will's response to Naumann's teasing makes it clear that in seeking to write such a heroine, the novelist needs the finest medium. He chides Naumann for the inadequacy of his 'painting and Plastik [which] are poor stuff after all. They perturb and dull conceptions instead of raising them' (p. 190), and though he goes on to defend language as a 'finer medium', his defence soon founders as he begins to recognise how far beyond language Dorothea is:

Language gives a fuller image, which is all the better for being vague. After all, the true seeing is within; and painting stares at you with an insistent imperfection. I feel that especially about representations of women. As if a woman were a mere coloured superficies! You must wait for movement and tone. There is a difference in their very breathing: they change from moment to moment. – This woman whom you have just seen, for example: how would you paint her voice, pray? But her voice is much diviner than anything you have seen of her. (p. 191, ch. 19)

Will looks with a hearing eye, the loving eye needed fully to realise Dorothea's greatness. Eliot's adoption of the synaesthetic suggestion in Shakespeare goes some way to articulating how Dorothea exceeds commonly available means of apprehension.

Dorothea's uniqueness is also conveyed through Eliot's referring to a Shakespearean heroine in describing her. This common nineteenth-century device relied upon readers' awareness both of Shakespeare's plays and, more importantly, of prevailing critical views of a certain part, and the ways in which it had been written into a Victorian rhetoric of femininity. Eliot does not often resort to this potentially ahistorical and homogenising strategy, and when she does so her references to Shakespeare's women are rarely other than provocative or ironic. Her allusions expose the casualness of Shakespearean heroines' incorporation into the Victorian period, and dem-onstrate what it means for society to make such allusions. Caterina Sarti is linked with Desdemona and Juliet, as well as Helen of Troy and Dido, as Eliot asserts her right 'to be a heroine' despite her lack of astronomical knowledge.[36] The allusion works ironically here to point up the nature of the tragic version of 'heroism' open to these women, and to assert the lack of a match between knowledge or experience and the tragic status foisted upon women. Their status depends not upon what they know, but upon the ambivalent talent for loving, in which it is probable, notes Eliot of Caterina, that 'the most astronomical of women could not have surpassed her' (p. 116).

There is, in Eliot's passing reference to Juliet and Imogen in describing Rosamond Vincy's schooling, an acknowledgement of the levelling out of the particularities both of the heroines and of the Victorian girl in their incorporation into a fixed scheme of appropriate femininity:

Mrs Lemon herself had always held up Miss Vincy as an example: no pupil, she said, exceeded that young lady for mental acquisition and propriety of speech, while her musical execution was quite exceptional. We cannot help the way in which people speak of us, and probably if Mrs Lemon had undertaken to describe Juliet or Imogen, these heroines would not have seemed poetical. (*Middlemarch*, p. 96, ch. 11)

Thus Eliot exposes the redundancy of both the aspirational education and the reference, as part of her critique of Middlemarch society's expectations of its women. That Rosamond colludes in her incorporation into a scheme of female romance rendered empty of much meaning is signalled in Eliot's comments about Rosamond's stifled and stifling imagination: 'in Rosamond's romance it was not necessary to imagine much about the inward life of the hero, or of his serious business in the world: of course, he had a profession and was clever, as well as sufficiently handsome' (p. 166, ch. 16). There is little hope here for a recognition of the specificities of Shakespeare's heroines, and particularly of the tragic endings of their stories. However, these tragic elements may resonate with the reader as Eliot signals the moral illiteracy to which Rosamond and her society are subject.

Eliot chooses to liken Dorothea to a Shakespearean heroine at one of the most overtly dramatic moments of the novel as she enters the drawing-room in which Rosamond and Will are playing music together. The moment is multiply dramatic, and its effect carefully managed. We are alerted first to the rather historically jarring effect of Dorothea's presence, then to its contrast to Rosamond's style, to the frisson of her presence in an alien social setting, to her appearance before the man who adores her, and finally to the complications of rumour and speculation that hasten Dorothea's exit. The reference to Imogen imports a specifically theatrical instruction to the reader, and also points up the distinction between Dorothea's apparently outdated, though still potent, qualities and Rosamond's manufactured attractions, thus participating in the novel's central debate about the available contexts for female heroism. Within those contexts, Shakespeare is a crucial factor:

When the drawing-room door opened and Dorothea entered, there was a sort of contrast not infrequent in country life when the habits of the different ranks were less blent than now. Let those who know, tell us exactly what stuff it was that Dorothea wore in those days of mild autumn – that thin white woollen stuff soft to the touch and soft to the eye. It always seemed to have been lately washed, and to smell of the sweet hedges – was always in the shape of a pelisse with sleeves hanging all out of the fashion. Yet if she had entered before a still audience as Imogen or Cato's daughter, the dress might have seemed right enough: the grace and dignity were in her limbs and neck; and about her simply parted hair and candid eyes the large round poke which was then in the fate of women, seemed no more odd as a head-dress than the godly trencher we call a halo. By the present audience of two persons, no dramatic heroine could have been expected with more interest than Mrs Casaubon. (p. 432, ch. 43)

The moment is rife with sexual tension, and marital complication, an effect heightened by the reinforcing reference to Cato's daughter Marcia, who was the subject of politicised marital negotiations in Addison's *Cato* (1713).

According to Anna Jameson, Imogen is 'the most perfect' of Shakespeare's heroines. Other heroines might exceed her in particular aspects, but:

> there is no female portrait that can be compared to Imogen as a woman – none in which so great a variety of tints are mingled together into such perfect harmony. In her, we have all the fervour of youthful tenderness, all the romance of youthful fancy, all the enchantment of ideal grace, – the bloom of beauty, the brightness of intellect, and the dignity of rank, taking a peculiar hue from the conjugal character which is shed over all, like a consecration and a holy charm. (Jameson, p. 226)

She is 'the angel of light, whose lovely presence pervades and animates the whole piece' (p. 158). Imogen is also, of course, one of Ruskin's 'perfect women'. However, in the mid-1860s, as Ruskin knew, the terms and possibilities of that perfection were being questioned. In 1864, Helen Faucit had made her return to the London stage – from which she had been absent for six years – in Samuel Phelps's production of *Cymbeline*, and was seen in that play by Eliot. Something of Faucit's conception of the role can be gleaned from her letter on Imogen in *On Some of Shakespeare's Female Characters* (1885), where she writes:

> It has been my happy lot to impersonate not a few ideal women … but Imogen has always occupied the largest place in my heart; and while she taxed largely my powers of impersonation, she has always repaid me for the effort tenfold by the delight I felt at being the means of placing a being in every way so noble before the eyes and hearts of my audiences, and of making them feel, perhaps, and think of her, and of him to whose genius we owe her, with something of my own reverence and love. (p. 160)

Though largely a critical success, Faucit's 1864 performance did have its detractors, as Carol Jones Carlisle records:

> An apologist for the newer school of acting, however, argued on the basis of changing political and social attitudes that her style, grounded in 'dramatic idealism,' was no longer in tune with the times. He maintained that, despite *Cymbeline's* admitted incongruity with modern realism, and despite Imogen's airy ideality in some passages, an infusion of human weakness was needed for a greater sense of reality. (Jones Carlisle, p. 12)

The ideality of Faucit's acting, and arguably of Imogen herself, clashes with the modernity of the critics, as does Dorothea against the levelling incomprehension of Middlemarch.

The figure and situation of Imogen contain potent parallels with those of Dorothea, and reveal something of the ways in which Shakespeare becomes transmuted in the fiction of Eliot. Of particular note is what Jameson describes as 'the conjugal tenderness' of Imogen, which 'is at once the chief subject of the drama and the pervading charm of her character' (Jameson, p. 230). In Dorothea's conjugal situation, Eliot takes the elements of Imogen's predicament and re-shapes, compacts and complicates them. Imogen's difficulties rest in the clash between her feelings and those of her father for the orphaned Posthumus, with whom she had been brought up. Imogen's subsequent marriage to Posthumus causes outrage to Cymbeline, who exiles Posthumus. Posthumus's situation echoes that of Will Ladislaw: both are orphaned and brought up by benefactors, whom they estrange by their love for a woman, respectively a daughter and a wife/daughter, deemed by their benefactor to be out of their reach. Eliot compacts the Shakespearean situation by combining the situation of the outraged benefactor with that of a fearful, jealous husband, perhaps articulating something of the jealously incestuous dimension to Cymbeline's anger. She removes the story from its situation in a royal court, as Shakespeare removed his play from its basis in the company of Italian merchants meeting in a Paris tavern in Bocaccio's *Decameron*, situating it instead within the contexts of small-town Midlands society, the larger European aspirations of both Casaubon and Will, and the small-mindedness of Casaubon's jealousies. This is a creative translation which keeps to the forefront of our minds both the historical distance travelled by the allusion, and the process of translation, rather than its naturalisation

Like Imogen, Dorothea is variously tested, before being able to effect a relationship with one whom many around her deem not good enough for her. Whilst Imogen finds a context for her existence in the play's resolution, in which her morality and virtue are not only confirmed to her husband, but upheld as a beacon for her society, Dorothea's fate is less obviously satisfying, as she faces a form of exile from Middlemarch, condemned by her aspirations to move to London. Curiously, the dimensions of her fate anticipate the conclusion of Imogen's story as imagined by Helen Faucit. In her series of letters on Shakespeare's heroines, Faucit takes up the common fictionalising practice of many contemporary commentators who wove fuller histories for characters than Shakespeare had supplied. While Cowden Clarke provided his women with girlhoods, Faucit imagined their lives after the plays had ended. For Imogen, she envisages not the realisation of a happy marriage, but her premature death, brought on by the physical and emotional suffering she had been through: 'Tremblingly, gradually, and oh, how reluctantly! the hearts to whom that life is so precious will see the sweet smile which greets them grow fainter, will hear the loved voice grow feebler!' (Faucit, p. 225). She continues, in words which signal something of the diffusive, distanced effect of Dorothea, that Imogen's

lovely soul will be to them
                    'Like a star
        Beaconing from the abodes where the Immortals are;'
inspiring to worthy lives, and sustaining them with the hope that where she is, they may, in God's good time, become fit to be. Something of this the 'divine Imogen' is to us also.   (pp. 225–6)

The Victorian actress anticipates that Imogen's exceptionality, like Dorothea's, cannot be sustained in her native context. Eliot's reference to Imogen, then, rather than passively invoking the terms of a heroine with whose character and whose predicament Dorothea has something in common, works instead to highlight her character's lack of situatedness in her own historical moment. Her appearance as an Imogen figure encapsulates Dorothea's dilemma throughout the novel: how to engineer a fit between her own aspirations and the conditions which cannot but misinterpret those aspirations, to the extent of effectively nullifying them through speculation and idle gossip.

In an early review under the name of Mary Ann Evans of Saint-Marc Girardin's *Cours de litterature dramatique* (1855), entitled 'Love in the Drama', the novelist demonstrates the appropriateness of using Shakespeare's heroines to signal such a dilemma. In his book, Girardin surveys 'the general expression of Love under the varying conditions of society, from antiquity down to the seventeenth century'.[37] The review spends some time on its consideration of those Shakespearean women, notably Juliet, Desdemona, Rosalind and Portia, who frankly 'avow their love, not only to themselves, but to the men they love … Then there are the women [the two Helenas, Sylvia, Viola and Olivia] who love without being loved in return, and some of whom even sue for love' (p. 255). Evans notes that this is 'inconvenient for those whose creed includes at once the doctrine of Shakespeare's infallibility and the doctrines of modern propriety', and argues that such frankness 'must be simply a natural manifestation which has only been gradually and partially repressed by the complex influences of modern civilisation' (pp. 254–5). In direct contradiction to Knox and Ruskin, Eliot suggests that in so far as they can be Victorian heroines, Shakespeare's women must be either misunderstood or understood in opposition to prevailing mores.

Like his heroines, Dorothea too frankly speaks, or sobs out, her love for Will, offending proprieties but achieving her match, and in her situation we see the clash of natural manifestations and modern civilisation, a clash which would reverberate in the broader international and spiritual movements of *Daniel Deronda*, but which reaches its most intense individual state in the case of Dorothea. The very words used by Dorothea in her declaration to Will move from the splendour of her overwhelming passion and the gesture of rejecting her wealth – 'Oh, I cannot bear it – my heart will break … I don't mind about poverty – I hate my wealth' (*Middlemarch*, p. 811, ch. 83) – to the financial exigencies of the modern moment – 'We could live quite well on my own fortune – it is too much – seven hundred-a-year – I want so little – no new clothes – and I will learn what everything costs' (p. 812). The Shakespearean-ness of Dorothea is both her triumph and the measure of her defeat, her greatness and that greatness's self-defining impotence within the world of Middlemarch.

There is no place, Eliot seems to be saying, for the truly Shakespearean heroine, or even for a properly understood Shakespeare, in the world of Middlemarch, and consequently at the end of the novel Dorothea leaves for London. Carol Siegel writes of this journey as Dorothea 'cross[ing] the border into the domestic plot because within the strictures of Eliot's realism that is the only place Eliot's Shakespearian fantasies can lead'.[38] Siegel's is a compelling argument for the impossibility of sustaining the Sonnets', and by extension, the Comedies', 'naturalization of multiple forms of desire' (p. 50) within the context of the Victorian novel, and of translating that desire into nineteenth-century heterosexual terms within *Middlemarch*. However, as we have seen, the existence of an emotional freedom and aspiration that might be termed Shakespearean is a crucial means by which Eliot can signal alternative lives and possibilities within the novel. That these possibilities and identities seem to remain primarily textual is an important part of the novel's meaning. Eliot's function as narrator is arguably to expose the interpretative gap between Shakespeare and Middlemarch, between Shakespearean tropes and the use made of them by Middlemarchers, for instance in Mrs Cadwallader's slighting reference to Will as 'Mr Orlando Ladislaw' (*Middlemarch*, p. 728, ch. 62). Characters' direct reference to Shakespeare and his characters are few, but telling in their limitations. Celia is made 'a little uneasy at [Dorothea's] Hamlet-like raving' (p. 776, ch. 77), and Mary Garth's comparison of herself to Ophelia and Juliet has a primarily ironising force (p. 138, ch. 13). Casaubon's use of 'who with repentance is not satisfied, is not of heaven or earth' from *The Two Gentlemen of Verona* (V.iv.79) is self-satisfied and emotionally self-deluding in shutting down the possibility of further communication with Dorothea. The use of Shakespeare amongst the novel's epigraphs goes some way to establishing a more symbiotic interpretative relationship between the worlds of Middlemarch and Shakespeare, but the most important bridge is arguably in the person and function of the novelist, and her recognition of the novel as the appropriate form of accommodating Shakespearean influences within the Victorian period.

In an 1867 article on Eliot, Peter Bayne had suggested that there was currently 'but slight precision of idea or dignity of character associated with this species of composition [i.e. the novel] in the public mind'.[39] His review of Eliot's work up to and including *Felix Holt* is an explicit attempt to achieve precisely that dignity for the novel. He uses the moral seriousness, the 'rare intelligence', the 'errorless accuracy [and] vivid precision' (p. 144) of Eliot's fiction as evidence of the novel's potential, but in some sense the whole review simply serves to back up his opening claim, and the main plank of his argument, that 'Were Shakespeare now alive he would write novels, and perhaps it would not be much to be regretted that the sovereign spirit of all literature should be technically definable as a novelist' (p. 141). He goes on:

Not only is it that superlative genius will contrive to give account of itself through whatever medium lies readiest to hand, but that the novel is really adapted in an extraordinary degree to afford play to a versatile, inventive, all-comprehending mind. What the novel, in contradistinction to other forms of literary art, specifically is, we shall not trouble our readers or ourselves to inquire; but we have yet to learn for what literary service the competent literary artist may not render it available. All that the old epic was in respect of narrative; all that the old drama was in respect of delineation of character by means of colloquy; all that the old lyrics and idylls were in respect of sentimental effusion and gay description of beechen boughs and milkmaids; this may the modern novel be. (p. 141)

In some sense then, Bayne suggests that Shakespeare would have found his most appropriate mode or medium in the novel, and implicitly that his artistry comes to critical fruition in the age of the three-decker, and gains its fullest appreciation and understanding in an age of viewers and readers trained by the Victorian novelist.

In his 1883 comparison of 'Shakespeare and George Eliot', Peter Bayne refers to their shared 'fondness for deep sayings', and more especially to a shared delight in 'psychological analysis … in tracing, stage by stage, the growth in the human mind of evil or of good'.[40] Bayne goes on to claim that no other Victorian novelist

was so inquisitively keen and close in observation of character as to feel so much interest as Shakespeare felt, and George Eliot could have felt, in the question started in 'All's Well That Ends Well,' respecting the unprincipled Parolles, 'Is it possible he should know what he is, and he be that he is?' Such a question, it is obvious, must be, comparatively speaking, thrown away on the stage. There is not time in the onward movement of an acted play for the reflection through which alone the significance of such a remark can be appreciated. (p. 525)

Shakespeare's work might, of course, be read, and Bayne quotes Goethe's belief that 'Shakespeare's works are not for the eyes of the body' (p. 526), but Bayne's principal point is that in the work of Eliot and in her characters, we find the most 'practically useful and philosophically profound commentary' (p. 527) upon Shakespeare and his characters, and in particular upon Shakespeare's women. Indeed he goes on to speculate about the kind of production that might have resulted had George Eliot been able to do for Helena (in *All's Well That Ends Well*) what she does for her own Dorothea, that is, to explain actions which might otherwise baffle an audience, as Dorothea's actions baffled that immediate audience in Middlemarch, and its descendants, for whom 'she could not have been "a nice woman", else she would not have married either' Casaubon or Ladislaw (p. 838, Finale). In Eliot's hands, Dorothea is exonerated, as Helena would have been, if Eliot had had the chance to '[level] hills of difficulty, [illumine] valleys of shadow and [put] in all those explanatory circumstances by which a brief and startling drama might have been worked out into the harmony and reconcilement of such a novel as Shakespeare himself need not have scorned' (p. 527). In order to be fully appreciated, Bayne suggests, Shakespeare needs an audience trained by the novelist.

Eliot is at her most Shakespearean when she is most successfully translating the kind of psychological profundity associated with Shakespeare into a form more appropriate to such profundity, and to an audience expecting gaps to be filled in, motives provided, and idiosyncrasies fully explained. In *Middlemarch* she develops and exploits such a form in telling stories not usually told, in giving behind-the-scenes narratives, such as that of Mrs Bulstrode's preparing herself for her new appearance as the wife of a disgraced man, and in telling the privacy of Bulstrode's thoughts whilst not estranging the reader wholly from that character. Her attempt to challenge and extend the reader's sympathetic vocabulary is an integral part of Eliot's aesthetic, and is perhaps most clearly marked in *Middlemarch*, where the reader finds herself aligned most closely with the narrator against the majority of the indigenous characters of the town, and is instead implicated in a form of identificatory aesthetic that works as much through textual as through empirical observations. *Middlemarch* is deeply aspirational. Will and Dorothea long for a world that they can embrace, in which they can find the fulfilment of their love and vocation. To the extent to which that world is unrealisable within the bounds of Middlemarch and the realist novel, it is Shakespearean. To recognise this is to qualify the significance of Shakespeare neither for the Victorians nor for Eliot, but simply to acknowledge the fullness of her own recognition both of Shakespeare's difference, and of her society's tendency reductively to appropriate that which is beyond it for its own resources.

Eliot's use of Shakespeare then works cunningly to educate her readers through the means of their own aspirational fantasies of identification with Shakespeare, as she exposes the grounds by which those fantasies are made impossible in the small-minded mercantilism and class-based discrimination of Middlemarch. In the projection of Will and Dorothea's future, there is the promise of at least a partial realisation of their Shakespearean potential, as mutually passionate lovers enjoying the prolongation of that courtship and education in conversation which is the lot of Shakespeare's comedic heroes and heroines. There is also, of course, in Dorothea's 'finely touched spirit [which] had still its fine issues, though they were not widely visible' (p. 838) an echo of Duke Vincentio's words to Angelo in I.i of *Measure for Measure*:

> Spirits are not finely touch'd
> But to fine issues, nor Nature never lends
> The smallest scruple of her excellence,
> But, like a thrifty goddess, she determines
> Herself the glory of a creditor,
> Both thanks and use.   (I.i.35–9)

But we leave Middlemarch rather with the uneasy promise of Dorothea and Will's being forgotten than with the promise of their being made immortal that Shakespeare's Sonnets had seemed to offer, and in which the Victorians' practice of adopting Shakespeare's characters as their own participates. If Dorothea's influence is to persist it will be because of her ongoing actions, rather than through a moment of identification with a character from a genre and time not her own. As Eliot's text moves through a variety of moments of contact with Shakespeare's work, it speaks not so much of that work itself, as of the multiple possibilities of the relationship between the new and old texts, between new readers and old texts, and between the play or poem and the Victorian novel. Eliot is not interested in memorialising or preserving Shakespeare, but in exploring what has become of him and his work over time, and in assessing the ways in which he and his work can still speak to a Victorian audience. As a translator herself, Eliot brings her practical knowledge about that process to *Middlemarch*. As such, the quality of her engagement with Shakespeare is complex and highly self-conscious. Eliot is interested in the nature of her society's relationship with the playwright, with the possible shapes it might take, rather than in herself assimilating particular effects, lines or characters for her own ends. *Middlemarch* is rather a text in which Shakespeare and the Victorians can speak to each other, engaging in that conversation which the best translations conduct, and after which Will Ladislaw hankered, albeit a conversation in which much is misheard over the distance of the centuries between Shakespeare and the Victorians.

CHAPTER 5

Socialism, nationalism and Stratford: Shakespeare and the New Woman at the fin de siècle

Eliot's unease over her contemporaries' appropriations of Shakespeare is mirrored in the 1890s, where a tension develops between official recognition of Shakespeare's status as pre-eminent English poet, through trappings such as his 'birthplace', and a number of women's defensive response to what they see as a form of nationalist usurpation. This tension manifests itself in a contest over the ownership – both legal and metaphorical – of Stratford-upon-Avon's Shakespeare sites, and the cultural resonances implicit in these geographical markers. Legally, the 1890s saw an incremental shift in the relationship between state and playwright. The Shakespeare Birthplace Trust had been established in 1866 with the remit to preserve both Shakespeare's birthplace and other associated buildings as national memorials, and to establish a library and museum (Wells, p. 317), but in 1891 the Trust was incorporated by Act of Parliament, thus establishing the preservation of Shakespeare's memory as of an importance deemed worthy of legislative guarantee. In a country reeling from the impact of Ibsen on its stages, the Act recognises and perpetuates an increased commitment to Stratford's place in the evolution of Shakespeare as both national poet and, thus, guarantor of culture and learning, and to the importance of the geographical and heritage dimensions of the memorialisation of Shakespeare.

It also, of course, gives official sanction to the status of Shakespeare as merchandising opportunity, and to the dimensions of the form of literary tourism parodied by Henry James in his story 'The Birthplace' (1903). James's central character, Morris Gedge, is appointed curator of the eponymous birthplace, and grows to dread the incautious tourists who, scarcely having read a word of the unnamed poet whom they profess to worship, have developed a compulsive interest in the house, the 'empty shell – or rather … the extraneous, preposterous stuffing of it', that is, in the legends and tales of its occupier that accrue over the years.[1] Gedge's patience is most tried by the particular feature of the ordeal that, by the time the lively season was with them again, had disengaged itself as the sharpest – the immense assumption of veracities and sanctities, of the general soundness of the legend with which everyone arrived … The form in which his irritation first came to him was that of his feeling obliged to say to them – to the single visitor, even when sympathetic, quite as to the gaping group – the particular things, a dreadful dozen or so, that they expected. (pp. 195–6).

Finally Gedge realises that his stories, and people's desire to believe in them, are all that there is, and all that there needs to be for the visitors whom he gradually learns to enthral.

Initially enamoured himself of the birthplace in which he comes to live, Gedge takes lamp-lit walks in the small hours to try to 'recover some echo, to surprise some secret, of the *genius loci*' (p. 190), for, as he explains to his wife, 'They're the only time, as I've told you before, that I'm really with *Him*. Then I don't see the place, He isn't the place' (p. 194). Gedge then comes to share James's scepticism about Shakespeare, in whom the American author found an 'unguessed riddle',[2] that is, the problem of who Shakespeare was and how he came to create his masterpieces out of such humble beginnings. Rather than subscribing to any of the available authorship theories, in his 1907 preface to *The Tempest* James attempts to resolve this dilemma by suggesting that the existence of Shakespeare the man scarcely mattered; what was important was his work as an artist, 'the monster and magician of a thousand masks'.[3] Shakespeare exists in his works for James, and in the influence of those works on his own writings, such as the moment when Gedge speaks of the tourists' insisting on his 'committing' himself to their delusions: 'It was the pound of flesh – They would have it' (p. 201). For James, the birthplace phenomenon is a blind, a simulacrum, bound up with the credulity upon which commercialism is based.

This is all very far removed from the experience of a number of women in the 1890s, for whom Stratford was the site of resonances which were both emotional and political, and which were embedded within an intriguing variety of forms of nationalism. So intense was their identification with Shakespeare that these women forsook the usual limits of literary tourism by actually going to live in Stratford, and thus investing in the town as a form of living memorial to the writer who was so crucial to both their lives and their writings. As will become clear, the oxymoronic quality of the term 'living memorial' denotes some of the ideological complexity of Shakespeare's significance for these women, who actually contested the submergence of both Shakespeare and Stratford within modern commercialism, and whose attachments themselves derive from a recognition of the very real previous existence of both Shakespeare and his Stratford.

MATHILDE BLIND

The evocation of place is central to the biographer, poet and translator Mathilde Blind's 'Shakespeare Sonnets', published in 1895 in her collection *Birds of Passage: Songs of the Orient and Occident*. In poems which evoke the presence of Shakespeare, such as 'Anne Hathaway's Cottage', 'Cleve Woods' and 'Evensong (Holy Trinity Church)', Blind uses the places associated with Shakespeare to conjure up his spirit in order that she can commune with the long-dead writer, even projecting herself into a vicarious romantic memory, as she fantasises about how Shakespeare might have come to woo Anne Hathaway:

> IS this the Cottage, ivy-girt and crowned,
>> And this the path down which our Shakespeare ran,
>> When, in the April of his love, sweet Anne
> Made all his mighty pulses throb and bound;
> Where, mid coy buds and winking flowers around,
>> She blushed a rarer rose than roses can,
>> To greet her Will – even Him, fair Avon's Swan –
> Whose name has turned this plot to holy ground!
> To these dear walls, once dear to Shakespeare's eyes,
>> Time's Vandal hand itself has done no wrong;
>> This nestling lattice opened to his song,
> When, with the lark, he bade his love arise
> In words whose strong enchantment never dies –
>> Old as these flowers, and, like them, ever young.[4]

In terms of extraordinary veneration, Blind rather cloyingly imagines the love-struck young Will and his Anne in a process of commemoration which is literally grounded in the bricks and mortar of the cottage, artefacts which act to guarantee the parallel perpetuity of his work and his renown. Nature and Time perpetually re-enact the scene of Shakespeare's domestic drama and remain, as do his words and love, 'ever young'.

In 'Cleve Woods', Blind invokes Titania in fantasising about finding 'a glowworm-lighted child, / Led far astray, and, with anointing hand / Sprinkling clear dew from a forget-me-not, / Hailed him the Laureate of her Fairyland' (ll. 11–14, p. 112). The river and woods are redolent of Shakespeare, and are created by him for future generations, just as he in his turn was created by them, born as a poet out of their inspiration for him when he was young. Blind's is a Shakespeare embedded fundamentally in the land in which he was born, and shaped and inflected inescapably by that topography. Similarly in 'The Avon', Blind writes of a leaning willow, 'That hath not ceased to weep, / Whence, hanging garlands, fair Ophelia sank; / Since Jacques moped here the trees have had a tongue; / And all these streams and whispering willows keep / The moans of Desdemona's dying song' (ll. 10–14, p. 114). The songs emitted by the willows have remained with them, a testimony in this case to the perpetuity of sorrow in love, and to Shakespeare's sympathetic witness of that sorrow. In 'Evensong (Holy Trinity Church)', Shakespeare's spirit is 'pervasive' round the 'old familiar things' (l. 14, p. 115) in the churchyard, and in 'Shakespeare' he is the ultimate cartographer, unrolling 'before our sight … the world of men', which

> Showed like a map, where stream and waterfall
> And village-cradling vale and cloud-capped height
>   Stand faithfully recorded, great and small;
> For Shakespeare was, and at his touch, with light
> Impartial as the Sun's, revealed the All.   (ll. 10–14, p. 116)

In a *fin de siècle* spin, Blind makes Shakespeare the mirror of nature; life imitates art as she accords to the poet a critical power so potent that it becomes a determining force.

The continuity between Shakespeare and place pervades these poems in a far from inert way. Nature and Shakespeare perpetually reinvest each other with resonance for the contemporary moment, albeit a resonance which has its affective roots in the past of Shakespeare's own day. This may at first sight appear to be a prime example of what Philip Dodd has described as the stabilisation of the growing conviction between 1880 and 1920 that

English culture was to be found in the past … The past cultural activities and attributes of the people were edited and then acknowledged, as contributions to the evolution of the English national culture which had produced the present. Nowhere was this more evident than through the establishment of a national literary tradition within the emergent discipline of English literature.[5]

Shakespeare may then conservatively be invoked as a form or manifestation of national consciousness which is simultaneously coercively present and out-moded. Yet this is far from articulating the visceral Shakespeare of Blind's poems, who is actively present in her work, as in so many Victorian women's accounts of him. Her Shakespeare is not a lapidary national treasure, but a lover, a lambent Laureate, a mapper of emotions, whose authority derives from, and is embedded in, the connotations of the geography which repre-sents a mode of anti-authoritarian, resistant identification.

In order fully to appreciate Blind's response to Shakespeare, we need to be aware of the ways in which her contemporary fellow thinkers were also invoking the notion of a pastoral ideal in the midst of late Victorian modernity, and to take account of her socialist affiliations. Blind was the stepdaughter of the German radical Karl Blind, who was an acquaintance of Karl Marx, a leader in the Baden Insurrection of 1848, and, like Marx, a political émigré who took refuge in London after fleeing several other European countries. Once in London, Karl Blind became a journalist, and his home was a natural meeting place for visiting radicals, including Mazzini, with whom Mathilde struck up a close acquaintance. As Simon Avery writes, 'Mathilde Blind was brought up in a household constantly involved in revolutionary and socialist discussion, where she was in continuous contact with many of Europe's leading political thinkers and activists.'[6] As an adult, Blind left behind the more radical affiliations of her youth: she became a great admirer of Gladstone, whom she called 'the grand old humanitarian leader of England'.[7] She moved primarily in literary, scholarly and artistic circles, and became a close acquaintance of the Pre-Raphaelites, most notably Ford Madox Brown and his family, and had her portrait painted by Lucy Madox Brown in 1872. The portrait is now in Newnham College, Cambridge, to which Blind left a large legacy for the promotion of women's education. Hers was a highly literary life, as she earned her living as a journalist, poet, translator (she translated the diary of the Russian artist Marie Bashkirtseff in 1890) and biographer (she wrote, amongst other works, the first life of George Eliot in 1883). Blind was also an active member of the radical Shelley Society, whose members included William Michael Rossetti, Eleanor Marx, Edward Aveling and George Bernard Shaw. Shelley was, according to the theosophist Annie Besant, the 'hero of the freethinkers' of London at the time (quoted in Avery, p. 179). Blind published criticism on the poet, and edited a collection of his verse in 1872, which included a memoir in which she champions him as a 'spiritual child of the Revolution' (quoted in Avery, p. 179).

Blind's life from childhood through to adulthood is one lived through a profound affiliation with concepts of stringent intellectual enquiry and social justice, and through a commitment to literature which could sound out those principles. Clearly she sees those principles as made manifest in Shakespeare, but her affinity with him has further personal dimensions. In September 1894, she writes to Richard Garnett, the Keeper of Printed Books at the British Museum:

The charm of Stratford grows upon me the longer I remain. I drove to Wilmcote this afternoon, and saw Mary Arden's house, a sweet old cottage said to be four or five hundred years old. The timbered walls and mighty oaken beams of roof and ceiling show that it must have been a place of some importance in Shakespeare's day. It strikes one everywhere hereabouts how plentiful wood must have been at that time, when all these villages and hamlets were still embosomed in the green recesses of the Forest of Arden. One seems to come upon Shakespeare's tracks here, and to get into closer touch with him and such plays as 'As You Like It' and 'A Midsummer Night's Dream'.

Memories and echoes of merry old England seem to have survived in Warwickshire longer than anywhere else … The inhabitants seem to be more cheerful than is generally the case in little provincial towns. They love the theatre.[8]

Blind's letters and the writings from the 1890s in her commonplace book attest to an enjoyment of nature, the rural world and small country towns, perhaps as a respite from the London where, as she quotes a friend as saying, 'one lives in too great a hurry … to taste life very finely'.[9] Stratford – and Shakespeare, who underwrites the town's effect – exemplify the relief from modernity.

Blind was briefly living in Stratford when she worked on the Shakespeare sonnets, the last poems she wrote. Their elegiac quality derives perhaps from her own age and declining health, and from her sense of sharing a last experience of Stratford with the Shakespeare who returned to the town at the end of his own life, but it also derives from a mournful sense of how the country had deteriorated since Shakespeare's day. In another letter to Garnett she records how, though she 'had some delightful boating on the Avon', the river was left to its own devices to such an extent that 'locks have fallen to pieces from disuse. In consequence of this there are rapids and shallows which produce quite an excitement'.[10] The excitement is an ironic outcome of something less than desirable, of a decline or decay since Shakespeare's day. A similar feeling is discernible in Blind's record of visiting Catherine's Court, 'a delicious Elizabethan house' near Bath in April 1895. Her Commonplace book records that in the house 'We find no mechanical repetition of ornament. The variety is endless. It looked as if every workman had loved his work and had had sufficient liberty to give play to his fancy. The balustrades of the steps were supported by delicate pillars and finished by roses and balls' (Commonplace book, p. 32). As she and her companion walk around the gardens of Catherine's Court, Shakespeare haunts their minds: 'Shield plucked a weed which he dubbed Titania's Flytrap … what infinite variety in the form and arrangement of the simplest of weeds' (p. 33). *A Midsummer Night's Dream* and *Hamlet* inhabit the minds of the visitors in a place which can make even weeds part of an idyll, and which celebrates a form of productivity and labour which is one with the rural scene. Earlier in the same Commonplace book, Blind had written of the labouring folk of Wendover that they 'have an air of quaint, old world rusticity … as if railways and telegraphs had never been heard of' (p. 6). The rustic setting enables the recuperation of labour for a pre-industrial ethic.

John Lucas has identified a tendency in socialist writers of the period to hanker after a rural vision with, as he puts it, 'its implicit politics of containment and hierarchical structures'.[11] Blind's hankering, however, like that of Eleanor Marx as we will see below, is for a countryside which was precisely not redolent of those structures and hierarchies, which were anyway probably less oppressive than the structures in place in capitalist, industrialised Victorian Britain, but which actively opposed by its very existence a capitalist ethos. In *Merrie England* (1894), Robert Blatchford describes the industrial counties of England as 'ugly, and dirty, and smoky, and disagreeable'. By comparison, he suggests that the Southern counties have

pure air, bright skies, clear rivers, clean streets, and beautiful fields, woods, and gardens; you will get cattle and streams, and birds and flowers, and you will know that all these things are well worth having, and that none of them can exist side by side with the factory system.[12]

The countryside takes on broader political, as well as literary and personal, connotations, as both Blind and Blatchford envisage a harmonising of nature and man's efforts, a harmony which for Blind had been achieved in Shakespeare, and of which she could find faint echoes in the countryside of the 1890s.

ELEANOR MARX

In many respects, Blind's affinity with Shakespeare echoes that of her contemporary and acquaintance Eleanor Marx, whose life is imbued with references to Shakespeare which have their roots in her émigré childhood, and their ultimate manifestation in the nature of her death. Marx's is a life which, like Blind's, demonstrates the centrality of literature to the lives of radical women of the 1880s and 1890s, both as a means of earning a living and also as a way of finding a historical voice which can work to articulate a contemporary sense of political disenfranchisement; even if the present proves uncongenial, a comradeship can be effected through readings from the past. A skilful translator, from a multi-lingual background, Marx was used to looking beyond England and the present for her work and inspiration.

The Marx family's love of Shakespeare involved them from the outset in the fabric as well as the language of their adopted country, for it was through the theatre in addition to their private study that their enthusiasm for the playwright was fed. In particular, the family were supporters of Henry Irving. They were initially attracted to him by his new interpretations of

Shakespeare's roles, such as his 1875 Hamlet, which involved him in some controversy. According to his grandson Laurence Irving, the actor stead-fastly refused to 'flatter the public taste' with the familiar 'points' of Hamlet's performance, being influenced instead by the more philosophical approach of the American Edwin Booth.[13] Such champions were they of Irving that Mrs Marx wrote an article defending him which Eleanor forwarded to Karl Hirsch for insertion in the *Frankfurter Zeitung*. Her accompanying note explains their interest in the actor, and adds that Karl Marx was himself a great admirer:

S'il avait eu le temps Papa aurait lui-meme fait une critique sur Mr. Irving qui nous interesse beuacoup (quoique nous le connaissons pas personnellement) d'abord parce que c'est un homme d'un rare talent, et ensuite parce que toute la presse anglaise, par suite des plus miserables intrigues, s'est acharnée contre lui, et a montré contre lui une vraie cabale. En faisant publier le critique de Maman dans la 'Frankfurter' vous nous ferez un grand' plaisir.[14]

The family's enthusiasm for Irving continued when he was no longer a persecuted young actor but the head of the Lyceum theatre, arguably in some respects one of the most designedly bourgeois institutions in the country, from the late 1870s to the late 1890s when Irving and Ellen Terry were its stars. In 'My Recollections of Karl Marx', Mrs Comyn recounts how the subscriptions to the Dogberry Club, which met most frequently at the Marxes' house, were spent on tickets to Irving's 'First Nights':

He used to let the club have the front row of the Dress Circle on these occasions – to my thinking, the best place in the theatre … Once, before my admission to it, the club presented him with a laurel wreath, and, on receiving it, he kissed the hand of Eleanor, who afterwards preserved the white kid glove his lips had touched as a precious, almost sacred possession.[15]

The Marx family's affiliation is witness to the irrepressibility of theatrical occasions in the Victorian period, and to their ability, matched by the power of Shakespeare's texts, to straddle political and class divides.

It is clear that for Eleanor Marx the playwright's significance was born out of a close-knit family life, and that her subsequent references to him are coloured by that inception. References to Shakespeare often crop up in her letters. She writes to her sister Laura on 19 December 1890 that Engels, like Macbeth, 'had screwed his courage to the sticking point', and in August of the following year she writes to the same correspondent, again of Engels and of 'Pumps', his controversial housekeeper: 'The General is happiest with his drunken enchanter … 'Tis a Prospero in love with a lower kind of Caliban; for Pumps hasn't Caliban's redeeming qualities.'[16] The references are warm, human and intimate, attesting to the depth of her affection for Engels, and also crucially providing a medium through which she can express her love for Laura, through a shared language and an implicit reference back to their childhood. It is arguable that Shakespeare's significance for Eleanor Marx never really exceeded its birth in the heart of her family, even when his significance was later to accrue more overtly political ramifications. Indeed, it is that coincidence of interests that seems to have determined the nature of Shakespeare's appeal and usefulness for her.

As an adult, Eleanor consolidated her interest in Shakespeare by being the only one of her family to join the New Shakspere Society, which was established in 1874 by the philologist and scholar of early texts F. J. Furnivall, also to be the founder of the Shelley Society in 1885, and which met weekly at University College, London. The Society was inspired in part by patriotic reasons: in Furnivall's opening address he announced that it was 'the duty of Englishmen to study Shakspere', and that he found it 'humiliating and lamentable' that 'not one in 20 – or shall we say 20,000' has a 'real notion' of the 'greatest author in the world'. The purpose of the Society was

by a very close study of the metrical and phraseological peculiarities of Shakspere, to get his plays as nearly as possible into the order in which he wrote them; to check that order by the higher tests of imaginative power, knowledge of life, self-restraint in expression, weight of thought, depth of purpose; and then to use that revised order for the purpose of studying the progress and meaning of Shakspere's mind, the passage of it from the fun and word-play, the lightness, the passion, of the Comedies of Youth, through the patriotism (still with comedy of more meaning) of the Histories of Middle Age, to the great Tragedies dealing with the deepest questions of man in Later Life; and then at last to the poet's peaceful and quiet home-life again in Stratford.[17]

Clearly, Furnivall has already mapped out the shape of the reassuringly coherent developmental chronology of Shakespeare's mind and work. The narrative of the life gives a framework for the chronology of the plays, and we might wonder whether the way in which those two aspects are taken to be synonymous was in itself appealing and even reassuring to Marx. There is a simplicity and optimism about the evolutionary progression to greatness and to understanding which might have appealed to any nineteenth-century reformer.

Marx is reported, under the name of Mrs E. Marx, as having become a member of the Society at its meeting on 21 May 1876. A few months later she volunteered to translate a lengthy German paper entitled 'Shakspere's Use of Narration in His Dramas', from the German of Professor Delius, and was commended by the Society for her work. The Society's lengthy *Transactions* record little by way of her contributions to discussions following papers read out at the Society's meetings. On 10 March 1882, she is recorded as having objected to Ruskin's classifying Viola and Juliet together, and as insisting that 'Cordelia must have been beautiful, or else her sisters would not have hated her so'.[18] (She was responding to Ruskin's suggestion, reported in the Society's proceedings, that had she been beautiful Cordelia would never have been so wilfully misunderstood as Shakespeare suggests.) The scarcity and nature of her responses may, however, reflect the Society's recording practices more accurately than they do Marx's participation in debate.

It was during this period too, of the late 1870s and early 1880s, that Marx's love of Shakespeare inspired her desire to be an actress. In June 1881, she made arrangements to take lessons from Mrs Hermann Vezin, and in March of the following year, having studied Juliet with the retired actress, felt sufficiently confident to be able to comment to her sister Jenny that Ellen Terry's Juliet was 'the most disappointing feature' of an otherwise 'exquisite production' at the Lyceum, and that the poison scene was particularly poor,[19] a comment that would have its own gruesome resonances in years to come. According to Engels, Marx 'modelled herself on Ellen Terry',[20] so she would have watched the performance of Juliet, arguably the nineteenth century's favourite Shakespearean female part, with particular interest. Prompted perhaps by Terry, Marx was compelled by what Jenny described, in a letter written in April 1882, as 'the prospect of living the only free life a woman can live – the artistic one' (quoted in Kapp I, 234–5). Had the sisters then known more of the actual conditions of the late Victorian stage, and the extent to which actresses' work, far from being a source of freedom, was profoundly bound both by economic considerations and their audiences' desires, their view of the potential of the actress's scope might have been different. However, apparently ignorant of these considerations, the progressive and excited view Marx took of the stage, and specifically of the actress's opportunities, was coterminous with her sense of the emotional freedoms and regenerative, liberating aspects represented by Shakespeare.

Marx's lessons with Mrs Vezin, which regrettably did not end in her working as a professional actress, heightened her awareness of a language and set of resources which, as her own writings show, were to remain of crucial importance to her, and indeed helped to determine her assessments of other writers. In the introduction to her 1886 translation of *Madame Bovary*, Marx-Aveling, as she was then known following her decision to live with Edward Aveling, constructs an introduction to and assessment of

Flaubert for her English readers which is largely based on an extended comparison with Shakespeare, most notably on the grounds of the enormous variety of each man's output, and in the quality of their both striving painstakingly for the 'ideal perfection' of the true artist.[21] In part, her assessment of Flaubert seems determined by his own regard for Shakespeare. She approvingly quotes an 1875 letter to George Sand: 'I am reading nothing, with the exception of Shakespeare, whom I have gone through again from end to end. It strengthens one, and puts air into your lungs, as if you were on some high mountain. All else seems mediocre by the side of this tremendous fellow' ('Introduction', p. xi).

Marx's understanding of the precise nature of this life-affirming quality is elaborated later, when she assesses the nature of Emma Bovary's reality. Emma Bovary is real, not because based on a real woman, but 'real as Hamlet or Lear, Goriot or Eugenie Grandet' are real. Emma's tragedy is that of Shakespeare's characters, who 'act as they do because they *must*. It may be immoral, contrary even to their own personal interests ... but it must be – it is inevitable' ('Introduction', p. xvi). This is a revealing interpretation of reality on the part of the social reformer. For her, it is a condition which inevitably contains the danger of self-destruction, in a world which is not necessarily equipped to assess sympathetically or properly actions which might incidentally act against the perceived good of society or common sense, in their more proper attention to the determining factors of integrity and honesty. Again Marx espouses for Shakespeare's characters an emotional commitment which is its own ineluctable reward, regardless of its seeming results in the social and political world.

We can begin to find in this introduction the seeds of a reading of Shakespeare which explores a fissure between the writer and a society which had come to adopt him as a national emblem. Although for both Eleanor Marx and her father Shakespeare always signified and was indivisible from a notion of English-ness, this was not necessarily coterminous with the England in which they lived. Their Shakespeare was deliberately acquired by learning, and through the mechanism of translation, rather than by their participation in the process which made Shakespeare the birthright, however neglected Furnivall perceived it to be, of every Englishman. Their Shakespeare could as readily be turned against, as employed to signify, the Victorian period, as George Eliot too had perceived.

Siegfried Prawer has shown, in his *Karl Marx and World Literature*, how crucial Shakespeare was to Karl Marx's thinking, suggesting indeed that Shakespeare's characters 'aid Marx in conceiving and formulating his own message'.[22] Rather than simply acting as a useful medium of illustration,

Shakespeare actually functions as part of the fabric of Karl Marx's writings, just as he was an acquired part of the fabric of his language. In Shakespeare, Prawer suggests, Karl Marx found access to a form of clarification which effectively helped him to assess his own world, and, more specifically, he found an 'image of England that once existed but now has vanished from all but literature; he then uses that image as a means of criticising the England of his own day.' He goes on to quote Karl Marx himself:

The emergence of sharp class divisions, extraordinarily complete division of labour, and a so-called 'public opinion' which is manipulated by the Brahmins of the Press have … brought into being a monotonous sameness of character that would make Shakespeare, for instance, fail to recognise his compatriots.[23]

For Karl Marx then, Shakespeare and his characters are redolent of a moment that is both potentially persistently desirable, and prelapsarian in specifically English terms.

The novelist and feminist Olive Schreiner, who was one of Marx's closest friends, responds similarly to Shakespeare. She champions him throughout her letters for the quality of life in his characters, and for his own humanity, writing to her husband in 1911: 'I've just been reading Shakespeare's *Measure for Measure*. How pure and beautiful and sweet he is, but *broadly human*, but with such a high sense of honour always. Never in one instance does he countenance falsehood or disloyalty between human souls.'[24] Later that year, she describes to Havelock Ellis the 'lived' quality of Shakespeare's characters, the extent to which he 'felt his characters'. Schreiner finds as well as purity a concentration of emotion in Shakespeare's characters which seems unavailable in contemporary society, and thus articulates the ways in which Shakespeare can be meaningful for women without their having to appeal to the kind of idealising tendencies associated with earlier Victorian society. We can see in Schreiner's writings the possibility of a Shakespeare who could become politically useful for the late Victorian woman who would read him from a position outside the parameters of conventional power structures.

This is more fully exemplified in Marx's publication (jointly with Edward Aveling), in the same year that her translation of *Madame Bovary* appeared, of *The Woman Question*, a pamphlet in which the Avelings protest against the contemporary situation of women, and most notably the prescription of chastity for those who were unmarried. The pamphlet embraces the kind of emotionally generous Shakespeare invoked in the Flaubert introduction through references to Miranda and to Helena in *All's Well That Ends Well*. In their critique of society's treatment of women,

Marx and Aveling refer to 'the rigorous social rule that from man only must come the first proffer of affection, the proposal for marriage', and use examples from 'our Shakespeare' to show that 'this is no natural law':

Miranda, untrammelled by society, tenders herself to Ferdinand. 'I am your wife if you will marry me: if not I'll die your maid:' and Helena ... with her love for Bertram, that carried her from Rousillon to Paris and Florence is, as Coleridge has it, 'Shakspere's loveliest character.'[25]

The examples are touching, and act in part as a measure of the degeneration of their own country, and its failure to advance the claims of women. In more personal terms, in the mismatch between Marx's own situation, and that which the examples conjure up, we see revealed most poignantly the extent of what can only be described as her 'belief' in the emotional structures of Shakespeare, and the gap between that aspirational faith and her own relationship with Aveling. Though the couple were living together, Aveling contracted a secret marriage with another woman, a young actress, shortly before Marx's death by poisoning in 1898.

The Avelings' relationship was in part based upon a shared enthusiasm for the theatre. Aaron Rosebury reports that she told a friend: 'Our tastes were much the same ... We agreed on Socialism. We both loved the theatre ... We could work together effectively' (Kapp, II, 204). In particular they shared a love of Shakespeare. The couple collaborated on a series of 'Dramatic Notes' for *Tinsley's Magazine* in 1890–1, which included an enthusiastic review of the Lyceum's revival of *Much Ado About Nothing*, and a more sceptical account of Lillie Langtry's Cleopatra at the Princess's.[26] Aveling's own writings on Shakespeare only serve in fact to show up the distance between them on this shared love. He produced a series of essays on 'Shakespeare the Dramatist' for the first two volumes of Annie Besant's *Our Corner* in 1883,[27] which are an extended version of his 'Hall of Science Thursday lectures' given on the 'Plays of Shakespeare' in the previous year. Nowhere in these writings can we see anything like the sympathetic, even empathic, commitment to Shakespeare espoused by Marx. Rather, Aveling uses Shakespeare as a means of insisting upon his own privileged access to the playwright which he is prepared to share with his listeners. He introduces his remarks with rather bombastic modesty by saying of Shakespeare that 'the innermost thought of him is only comprehended by those rarer minds, to whose fuller comprehension of his words and works haply some of us here may in good time attain'.[28] Havelock Ellis wrote of Aveling: 'His mental powers were certainly vigorous, though he was devoid of any intellectual originality. All his writings exhibit a receptive power of comprehension and of lucid exposition.'[29] His powers, never very pronounced in these lectures, are those of analysis and tabulation, rather than the more profound and committed form of understanding shown by Marx. Aveling was speaking under a socialist banner, but his reading of Shakespeare is effectively based on exclusivity. Nowhere in his lectures is there the emphasis on a shared access, on the kind of inclusivity espoused by Eleanor and Karl Marx in their writings on Shakespeare. Aveling's Shakespeare has always to be filtered through his own mediating presence. At no point does he suggest ways in which Shakespeare might be directly enabling to his readers, whereas in Eleanor Marx's critiques of contemporary society, particularly of the place of women and workers in that society, Shakespeare represents a prelapsarian, pre-industrial voice signalling possibilities of regeneration for all through the recuperation of a past characterised by emotional integrity and generosity.

For Marx, however, the recuperation of that past is also tinged with a poignant personal longing. She found a brief taste of such a recovery in the cottage which she and Aveling found, just outside Stratford, in 1887:

One day, walking from Stratford to Bidford, (one of Shakespeare's well-known walks) we saw a farm – near the farm two cottages, one unlet. We inquired, found the rent was two shillings a week and … decided to rent this lovely little place. It is two miles from Stratford and Dodwell and consists of this farm and its two cottages. The farmer at first tried to explain these were only for … labourers – he could not understand our wanting to come. You would. Downstairs we have a large kitchen – stone-flagged of course, a back kitchen and wash-house in one and a pantry. Upstairs three rooms – two, of course, very small. Besides this we have a quarter of an acre of garden … Ed. goes out and digs up our potatoes as we need them and we have been sowing all sorts of things. Next spring our garden will be not only ornamental but useful … There's plenty of room … I can't tell you how charming this country life is after the hurry and worry and tear of London … Think of it Laura, Shakespeare's Home! We work two or three times a week at his 'birthplace' (by permission of the Librarian of the place) and we have been over this home, and seen the old guild Chapel that stands opposite 'New Place', and the old grammar school – unchanged – whither he went 'unwillingly to school'; and his grave in Trinity Church, and Ann Hathaway's cottage, still just as it was when master Will went a-courting, and Mary Arden's cottage at Wilmecote – the prettiest place of all. Now that I have been in this sleepy little Stratford and met the Stratfordians I know where all the Dogberries and Bottoms and Snugs come from. You'll meet them here today. Just near our 'Kastle' is a bank – many think it Titania's for it is covered with wild thyme and oxlips and violets … I never knew before how Stratfordian Shakespeare was. All the flowers are Stratford ones and Charlecote I would wager is Rosalind's Arden … we are settled here till our lessons and other work call us back to London … Then we get back to Chancery Lane to our teaching and usual dreary round of work. (quoted in Kapp, II, 209–10)

Marx joins a number of late Victorian women who find in Stratford a redemptive quality. The potential sentimentality of this letter is redeemed by the anguish which underlies and even impels it. This injects an extraordinary pathos into the personal relief afforded by the cottage, a relief clearly made possible for Marx by its Shakespearean connections. Her rural vision confirmed her access to Shakespeare as a poet who gave voice to the 'Dogberries and Bottoms and Snugs' as well as Helena, and enabled a visceral satisfaction in shared labour which temporarily overcame her emotional isolation.

Marx's final engagement with Shakespeare is a posthumous one, generated by Yvonne Kapp, who ends the second volume of her biography with Macbeth's words about his wife: 'She should have died hereafter' (V.v.17) The Shakespearean quotation in reference to Marx's suicide, an act which has been more often seen in the context of the *fin de siècle* and the heroines of Ibsen and Flaubert, is striking. Marx's suicide, and indeed her life, are far from the images of world-weary lassitude and ineffectualness experienced by such nineteenth-century literary characters as Emma Bovary, Hedda Gabler and Rebecca West. Rather her suicide might seem to have been generated by the perception of lost love, wasted sacrifice and thwarted ambition, arguably experienced by such heroines as Ophelia, Cleopatra and perhaps most notably Lady Macbeth. We might also look to Wilde's *The Picture of Dorian Gray* (1891) and to Sybil Vane for an example of a character who, like Marx, believed in the possibility of finding and living out the emotional intensities of Shakespeare, but who is disappointed in the man with whom that dream and that emotional rhetoric had seemed to be a possibility. 'Suicide in Shakespeare' had been discussed at the New Shakspere Society meeting of 13 January 1882, when the Reverend J. Kirkman suggested that in women 'emotion became uncontrollable, and gave a final momentum' to their action, and further implies that in the case of Lady Macbeth her moral strength was partly responsible for her act. Comparing her with Richard III, he suggests that it was the latter's 'moral cowardice [that] retained him for punishment this side of the act'.[30] Lady Macbeth's suicide thus indirectly becomes a condemnation of a world unfit to appreciate her integrity, rather than an act of despair more appropriate to one of the *fin de siècle*'s degenerates. It is at this point, however, that the critic has to stop short of insisting on a final identification of Eleanor Marx as one of Shakespeare's heroines. However tempting the chance to explain, define, confine the act of suicide, it has surely to be resisted, lest in the cause of one's own anxieties one denies Marx's autonomy, and the very things which attracted her to Shakespeare.

The analogy with Lady Macbeth does, however, bear examination in its own right beyond the circumstances of the character's death, for she was a figure with whom Marx had previously been compared. An article in the *Radical* journal of December 1893 describes Marx at a meeting to discuss the possibility of a demonstration in Hyde Park, in the face of the threat of violent suppression, as 'Lady Macbeth Aveling', and goes on to picture the 'lofty scorn' with which she responded to peaceful suggestions. The journalist goes on: 'When the resolution proposing the Hyde Park meeting was read Lady Macbeth turned to Edward, D.Sc., and hissed "C-o-w-a-r-d-s!" between her teeth. It was very fine indeed: something of the "Infirm of purpose! give *me* the daggers!" school of acting' (quoted in Kapp, II, 233–4). What was it about Lady Macbeth that tempts both Kapp and the *Radical* journalist to liken Marx to her?

Lady Macbeth was a famously controversial figure during the Victorian period, and was often discussed by the New Shakspere Society, whose recorded opinions were often split along gender lines. A paper by the Countess of Charlemont in 1876, claiming that Lady Macbeth's devotion to her husband was her sole motivation, was rejected forcibly by Dr Furnivall.[31] A further paper on Lady Macbeth given in 1889 by Beatrice Lamb argued that 'Lady Macbeth was of an unselfish and noble nature, and did what she did only that [Macbeth] might be king'.[32] The *Transactions* record that 'an animated discussion followed, in which almost every one of Miss Lamb's points and conclusions were denied, and declared to be in direct contradiction to Shakespeare's text, though a few speakers defended her'. Ellen Terry, whose performances held a particular interest for Marx, played Lady Macbeth as a devoted wife to mixed responses in 1888. Terry sought to convey the idea that Lady Macbeth was no fiend, but was motivated in her actions by her love for her husband. The part was something of a turning point in the actress's career, her triumph in that role lying not in being found charming, as was her usual critical fate, but in exciting critical dissension and discussion. She herself wrote: 'The critics differ, and discuss it hotly, which in itself is my best success of all' (Terry, *Story*, p. 306).

An earlier view of Lady Macbeth is given in Jameson's *Shakespeare's Heroines*. In her comments on Lady Macbeth, she argues that we see in her 'the possible result of the noblest faculties uncontrolled or perverted' (Jameson, p. 361). The paradigm informing Jameson's reading is based on what she describes as a fundamental divisibility between person and context, a divisibility which she suggests is camouflaged in the study of history, but which is evident in Shakespeare:

In history we can but study character in relation to events, to situation and circumstances, which disguise and encumber it: we are left to imagine, to infer, what certain people must have been, from the manner in which they have acted or suffered. Shakespeare and nature bring us back to the true order of things; and showing us what the human being is, enable us to judge of the possible as well as the positive result in acting and suffering. (p. 360)

Jameson's reading of Shakespeare, which she employs in order to illustrate what women are capable of, has much in common with Eleanor Marx's responses to the playwright, and her turning to him as one who might articulate possibilities apparently unavailable to her elsewhere in contemporary society. Marx's enthusiasm for and commitment to Shakespeare ultimately confirm for herself and for the playwright a revolutionary, critical potential in the late Victorian period.

MARIE CORELLI

Yet Shakespeare was not solely the preserve of the New or Socialist Woman at this time. Arguably Shakespeare's best-known female champion at this period was Marie Corelli, best-selling author, self-determined scourge of the new, dedicated controversialist, and a leading figure in Stratford in the 1890s. Corelli was renowned for the personal gondola – and gondolier – she maintained on the Avon, for her daily promenades amongst her adoring fans, and for the celebrities she entertained at her home, Hall's Croft, now appropriately part of the Shakespeare Institute at Stratford. Corelli and her friend Bertha Vyver fell in love with Stratford when they recuperated there following the final illness of Bertha's mother in 1890. A few years later Corelli wrote to a Mrs Corker, the then owner of Hall's Croft, from whom she hoped to rent the house: 'I ... am only seeking peace and comfortable surroundings in dear Shakespeare-land in order to finish my new book'.[33] Once installed in Stratford, Corelli became an indefatigable campaigner for the protection of the relics and memorials in, through and by which the town remembered its playwright. Part of the attraction of Hall's Croft itself was its associations with Shakespeare's family. His daughter Susanna had lived there during her marriage to Dr Hall. On discovering a debt being carried by Holy Trinity church, where Shakespeare is buried, Corelli wrote to Ellen Terry to enlist the actress's help in paying it off. Terry replied in characteristic fashion:

I'll do what I can to help, but at the moment I am ill and confined to my bed, but what a disgrace ... I don't quite know how to beg, but I'll try. People should rush forward longing to do each a little in such a case. Shakespeare! (quoted in Ransom, p. 107)

A friend of Terry and Irving's, Corelli was less enamoured of Helen Faucit, or rather of the efforts made shortly after her death by her widower to cement a posthumous alliance between the actress and Shakespeare. Sir Theodore Martin presented Holy Trinity Church with a new green marble pulpit in 1900, which was decorated with five full-length images of female saints in white marble. The figure of St Helena was held to resemble the young Helen Faucit (Jones Carlisle, p. 269). In the eyes of Corelli, however, Martin threatened to go a step too far in seeking to install a marble tablet in memory of his wife opposite that memorialising Shakespeare. This would have involved removing a tablet commemorating a former vicar, which Martin gained permission to do. However, on Corelli's discovering that the vicar's widow had not been consulted, Martin withdrew his plans amidst accusations from Corelli that he had attempted, by means of promising a substantial contribution to the church, to buy his way into favour with the church authorities (p. 270). Corelli seems to have shown little sympathy for the grieving widower, and rather relished the episode as an opportunity to carry out the campaigning role for which she was increasingly becoming renowned.

As well as being a popular novelist, Corelli was a polemicist whose arguments could ally her with those new women who were otherwise one of her favourite targets. In an outspoken piece, 'The Modern Marriage Market', for instance, she likens Istanbul's slave markets to the London season:

> when women are as coolly 'brought out' to be sold as any unhappy Armenian girl that ever shuddered at the lewd gaze of a Turkish tyrant … It is an absolutely grim fact that in England, women – those of the upper classes, at any rate – are not today married, but bought for a price.[34]

However, rather than advocating a thorough examination of the basis of marriage, as writers such as Mona Caird or Sarah Grand did at the time, Corelli ends by suggesting that the solution lies in women's own hands; that if they hold on to the ideal of love they will not go wrong and will not contract a purely mercenary marriage. Poverty is advocated as helpful in that it can strengthen a married partnership through adversity. The state of contemporary marriage clearly provides a vehicle, as did Corelli's championing of Shakespeare, for a form of energy which craved the outlet of publicity, albeit through a sublimated form, and which needed authorisation through a greater good, whether that be the protection of young women, or the protection of Shakespeare.

In Corelli's popular 1895 novel , *The Sorrows of Satan*, the two issues come together as Corelli writes of the dangers of improper literature which

corrupts the innocence of her character Sybil Tempest, and advocates
instead the more idealistic fiction produced by Mavis Clare (her initials
the same as the real novelist's pseudonym), whose inspirations are the
literary and Classical figures commemorated in the busts and quotations
which adorn the writing room of her modest but cosy cottage, nestling on
the banks of the Avon in 'poet-haunted Warwickshire'.[35] One of the panels
in Mavis's study is of 'a fine engraving of Shakespeare', under which are to
be found Polonius's words: 'to thine own self be true, And it must follow,
as the night the day, / Thou canst not then be false to any man' (*Hamlet*,
I.iii.78–80). It is one of a number of references to *Hamlet* in the text, not all
of which are so fully acknowledged, and which unequivocally unite Mavis
Clare and Shakespeare in alliance against the forces of a newly degenerate
form of literature which has lost its integrity in its twin aims of trying to sell
and to shock. As Lucio Rimanez, who is ultimately discovered to be the
Satan of the title, declares to Geoffrey Tempest, an aspiring author:

Not one author in many centuries writes from his own heart or as he truly feels –
when he does, he becomes well-nigh immortal. This planet is too limited to hold
more than one Homer, one Plato, one Shakespeare. Don't disturb yourself – you
are neither of these three! You belong to the age, Tempest – it is a decadent
ephemeral age, and most things connected with it are decadent and ephemeral.
(Corelli, *Sorrows*, p. 62)

It is a measure of the decadence, the apostasy of the age that, through the
agency of Rimanez, several critics are secured to review favourably
Tempest's novel, and will praise him as 'the newest discovered "genius" of
the day, only a little way removed from Shakespeare himself (three of the big
leading magazines are guaranteed to say that)' (p. 141). In due course,
Tempest does indeed find himself compared to 'a new Aeschylus and
Shakespeare combined' (p. 146).

Mavis Clare and the Devil effect an initially unlikely alliance in their joint
apprehension of the greatness of Shakespeare, and of the extent to which
that greatness had either gone unrealised or was misused in the 1890s. In the
unacknowledged borrowings from Shakespeare which are scattered liberally
throughout her work, such as Rimanez's observation that 'Everything in
the Universe is perfect ... except that curious piece of work – Man' (p. 68),
which recalls *Hamlet*, and in her more direct tributes to Shakespeare, such as
Rimanez's calling him 'the uncrowned but actual King of England' (p. 174),
Mavis Clare and her creator ally themselves directly with the genius of
Shakespeare in such a way as to suggest that Corelli is, if not his living
representative, then the next best thing, his most sympathetic and forthright
witness. Crucially she is a witness to him in an age which seems to have

forgotten not only him, but the integrity and moral worth which he represents to her, the scale of values, discernment, and wisdom upon which Corelli can draw in describing Tempest's publisher as 'not, like Shakespeare's Cassio, strictly "an honourable man"' (p. 78),[36] and in giving Lady Sibyl her only moment of true wisdom immediately before her self-inflicted death in having her repeat Hamlet's final words – 'The rest is silence' (V.ii.372) – as her own.

Following a disastrous voyage and subsequent shipwreck spent in the company of the devil, a reformed Geoffrey Tempest can welcome his return to Shakespeare's 'happy isle', invoking the 'sceptr'd isle' of *Richard II*, II.i.4. But such a joint recognition of England as distinctively Shakespeare's land, and of Shakespeare's authority, is hard won and places him, in the novel's terms, in a discerning, anti-contemporary minority with whom Shakespeare is allied in a spirit informed by the kind of restless social antagonism experienced by both Eleanor Marx and Mathilde Blind. All three women, in their different political, financial and literary positions, find themselves at odds with their age, and find in Shakespeare their most natural resource in attempting to articulate that sense of unease. Though highly popular in England, and indeed throughout the Empire, Corelli never achieved the critical recognition she craved, and her use of Shakespeare becomes both her claim to that recognition and a measure of her superiority to her critics. Throughout the century, we have of course seen numerous women resorting to Shakespeare in their disaffection with aspects of their contemporary moment, but in the unexpected alliance of these women of the 1890s we see the extent of the strength of Shakespeare's resonant language, articulating as it does the intensity of the women's disaffection with their age, and the flexibility, or rather the depth, of the emotional articulacy of a playwright whose words can cut through the actual differences in these women's positions and beliefs to express the recognisably common root of their experience of contemporary disenfranchisement, be it emotional, political or literary. The women's allegiance to Shakespeare, and his usefulness to them, is figured partially through their extensive use of his language and images to give form to their feelings, through which strategy is created a compensatory form of solidarity, both with him, and with their female contemporaries at a moment in which the evolution of a shared literary language was part of the repertoire of the New Woman. But the connection with Shakespeare is also made through these women's affiliations to Stratford, and their recovery of a form of artistry and industry which, certainly for Marx and Blind, pre-dates their own century.

Jonathan Bate has convincingly demonstrated the ways in which the burgeoning concepts of the 'genius' of Shakespeare and of his status as national poet were ineluctably linked with his roots in Stratford and the Warwickshire countryside. His strategic embedding in his native environment, argues Bate, enables the construction of Shakespeare as one distinguished by his epitomising Englishness:

The Shakespearean temperament was seen to match the English temperament: empirical, sceptical, unsystematic, ironic. Shakespeare's rural origins proved invaluable to this process whereby he was reconstituted as the national poet. In the eighteenth century the Bard was seen as a country boy, a genius of the English earth, not a city man.[37]

The English countryside becomes the root of creativity and of the imagination, especially in the late eighteenth and early nineteenth centuries, when the 'Romantic idea of authorship locate[d] the essence of genius *in the scene of writing*' (p. 82). In some ways then, Blind, Corelli and Marx, in their specific affiliations to the countryside, might seem to be reviving an earlier understanding of the significance of Stratford and its environs in the face of the town's increasingly commercial status at the hub of a developing tourist industry. Yet the oppositional nature of the affiliation which is created fundamentally disrupts the harmony Bate cites between poet, rural identity and nation. Rather the women find in Shakespeare a voice out of tune with their times, although not their own aspirations. What had previously signalled the poet's national standing and identity now becomes a measure of his, and the women's, lack of affiliation with their late nineteenth-century moment. Variously disenfranchised by romantic disappointment, ill health and the disdain of the literary establishment, late Victorian women could make Shakespeare into an ally in a manoeuvre which simultaneously bereft the establishment of one of its cornerstones.

Marx and Blind did so, as we have seen, by effecting their own alliance in nature with a poet who seemed to them able to voice an anti-capitalist identification with their contemporary dissatisfactions. Corelli did so rather by taking on the forces of capitalism, as manifested in the local interests of tourism and civic identity, and exposing their inadequacy as guardians of the memory of Shakespeare as it was manifested in the buildings which his presence had sanctified. Taking confident advantage of her own fame and the extent of her popularity, Corelli took on the Trustees of Shakespeare's birthplace in their attempts to create a new Carnegie library for the town in Henley Street on the site of some cottages which were contemporaneous with Shakespeare, and which thus, as she believed, should not be altered. Corelli published her version of events in:

THE PLAIN TRUTH OF THE STRATFORD-ON-AVON CONTROVERSY: CONCERNING THE FULLY-INTENDED DEMOLITION OF OLD HOUSES IN
HENLEY STREET, AND THE CHANGES PROPOSED TO BE EFFECTED ON THE

National Ground of
Shakespeare's Birthplace
MARIE CORELLI
'Fear not my truth; the moral of my wit
Is "plain and true".'

SHAKESPEARE
Troilus and Cressida[38]

Corelli's is an exhaustively detailed narrative of the attempts of the members of the Shakespeare Birthplace Trust to enable the demolition of two houses on Henley Street (also the street on which the birthplace was to be found), and the alteration of a third in order to enable the construction of a Carnegie library for Stratford. During the ensuing controversy, Corelli set herself firmly against both the Trustees, many of whom were also councillors in Stratford, and the substantial wealth of Andrew Carnegie, whose generosity had seen free libraries established throughout the United Kingdom and Ireland. In all, Carnegie would finance the building of 660 libraries in these countries (out of a total worldwide of 2,811), at the cost of nearly $12 million. Corelli's opponents are chided for their lack of respect for their Shakespearean heritage, which is shared by both English and American alike, and in Carnegie's case, for the vulgarity of his attempting to use his substantial wealth to ride roughshod over local opinion. The most xenophobic and frankly snobby objections to Carnegie are articulated by Lady Vera Campbell, in a letter fully quoted by Corelli:

Dear Miss Corelli, – Can you, who have already done so much for Shakespeare and for Stratford [presumably an allusion to the Faucit Martin affair], not raise your voice once more to save the old houses next to Shakespeare's, which are apparently doomed to make way for Mr Carnegie's new library?

Surely it is far more important that Stratford should keep the houses that must surely have formed part of Shakespeare's early life, as much as his own abode, rather than that they should be wiped out to please a modern American Millionaire? …

I do hope that you with your all-powerful pen and influence, will do something to prevent this ruthless act of destroying what it is impossible for all the Carnegies in the world to replace! – Truly yours Vera Campbell (*Plain Truth*, p. 4)

The newness of American money blunts the appreciation of time-hallowed associations which nothing can replace, and modernity threatens the authority of history in a contemporary battle for culture which sees the socially aspirational author opposing the free libraries which might have benefited some of her own readers, and arguably even augmented her readership. Such is Corelli's desire to ally herself with aristocracy and Shakespeare in a rejoinder to the American philanthropist and his supporters that concepts of social justice are submerged. Corelli was, however, careful to position herself as a voice of the people in opposition to both Carnegie and his local representatives. Using the local and national press to maximum effect, and even briefly setting up her own newspaper to promulgate her views to a local readership, Corelli professed to express 'a very general and deeply-felt opinion by saying that when there are so few old-world towns remaining unspoilt in England, the Birthplace of Stratford should at least be guarded more sacredly for the nation at large than that a portion of its most historic street should be left open to the easy purchase of the mere millionaire'.[39] Authorised by her affiliations with Stratford itself and its people, Corelli goes on to contend that 'I do not think I am mistaken in believing that the smallest and most traditional scrap of Shakespearean times is dearer to the world than a wilderness of Free Libraries' (*Plain Truth*, p. 45).

And it is indeed the case that the controversy was over a 'scrap' of Shakespearean times: two cottages adjacent to and contemporaneous with the Birthplace, and which Corelli suggests 'must' have been familiar to the young Will. The cottages are hallowed by an association which Corelli suggests Carnegie and the local Trustees are too callow to appreciate. Eventually, through skilful manipulation of public opinion and a consistent insistence on the validity of her heightened appreciation of the two tumble-down cottages, as well as a detailed demonstration of the ways in which she felt that the Trustees had been willing to pull the wool over local residents' eyes, Corelli won the day: the cottages were saved, and Henley Street remained intact. The whole exercise had proved Corelli's energy, her skills in managing public opinion, and a degree of combativeness which was also in evidence in her public controversies with a literary establishment which kept her firmly positioned as a popular rather than serious author. Much of the *Sorrows of Satan* is taken up with this debate, as Corelli exposes contemporary reviewing to be a venal trade and critical opinion ready to be cheaply bought. Luckily for her and her alter ego Mavis Clare, public opinion is too wise to be similarly easily swayed and retains its integrity in preferring the works of the woman writer to those puffed by periodical reviewers. As we have seen, this form of demotic authorisation is also in evidence in the Henley Street controversy, where Corelli purports to speak for and of the people of Stratford and to make them the most virtuous and proper protectors of the name of Shakespeare in the face of the philistinism of local leaders and the national press. Curiously then, Corelli espouses a form of radical democratisation, albeit for a fundamentally conservative end as she and the 'people' of the town set out to protect Shakespeare. Shakespeare commensurately becomes a popular rather than an establishment figure, joining Corelli in her oppositional state. There may then be more common ground between the radical Eleanor Marx, Mathilde Blind and Marie Corelli than has previously seemed apparent, united as all three are in their attempts to realise Shakespeare and his continuing presence in the late Victorian and early twentieth-century periods.

'THE BIRTHPLACE'

The Henley Street controversy coincides historically with 'The Birthplace'. Whose birthplace is not specified, but the implications are clearly that Shakespeare lies behind the shrine, 'the early home of the supreme poet, the Mecca of the English-speaking race' (p. 181), which is at the centre of story. In a number of ways, the story speaks directly to the Henley Street controversy and its conflict between modernity and heritage. Gedge is even originally in 'charge of the grey town-library of Blackport-on-Dwindle, all granite, fog and female fiction', a 'narrow prison, so grim with enlightenment' (p. 181). The conflict of this story hinges on Gedge's being unable to sustain his guardianship duties sufficiently enthusiastically in the face of his growing dissatisfaction with his own role as perpetuator of what might be a fraud ultimately damaging to the actual renown of the playwright. Yet for many people in addition to James's tourists, Shakespeare precisely was Stratford, from the New Shakspere Society, who evolved their narrative of the playwright's progression from their sense of his personal history, to those critics who, as Gordon McMullan has pointed out, came specifically to associate late Shakespeare with his return to Stratford late in life:

The final period of Shakespeare's life in Stratford thus complements the final period of his work, allowing lateness to be defined synecdochically, through the location of the last days of the National Poet, with England: it is Stratford's quintessential rural Englishness, finally, rather than cosmopolitan London, which embodies the later serenity of the master.[40]

James is deeply fearful of the implications of a posterity based in geography, in space and relics, for, as Gedge suggests to the sympathetic American visitor Mr Hayes, to locate a long dead and revered author in such a way is to render him less achievable and knowable than ever, as it obscures the work in an attempt to revive the man.

It is only possible to speculate about what James might have made of Corelli's zealously aggrandising efforts to protect the Shrine, or of Marx and Blind's more private experiences of making contact with something fundamentally Shakespearean in believing that they were experiencing the natural world that he grew up in. They might for James simply have been variations on the kind of literary tourist, creeping parasitically and destructively around the shrine at which they professed to worship and which he creates in 'The Birthplace'. One might argue that Corelli was such a parasite in using the renown and stature of Shakespeare to increase her own status and standing, but for Marx and Blind, and those other women throughout the century, such as Barrett Browning, who had revered the possibility of Shakespeare's relics, these were significant not in their own right but because they enabled an act of connection which was transhistorical, rather than ahistorical, a connection which went beyond the material in an attempt to connect emotionally with a form of authenticity that Shakespeare could provide. For them the relics and places are a form of visceral reminder of the words which had brought Shakespeare alive to them in the first place, and as such I would suggest that James would do a disservice to Blind and Marx in bracketing them with other literary tourists of his day. Far from disregarding Shakespeare's words, it was those words themselves which acted as the stimulus to trying to find a relic of the man and of the moment in which those words were created, and thus effecting a more concrete connection with a more sympathetic time than their own. James overlooks the fact that literary relics, literary tourism, are about more than a spatial connection, that they can involve a temporal connection too, and that as such they can retain intact at their heart the figure of the inspirational writer.

CHAPTER 6

Shakespeare and the actress in the 1890s

During most of the Victorian period, the concept of the 'Shakespearean actress' was one which carried transparent cultural connotations of an actress defined primarily by, and known mainly for, her work in Shakespeare's plays. The best-known of these figures were Helen Faucit, Fanny Kemble and Ellen Terry, with Sarah Siddons their most illustrious eighteenth-century predecessor. Such actresses were not, of course, only to be seen in Shakespeare, but their grounding in his work coloured appreciation of their other performances, and conferred upon those appearances something of the legitimacy that their Shakespearean reputation entailed. The term was most redolent when the Shakespearean heroine being played and contemporary ideologies concerning the feminine were made most synonymous, that is, when the Shakespeare woman and the Shakespearean actress most closely coincided. Thus the stage and Shakespeare's works were embedded within a symbiotic relationship with contemporary gender politics. As we have seen throughout the century, the complicity of that relationship was continually being tested by women who found in Shakespeare a far from conventional voice, and whose language and women might offer a form of dissent rather than of assent. But on the legitimate stage the story is very different, being rather one of containment: within the economic imperative to please an audience; within the company and its dynamics; and within a text which was rather moulded to its theatrical and cultural moment than representative of Shakespeare's own writing. Indeed, Helen Faucit was one of the period's most significant promoters of an institutionalised Shakespeare.

In the 1890s, however, this narrative is challenged, as the stage achieves a cultural and political centrality through a dissonance which puts it at the nexus of a range of contemporary discourses and concerns, not least of which were the issues concerning the New Woman, herself a profoundly literary figure, both in the sense of being created through literature and in using literature as a crucial tool in her attempts to win greater political, cultural and personal autonomy. Within this context, the possibility, and legibility, of the 'Shakespearean actress' becomes occluded, as actresses of the 'New' theatre tackle Shakespeare alongside Ibsen, as Ellen Terry's visibility declines along with the fortunes of the Lyceum, and as Shakespeare himself is written more explicitly into controversy through the criticism of George Bernard Shaw. Shakespeare continued to be performed to large audiences in the 1890s, in the Lyceum, which was Shaw's favourite target, as well as in the theatres of Beerbohm Tree (Her Majesty's, and later the Haymarket), Augustin Daly (Lyceum and Daly's) and Charles Calvert in Manchester, to name but three. But his plays were also the subject of more innovative forms of theatre, as demonstrated by the experimental theatre of William Poel, who aimed as far as possible to recreate sixteenth-century stage conditions in his productions with the Elizabethan Stage Society, and by a number of all-women productions which experimented with the well-established tradition of travesti performances in Shakespeare. Indeed, far from being a spent force in nineties theatre, and one that, Shaw would hold, had been superseded by Ibsen and the new drama, Shakespeare prospered with newly energised practitioners and the theatre-going public.

So what of the 'Shakespearean actress' in this period? Despite the continuing presence in the theatre of Ellen Terry and the emergence of Ada Rehan, both most noted for their Shakespearean roles, it seems more difficult to use the appellation 'Shakespearean actress' of this decade, given the variety of types of performance being produced, and theatrical experiences on offer, and the often oppositional responses to that figure. Rather, I would suggest that, in this decade, the legitimate theatre and its women are fully initiated into the possibilities of the radical Shakespeare whom other women had long been hearing and reading. The deaths of Kemble and Faucit in 1893 and 1898 signal the generational shift being effected as actresses emerge out of the control of the actor-manager to put themselves centre stage, and thus to enter into fundamentally new relationships with Shakespeare.

ELLEN TERRY

Ellen Terry's work with Shakespeare was an ineluctable part of both her persona and of the professional work which had, since 1856, made her into probably the best-loved and most famous British actress of the century. That work has been amply examined in numerous biographies and essays, most effectively by Nina Auerbach, Roger Manvell and Michael C. Booth.[1] I am mainly concerned here with the ways in which Terry negotiated the end-of-century conditions affecting Shakespearean productions, how she herself moved away from the cultural centrality of the Lyceum stage, and with her writings on Shakespeare, which offer a new dimension to his role and availability for the actress beyond the confines of the spectacular Lyceum stage.

Terry's own account of herself positions her as one who had always felt a considerable affinity for the dramatist. Her autobiography provides a narrative of one literally born, as she notes with great rejoicing, into Shakespeare's Warwickshire, and destined soon to appear on stage in 1856 as Mamilius in Charles Kean's *The Winter's Tale* at the Princess's Theatre. She writes gleefully of this role: 'a real Shakespeare part – a possession that father had taught me to consider the pride of life!' (Terry, *Story*, p. 8). Mamilius is just the beginning of a professional life spent interpreting Shakespeare, first with Charles Kean, and most famously with Irving at the Lyceum. Christopher St John notes the intimacy of the terms upon which Terry lived with Shakespeare and his characters in her introduction to Terry's *Four Lectures on Shakespeare*, which were published in 1932:

> She told Henry Irving once that Shakespeare was the only man she had ever really loved. 'When I was about sixteen or seventeen, and very unhappy, I foreswore the society of men … Yet I was lonely all the same. I wanted a sweetheart! I read everything I could get hold of about my beloved one. I lived with him in his plays.'[2]

The romantic metaphor she used to Irving, similar to those images of domestic or sentimental attraction used by and of many Victorian women in relation to Shakespeare, prolongs the performed rhetoric which made Terry the century's most enduring and 'charming' Shakespearean performer, but also articulates the beginning of the professional and scholarly commitment which lay behind her status as a leading interpreter of Shakespeare's women. During much of her career it was that narrative of perpetual romance, which constantly eludes or avoids closure, which informed audiences' reception of her own acting, for responses to Terry throughout her career remain remarkably static. Her perpetual charm is precisely that, a perpetuation of her audiences' initial enamoured response. That stasis begins to explain why it is not only possible, but necessary, for Terry to play the parts of much younger characters, or to reprise some of her earlier successes in later life: it enables the repetition of the terms of her success, reminds her audiences of why they have adored her, and enables them to keep on loving her, and watching her play. Even when she takes on a new role – for instance, Imogen in Irving's 1896 production of *Cymbeline* – reviewers' responses articulate the grounds of her success in a reiteration of the terms of her previous popularity, sometimes self-consciously:

Miss Terry plays the part with a radiance and a charm all her own, with a pathos and a grace of which she, among modern actresses, seems to possess the unique secret ... It is long since we have seen such girlish *abandon*, such womanly tenderness, as that elicited by the reading of the letter from Posthumus announcing his arrival at Milford Haven. Time seemed suddenly to be effaced, the years to roll back, and before us stood Miss Terry as young, as fragrant, and as bewitching as ever she was in the seventies.[3]

The *Times* reviewer writes that

Imogen is a very beautiful character, and Miss Ellen Terry (for whom it might have been designed) plays it with rare grace and charm ... with her airy grace and tender womanliness [she] is Imogen to the life ... it is in the true womanliness of Imogen that the actress excels, and here voice, manner, looks and temperament combine to help her.[4]

Any sense of history to be found in the latter review derives from the production history of the play, in which Siddons and Faucit had distinguished themselves. There is no sense to be gained of the play's status as a relatively late performance from Terry, who, by that time, had almost twenty years' experience of acting at the Lyceum behind her, though Archer's review in the *Theatrical 'World'* writes interestingly of the play as a late-Shakespeare production, in which he finds that 'the wheels of Shakespeare's intellect were whirling a little faster than is quite consistent with what we call the sanity of genius'.[5]

Critics and audiences were, on the whole, reluctant to allow Terry to grow up. To do so, would of course, have been to expel her from the theatrical space that she so happily occupied, and in which she was still enthusiastically received by audiences. It was perhaps from this state of perpetual youth that Bernard Shaw sought to rescue Terry when they launched, initially somewhat tentatively, into a correspondence which would see him attempt to woo her instead for his own theatrical vision of her. Terry's predicament was for Shaw endemic in the predicament of the female performer in Shakespeare at the end of the century. He saw the continued attendance of British audiences at Shakespeare performances in the 1890s as

sheer hypocrisy, the proof being that where an early play of [Shakespeare's] is revived, they take the utmost pains to suppress as much of it as possible, and disguise the rest past recognition, relying for success on extraordinary scenic attractions; on very popular performers, including, if possible, a famously beautiful actress in the leading part; and, above all, on Shakespeare's reputation and the consequent submission of the British public to be mercilessly bored by each of his plays once in their lifetime.[6]

The review is typically, mischievously Shavian. He would later write that 'the literary side of the mission of Ibsen here has been the rescue of this unhappy country from its centuries of slavery to Shakespeare' (*Our Theatres*, III, 343–4). However, in his correspondence with Terry he shows himself a sympathetic and knowledgeable reader of Shakespeare who tries simultaneously to rescue Shakespeare from the Victorians, and Terry from the Victorians' Shakespeare.

In their extended discussion of *Cymbeline* we see the exchange of views of theatre professionals, but we also see revealed the terms of *Cymbeline*'s success, the extent to which Terry's own success as Imogen relied upon her toleration of her audiences' unrealistic preconceptions concerning herself, and the ways in which, according to Bernard Shaw's account, Imogen reveals both the grounds upon which Shakespeare's heroines had occupied a privileged and often contradictory position on the Victorian stage, and also the reasons why that position was becoming untenable in the 1890s. Shaw wrote to Terry on 6 September 1896:

I really don't know what to say about this silly old Cymbeline, except that it can be done delightfully in a village schoolroom, and cant be done at the Lyceum at all, on any terms. I wish you would tell me something about Imogen for my own instruction. All I can extract from the artificialities of the play is a double image – a real woman *divined* by Shakespear without his knowing it clearly, a natural aristocrat, with a high temper and perfect courage, with two moods – a childlike affection and wounded rage; and an idiotic paragon of virtue produced by Shakespear's *views* of what a women ought to be, a person who sews and cooks, and reads improving books until midnight, and 'always reserves her holy duty,' and is anxious to assure people that they may trust her implicitly with their spoons and forks, and is in a chronic state of suspicion of improper behavior on the part of other people (especially her husband) with abandoned females. If I were you I would cut the part so as to leave the paragon out and the woman in; and I should write to The Times explaining the lines of the operation. It would be a magnificent advertisement.[7]

Shaw reveals the potential for Victorian idealisation in the role, a potential which had of course been realised on stage and in print by Helen Faucit, but also gives a clue as to why Faucit might have felt compelled to envisage the killing off of Imogen in a late-Victorian context which could now apprehend – through the work and example of the New Woman, and her critics – the conditions and compromises by which an idealised form of Victorian femininity had been allowed to persist, but in which her dissection was now inevitable. The only way in which she might remain on stage was through the turning back of the theatrical and social clock, which the illusion of an ever-youthful Terry enabled. She herself writes of her audiences as critically undiscerning, and as loving her, 'Not for what I am, but for what they imagine I am' (23 September 1896; *Terry–Shaw Correspondence*, p. 70). Her realisation of herself as 'being fat and nearly fifty' (7 September 1896; *Terry–Shaw Correspondence*, p. 48) was impossible to an audience determined on a theatrical and social nostalgia which the figure of the actress and the character of Imogen served well.

It is possible, however, at this period, to see a fissure opening up between Terry's sense of her own professionalism, her Shakespearean roles, and the possibilities for Shakespeare's conservative social appropriation through the work of the Lyceum. Edwin Wilson writes of Shaw's 'passion' for contesting popular concepts of Imogen that it was more than 'a personal eccentricity', but rather articulated 'all the growing aggression towards an earlier Victorian idealisation of women' which found its best expression in the figure of the New Woman, none of whose causes 'Shakespeare's Imogen could be imagined as supporting'.[8] In the 1890s, however, Ellen Terry might be imagined absolutely as supporting the New Woman, who was becoming such a force for change on the stage. And in her lectures on Shakespeare, delivered between 1911 and 1921, Terry does precisely that in declaring: 'Wonderful women! Have you ever thought how much we all, and women especially, owe to Shakespeare for his vindication of woman in these fearless, high-spirited, resolute and intelligent heroines?' She goes on in more explicitly political mode: 'Don't believe the anti-feminists if they tell you, as I was once told, that Shakespeare had to endow his women with virile qualities because in his theatre they were always impersonated by men! ... They owe far more to the liberal ideas about the sex which were fermenting in Shakespeare's age' (Terry, *Lectures*, p. 81). Terry comes out here, perhaps helped by the mediating force of her explicitly feminist and suffragist editor and secretary Christopher St John, in a radical vein at odds with the terms of her reception, which puts her later work in a new light, as does the evidence of her own writings and her library at Smallhythe, Kent, where she lived after retiring from the London stage.

The library is an extensive collection of scholarly material on the stage, including Jameson's work on Shakespeare's heroines, and the criticism of Georg Brandes:[9] 'the Shakespeare commentator I have found of most use to me as an actress'. In her lectures she chooses specifically to write of Brandes's sense that in Portia, 'in spite of her self-surrender in love there is something independent, almost masculine in her attitude towards life' (*Lectures*, p. 117). Her Jameson edition is heavily underscored throughout as she engages with the writer and her interpretations, noting approvingly at one point in the margins of the chapter on Cleopatra, 'Mrs Jameson must surely have been an Actress!'[10] Terry also engages with Jameson in the form of her own lectures, in which the taxonomy of female characterisation in lectures on 'The Triumphant Women' and 'The Pathetic Women' mirrors Jameson's attempts to classify the female characters, with some thought-provoking results, such as the inclusion of Lady Macbeth – 'a delicate little creature, with hyper-sensitive nerves' (p. 125) – in the category of pathetic heroine.

The lectures on Shakespeare were originally given, or performed, to British, American and Australian audiences following her official retirement from the stage, after fifty years of professional performances, in 1906. Published posthumously by St John as *Four Lectures on Shakespeare* in 1932, the talks, on 'The Children in Shakespeare's Plays', 'The Triumphant Women', 'The Pathetic Women' and 'The Letters in Shakespeare's Plays' allow the more complex and intellectual aspects of Terry's work as an actress, and specifically as a Shakespearean interpreter, to be made public. Within the lectures, both as given and as reproduced on the page, Terry can be all the parts she had never had the opportunity to play: the Rosalind whom she and critics mourned for, but whom Irving would not produce; the male characters, such as Henry V and Macbeth, her impersonation of whom would have been unthinkable in late-Victorian London, despite the example of Sarah Bernhardt's Hamlet in 1899, and of numerous other actresses throughout the century. In her lectures a complicating voice is given specifically to the Shakespearean heroines who had long been favourites of the Victorian age. She celebrates Shakespeare's 'predilection' for 'women of strong character, high-mettled, quick-witted, and resourceful' (Terry, *Lectures*, p. 103), and even in her lecture on the 'Pathetic' women is unable to help giving a reading of a feisty Desdemona, one who is unconventional, and 'not at all prim or demure' (p. 130). In the same lecture, she celebrates Emilia's anger, her chivalric championing of her dead mistress, and her moral courage. She goes on: 'Shakespeare is one of the very few dramatists who seem to have observed that women have more moral courage than men' (pp. 137–8).

Terry ends the volume of lectures, on which she worked closely with St John before her death in 1928, by asserting the value of friendship in Shakespeare: 'It is impossible to study Shakespeare's plays closely without noticing that to him friendship was perhaps the most sacred of all human relations' (p. 177). Coming from the actress who had done so much to popularise Shakespeare's tragic and specifically romantic heroines, this is an important revisionist judgement, and one which potentially recasts both her and our understanding of the romantic imperative, and the adoring gaze, which was at the heart of Terry's reception by contemporary audiences and critics, and upon which the professional life of the spectacular actress depended. In a way that was not possible within the mechanics of the spectacular stage, Terry used her writing to assert a new dynamic of reading and of spectatorship which could exceed the heterosexual imperative of her on- and off-stage relationship with both Irving and her audiences. The emphasis on friendship, which was a crucial, and well-attested part of the actress's own life, reconfigures the popular incorporation of Shakespeare's plays within Victorian culture, and realigns the audience's participation with the spectacle, and with the actress, on stage. It also, of course, privileges the female spectator in a new theatrical aesthetic which only became possible in the freedoms of the 1890s.

The lectures, and Terry's more explicitly autobiographical writings, sit in her library alongside her annotations of play scripts and critical texts, and show an actress ever engaged in the processes of interpretation, retrieval, intervention and disputation. Almost every book in Ellen Terry's library in Smallhythe is heavily annotated, and demonstrates Terry's entering into discursive relationships with playwrights, critics, her partner Henry Irving, and her younger selves. Her ebullient and bracing comments, scrawled in a highly distinctive script, are a means of self-conscious engagement with the matter and means of representation which enact an ongoing contesting of the containment of the theatrical spectacle, and of the concomitant authority of managers, playwrights and audiences over the actress. These annotations take on, in the wake of the 1890s, a newly resisting aesthetic and function, and offer a model for reading her published works too, all of which might be seen in some sense as annotations to a public life spent in speaking the words of others. Most fundamentally, they comment on her self-positioning in relation to the ideal of the Shakespearean heroine, and to the notion of the text itself.

The practice of annotation is an engagement with concepts of power and alienation. As Laurent Mayali writes:

In Western culture, the relationship of annotation to the text is less a relation of meaning than it is a relation of power. This relation of power has its source in a conception of knowledge in which the written text has become the fundamental legitimising instance. In our culture it might be said that the text is the dominant image of knowledge. The annotation achieves its political function by fulfilling a need for knowledge that is first of all an essential need for authority.[11]

Within the particular dynamic of Terry's annotations, which were not of course intended for public display, her interventions become frustrated cries against an aesthetic that would consign her to a form of public silence. Her annotations dispute that linguistic relationship, and indeed might seem to represent a degree of 'alienation' from the text,[12] perhaps even, as Mama suggests, 'a form of aggression' against that text and its originating context or intended audience (p. 179). In a sense, as Mama argues, the annotator creates him or herself anew as a reader of the text, and indeed creates a new reading community for the text itself. As an annotator, Terry might even be seen to be recreating the text, 'enveloping [the] author, always in the act of invading him, of delimiting his possible meaning and relevance' (p. 182). As an actress, Terry's opportunities for intervening within the public remit of her texts was limited to appearances, and to her appearance, on stage. As a writer or annotator she might legitimately hope to influence more effectively and strategically how those plays might be read, and her own role might be understood. It is striking that, in seeking to explain her work in transmitting Shakespeare to an audience, she combines the models of translation and scholarship which have been so enabling for women throughout the century:

[The actress's] task is to learn how to translate this character into herself, how to make its thoughts her thoughts, its words her words. It is because I have applied myself to this task for a great many years, that I am able to speak to you about Shakespeare's women with the knowledge that can be gained only from union with them. (Terry, *Lectures*, p. 80)

SHAKESPEARE, THE NEW ACTRESS AND THEIR CRITICS

Popularly conceived of as working in necessary opposition to the new theatre, Terry and Ada Rehan were trapped in that oppositional mode so long as they worked within the confines of the traditional actor-manager company. Elsewhere, however, other Shakespeare productions and performers benefited from the context of challenge and innovation that Ibsen's work initiated in the theatre. The work of Poel and serious amateur dramatic companies such as the Irving Amateur Dramatic Club did much to challenge the prevalent and distracting practices of the spectacular stage and to extend Shakespeare's theatrical repertoire. In a review of *All's Well That Ends Well* given by the Irving Amateur Dramatic Club at St George's Hall in January 1895, William Archer ponders the dilemma 'As I enjoy the privilege of being an Englishman (à peu prés) and not a German, I shall certainly go to my grave without having seen anything like the full cycle of his playable plays', and goes on:

Far be it from me to maintain that all or any of these plays ought to be constantly represented; but is it utterly chimerical to dream of a theatre at which no year should pass without a revival for a few nights of one or two of the lesser known Shakespearian plays, so that the whole repertoire should be passed in review once in ten years or so?'[13]

Such a desire was based in part, as Archer acknowledges, upon the reproach offered by Germany's more serious and scholarly appreciation of Shakespeare, of which Archer had been aware since the visit of the Saxe-Meiningen company to London in 1881, when they had included *Julius Caesar, Twelfth Night* and *The Winter's Tale* in a season of ten plays given in German.[14] *All's Well That Ends Well*, felt Archer, was no great loss to the public: 'In plain latter-day English, Bertram is a snob, Helena an adventuress' (pp. 39–40),[15] but its importance lies in its assertion of the worth of seeing an extended Shakespeare repertoire performed to a discerning audience.

Within the theatre criticism of William Archer, translator and exponent of Ibsen, champion of the new literary drama, and Elizabeth Robins's lover, Shakespeare's role is entirely different from that articulated by Shaw. For Archer, Shakespeare remains the measure of theatrical significance, of cultural weight, and of acting skills, and it is around the figure of Shakespeare that Archer's long-held ambitions for a national theatre coalesce at the end of the nineties. Archer's reviews of Shakespeare in the 1890s feed into the prospectus for a National Theatre that he developed with Granville Barker. *Scheme and Estimates for a National Theatre* (1904) has Shakespeare at its very heart, partly, as Peter Whitebrook rightly notes, so as not to alarm traditionalists with the spectre of an advanced, subsidised state theatre, but also to confirm the ambition of such a theatre to be 'national, representative, and popular' (Whitebrook, p. 231). Their plans for the first year of the theatre have it opening with four nights of Shakespeare: *Richard II*, *Henry IV*, parts 1 and 2, followed by *Henry V*. The rest of the year (363 performances in total, made up of 34 plays), would also include *Romeo and Juliet*, *Hamlet*, *The Taming of the Shrew*, *The Tempest* and *As You Like It*, the latter Archer's own favourite Shakespeare play. Denounced by Shaw as a scheme which sold out the principles of the New Theatre previously championed by Archer, it shows up the fault lines between their two positions on Shakespeare in the modern theatre, and also something of Archer's own difficulties in reconciling Shakespeare with the New, and specifically with the New actress. His avoidance of a more avant-garde repertoire for this national theatre was not simply a canny ploy to avoid antagonising conservative detractors, but represented a real tension in Archer between his veneration for 'an art that I am old-fashioned enough to love – the art of Shakespearian acting',[16] and the tenets and performers of the new theatre.

This was most comically expressed in his response to a matinee performance of the all-female *As You Like It* at the Prince of Wales Theatre in 1893. He begins jocularly enough in positioning himself by establishing his impeccable credentials:

For a man to lay down laws as to what is and is not 'womanly' and 'seemly', appears to me, theoretically, a piece of impertinent Helmerism … Nowadays, at any rate, women are perfectly capable of looking after their own dignity, and are even beginning to turn the tables and lay down laws for men.[17]

And yet, he goes on, even despite these credentials, he sees 'neither the use nor the beauty of such an exploit':

The performance had not even the comprehensible attraction of burlesque, that appeal to the average sensual man which lies in the display of 'shapely' limbs; for jack-boots were the only wear in the Forest of Arden. The whole thing, then, was a purposeless curiosity, and rather ugly than beautiful. (p. 70)

It is interesting to see Helmer, who is nothing if not an average sensual man, haunting these comments too.

The ugliness Archer refers to is very specifically suggested to him by the appearance of bearded women on stage, which prompts him to recount a catalogue of cross-dressing women in Shakespeare who have not had to resort to that apparently genuinely distasteful means of disguise. In this most intriguing of cross-dressing comedies, it seems strange that Archer could not entertain some notion of the intrigue and interest of extending the licensed cross-dressing still further by using an all-female company to interrogate the games Shakespeare was playing with actor and audience alike. Archer seems to find himself confronted in Shakespeare by his own expectations of theatrical femininity, and finds the reality lacking. For all his radical credentials, Archer sounds curiously conservative in this aspect of his career.

This is a tension most in evidence in his reviews of the New actresses' appearances in Shakespeare, and is further nuanced by the overlapping of those actresses with the international performers, the new celebrities of the stage, represented in the 1890s by Eleanora Duse and Sarah Bernhardt, the former of whom was elsewhere much championed by Archer. What becomes clear throughout this decade is the extent of those new actresses' fascination with Shakespeare, as we see in this 1899 letter from the American actress Elizabeth Robins to Henry Irving:

My Dear Sir Henry,
It just occurs to me: since the opportunity hitherto of doing any Shakespeare in London has been barred to me, & since I cannot hope

you will realize that such parts are what I do best – would it simplify matters at all if I got up ... say Portia, & and came & rehearsed her for you on approval? I've never done such a thing but why not try to show you?

I am conscious that I must seem to you like the hundreds of cocksure young women who haunt your door – but think! ever since I came to England it has been my dream to work with you. And I have waited, waited – hoping you would ask me. And now, at the eleventh hour, I am putting a pressure upon myself very foreign to my nature in striving to show you that what I want would not be ill-bestowed.

I am

Yours very sincerely;
Elizabeth Robins[18]

Irving's reply is not known, but certainly Robins never took on the mantle of Ellen Terry in the way that she hoped.

Given their respective positions in the theatre of the 1890s, the letter is extraordinary. Robins was one of the prime enablers of the Ibsen revolution in the English theatre. She had translated, produced and starred in pioneering productions of Ibsen including her own company's *Hedda Gabler* in 1891 and *The Master Builder* in 1893. Irving, by contrast, was Britain's first theatrical knight (he was honoured in 1895), and one of the actors chiefly responsible both for the increased late Victorian respectability of the stage and for the prominence and appeal of Shakespeare on that stage. What they both have in common, however, in 1899, is a shared experience of having already known their greatest theatrical moments. Irving's relationship with Terry had effectively dissolved, though the two remained friends, and he had lost the lease of the Lyceum which he had occupied since 1878. Robins was also experiencing a form of unease with the theatre. Ibsen had lost his thrilling attraction, and Robins could not bear to go back to wearing the leading lady's 'leading strings' within conventionally popular plays, once her own company wound up.[19] Irving was similarly anchorless at this point, yet it was to him – and to Shakespeare – that Robins turned in a last attempt to extend her occupation of the London stage.

Her letter is most intriguing in its reference to Shakespeare as the means by and through which these two performers might unite professionally. It marks the end of a decade which had seen the emergence of Ibsen to shocked British audiences, the end of Robins's career as a theatrical innovator and radical, but attests also to the prevailing popularity of Shakespeare in the theatre, to his status as a measure of the actress's worth – Robins after all offers to be judged by her Portia – and the extent to which the new actress still sees in Shakespeare a resource worth exploring, perfecting, and practising, despite, or perhaps because of, all the innovations of the theatrical nineties. At first it seemed to me that Robins was simply desperate not to leave the theatre, and that she would try any means to remain on the stage. However, it seems to me now rather that Robins's letter acknowledges unfinished business in the Victorian theatre. It might have been possible for Terry, Faucit, Marx, Schreiner and numbers of other women to write their own Shakespeares, appropriate to the 1890s, and to the social context that Robins had helped to create. On the stage, however, that ambition had not yet been recognised. Robins's 1899 letter is her final plea to be allowed to participate in the amalgamation of the theatrical practice of the New Woman and Shakespeare.

Eleanora Duse was a central part of that process. She arrived in Britain in 1893 with a reputation for playing the heroines of what Bernhardt had famously dismissed as 'Nordic trash'.[20] Duse had been Italy's first Nora, in Milan in February 1891, and had followed up that performance with work in *Rosmersholm*, *John Gabriel Borkman*, *Ghosts* and *The Lady from the Sea*. Her first London season was in the spring and summer of 1893, an important year for English theatre, in which *A Woman of No Importance* and *An Enemy of the People* were both seen at the Haymarket, J. T. Grein's Independent Theatre had produced Elizabeth Robins and Florence Bell's *Alan's Wife*, Robins had premiered *The Master Builder*, and there was a well-received series of Ibsen performances at the Opéra Comique. The most sensational event of the year, however, was arguably the appearance of Stella (or Mrs Patrick) Campbell as *The Second Mrs Tanqueray*. In its 'Dramatic Notes' for 30 May, the *Pall Mall Gazette* recorded that the two dominant topics of the theatre were 'The Second Mrs Tanqueray' and Duse.[21] Duse's own participation in that season was highly eclectic. She appeared first as 'Fedora' and as Margaret Gautier in *Camille*, an Italian version of Dumas's play. She followed these roles, primarily associated with Sarah Bernhardt, with Nora in *A Doll's House*, and Cleopatra. In the former, Duse achieved a qualified success, in which Archer most appreciated her 'natural acting, her gaiety being spontaneous, effervescent, iridescent', and her 'wonderful variety of facial expression'.[22] He reviewed her Cleopatra, however, with conspicuously less warmth.

The play had been translated and heavily cut for Duse by Arrigo Boito, her then lover, and the librettist for Verdi's *Otello* of 1887. As Boito later wrote to Duse: 'We only thought about one thing and that was: taking from this powerful poem all the divine essence of love and pain and we shut our eyes to everything else. That was a mistake.'[23] William Archer was quick to point out the ineptitude, specifically the lack of poetry, in the Italian translation, and the radical textual cuts that were of the essence of Shakespeare in the 1890s, at least in the popular theatres of Irving, Augustin Daly and Beerbohm Tree, and which were a regular target of Archer's. He begins his review in damning terms:

It is said that Signora Duse understands no English; and this fact, if fact it be, is the explanation and excuse of her Cleopatra. If she could read Shakespeare's *Antony and Cleopatra*, she would either drop the part altogether from her repertoire or act it very differently. She would realise that the play is not a badly constructed domestic drama in outlandish costumes, but a glorious love-poem, portraying and celebrating that all-absorbing passion for which the world is well-lost.[24]

Along with the lack of poetry in this version of the play, Archer also finds a lack of passion:

Her Cleopatra is a paradox incarnate, a contradiction in terms; for cold fire is not more inconceivable than a passionless Cleopatra. There is nothing in the least voluptuous, sensuous, languorous about her performance. Her very embraces are chilly, and she kisses like a canary-bird. (p. 175)

Despite her greatness as the tortured heroines of the *fin de siècle* stage, Duse cannot perform Shakespeare, partly because of the inadequacies of her translation, but partly also because, one is led by Archer to suspect, the modern stage fundamentally works against the interests of Shakespeare and those actresses who would perform him:

Signora Duse is never for an instant that incarnation of love and luxury, of all that is superb and seductive in womanhood, which has haunted the minds of men for nineteen centuries. She is simply a bright little woman, like her Nora … She is not Cleopatra, but Cleopatrina, Cleopatrinetta. (p. 176)

Duse was a highly distinguished actress, and yet even she fell short of what was clearly Archer's imagined ideal of the Shakespearean role, and was consigned to her newness as the marker of her failure.

We cannot of course know precisely how these performances played – crudely speaking, whether they were any good or not – but we can examine the terms used by critics such as Archer and Shaw in assessing the Shakespearean work of actresses whom they had previously championed in the New Drama. In 1897, for instance, the Independent Theatre produced *Antony and Cleopatra* in Manchester, with Janet Achurch, Britain's first Nora Helmer, in the lead role. Shaw opens his tirade thus:

Of the hardihood of ear with which she carries out her original and often audacious conceptions of Shakespearean music I am too utterly unnerved to give any adequate description … I have only seen the performance once; and … I am a broken man after it

…

I need not say that at some striking points Miss Achurch's performance shews the same exceptional inventiveness and judgment in acting as her Ibsen achievements did, and that her energy is quite on the grand scale of the play. But even if we waive the whole musical question – and that means waiving the better half of Shakespear – she would still not be Cleopatra.[25]

Shaw goes on to add that she simply looks wrong, that she is too much of 'the broad-browed, column-necked, Germanic type' (p. 79), she is too bourgeoise, she is 'Brynhild-cum-Nora Helmer' (p. 80), and not Cleopatra. This is harsh, but of Louis Calvert's Antony, Shaw simply records that he is 'inexcusably fat' (p. 81).

William Archer is more temperate – he finds Calvert 'rugged, forcible and effective' – and more detailed, but is scarcely less fundamentally disparaging of the production. He too is troubled by Achurch:

To say, then, that Miss Achurch is not the Cleopatra of the imagination is only to say that she is human. But I think she might, in the earlier acts, come nearer the ideal, if she would seize upon the poetry of the part, and let the comedy take care of itself.[26]

Amidst the precision of his advice to the modern actress, such an invoking of the ideal is striking and betokens the extent to which, in Shakespeare, the actress of the 1890s had to contend not only with the theatrical conditions of the time, but also the imaginative projections and firmly held beliefs of one of their champions. In his reviews of nineties Shakespeare, Archer never achieves the desired assimilation of new acting talent and time-honoured expectations. His reviews constantly return to the fissure he finds in Shakespeare productions between the contemporary achievements of the actress and his time-honoured expectations of the plays and their poetry.

He is self-defensively aware of his predicament, and is at pains in his review of Mrs Patrick Campbell's 1895 Juliet, which she played opposite Forbes Robertson at the Lyceum while Henry Irving and Ellen Terry were touring America, to stress that he does not wish to 'erect tradition into a law, but simply assert its uses as a guide' ('*World' for 1895*, p. 294). The tradition he writes of is 'the art of Shakespearian acting', which I mentioned earlier, and which he fears is being lost in a theatre which can rely on its audiences' taste for celebrity to disguise an actress's lack of proficiency. He writes: 'every one is eager to see a beautiful and very popular actress in a character of traditional renown, and every one is (quite literally) eager to applaud her' (p. 293). In such a response, he suggests, is heralded the death of not only

Shakespearean acting, but acting per se. So distressed was he by the success accorded Mrs Campbell by other critics, that he returns to this production of *Romeo and Juliet* a week later to denounce her again:

> We have not only traditional standards, but the clearest internal evidence as to the order of effects at which Shakespeare aimed; and when these effects are not attained, are not even attempted, we have a right to say not only 'This performer impresses us thus and thus,' but 'This performer does not know the rudiments of the complex and difficult art he or she is essaying.'[27]

He admits that Mrs Campbell's success is symptomatic of a commercial situation which necessitates the long run that minimises the chance of seeing Shakespeare on stage, and which means that audiences and actors alike lose sight of the standards that the Shakespearean stage represents – 'The result is that we literally forget our Shakespeare' (p. 298).

There is then in Archer, unlike in Shaw, a love of Shakespeare which he feels to be endangered by a combination of the commercial conditions of theatre in the 1890s, by actor-managers' attitudes to the plays themselves, and their willingness to cut and edit at will, and by the distorting effect of the celebrity, even notoriety, conferred upon a group of 'new' actresses which significantly affects audiences' responses to them and the plays in which they appear. Yet it is also the case that Archer, again unlike Shaw, seems to find himself imaginatively hampered by the other 'New' roles in which the Shakespearean actresses have appeared. In his review of *Romeo and Juliet*, he finds Mrs Pat most effective in those parts of the play where she can display petulance, one of the most important emotions of Pinero's *The Second Mrs Tanqueray*, the role in which Mrs Pat made her name. It might of course be that she did do petulance very well, and that it suited one role and not the other, but in his response to the more eminent Eleanora Duse's Cleopatra, the same critical impasse was reached. This is particularly shown up by comparing Archer's views on Duse's Cleopatra with Shaw's. In a letter to Ellen Terry on her forthcoming Imogen, Shaw attempts to quell her fears that the part might be too much for her, by suggesting that there might not be

> *enough in it* – not enough to absorb your whole power of work and fill your embrace and occupy every corner of your energy and affection – that Imogen, an old, mechanical thing with a few touches of simple nature, is too cheap for you instead of too big? Good Lord! did you ever see Duse play Shakespear? I did – Cleopatra! It was like seeing her scrubbing a scullery. (*Terry–Shaw Correspondence*, pp. 57–8)

There is no recognition here that the part in fact was not Shakespeare's, as Shaw uses Duse's disappointing performance to fuel his own campaign to woo Terry away from Irving and Shakespeare. By comparison, these actresses of Shakespeare seem to have confronted Archer, the most forward-thinking and ardent champion of Ibsen and the new actress, with a considerable challenge to his sense of an appropriate theatrical femininity, and to have entered into a relationship with Shakespeare which enables them to represent their, and Shakespeare's, theatrical modernity.

SARAH BERNHARDT

Arguably the most high-profile actress of the decade was Sarah Bernhardt, long both adored and reviled by the British public since her debut in London in 1879 with the Comédie Française, when she arrived in London, as Henry James notes, as an acknowledged celebrity whom the British were eager to admire. Her success, he writes:

> has been the success of a celebrity, pure and simple, and Mlle. Sarah Bernhardt is not, to my sense, a celebrity because she is an artist. She is a celebrity because, apparently, she desires with an intensity that has rarely been equalled to be one, and because for this end all means are alike to her.[28]

He goes on to suggest that she may justifiably be called 'the muse of the newspaper' (p. 129), and that so potent is her celebrity that it has made her into 'a sort of fantastically impertinent *victrix* poised upon a perfect pyramid of ruins – the ruins of a hundred British prejudices and proprieties' (pp. 128–9). The power of her allure, her French exoticism and subsequent hint of immorality, would determine her reception in England for the next two decades as she repeatedly imported a repertoire of her tragic heroines, such as Fedora and Marguerite Gautier, and, like many of her continental tragedienne predecessors, tried her hand at Lady Macbeth.

The part seems to have had something of a talismanic quality for the international actress, and was attempted by Charlotte Cushman in London in 1845, by Adelaide Ristori for the first time in 1857, and by Bernhardt in 1884.[29] The role had a recognised part in an English theatrical tradition going back to Sarah Siddons, but it did not have a similar role within expectations of English femininity. Audiences and critics felt less protective about this role than, say, that of Juliet, and it gave them more to assess in theatrical terms. Reviews of Ristori's 1857 Lady Macbeth certainly engage with the English stage tradition of Lady Macbeths: 'To be able to act Lady Macbeth is to come up to the English traditionary standard of excellence in an actress', and her interpretation varied from the English tradition and was 'slightly coloured by the habits of Southern life'.[30] The references to tradition, and the comparisons to Siddons, which Ristori had feared would be made,[31] are, however, a measure of her success. Despite, or perhaps even because of, the visibility of a 'fundamentally Italian' (*Saturday Review*, p. 37) aspect to her acting, Ristori is eligible to become part of a tradition of playing Lady Macbeth which may supplement, but will not supplant, her English predecessors, most notably Siddons. This 1857 production was, however, just the first stage of a career-long assault on this part, and perhaps on the sensibilities of an English audience whom she and the Polish actress Helena Modjeska both found lacking in respect to Shakespeare.[32] In 1873, Ristori gave the sleep-walking scene in English, and in 1882, once assured of the 'perfection' of her acquisition of an English accent, she performed the whole role in English at Drury Lane, and claims that she was acknowledged a 'splendid success' (Ristori, p. 107). Other critics were, however, less enthusiastic, mainly on account of the poor cast with whom she acted, who undermined her performance, and who gave some cause to bewail both the star system and the lack of systematised theatre training in Britain.

Bernhardt appeared in Jean Richepin's version of *Macbeth* in 1884, first in Edinburgh in June, and in the following month in London. *The Times*'s reviews of both productions are revealingly contradictory, and invoke their own nationalist sympathies in response to Bernhardt. In Scotland, in the country with which the play was associated, and which, it is suggested, has its own distinct stage traditions, Bernhardt is allowed to have the courage 'to challenge comparison' with her illustrious predecessors, and to create a Lady Macbeth which is 'doubtless ... one of her most original and most carefully elaborated characters, and which is recognised as being for her, as it was for Ristori, 'the one character in the list of Shakespeare's heroines that exactly and completely suits her idiosyncracies'.[33] This review praises the ways in which the softer touches of the character, her tenderness for her husband, and the spark of love which animates her even when Macbeth has most need of her 'diabolical determination', are in evidence throughout, and play alongside 'the extraordinary energy of her concentrated devilry'.

The later review of Bernhardt's London production recasts this energy as a specifically sexual one which, allied with a translation which is deemed unworthy of the original, makes for a performance which is 'more inadequate and unsatisfactory' than any Shakespeare play seen in London by the reviewer.[34] Where the Scottish reviewer saw feminine wiles, the London writer sees 'an unromantic Cleopatra, who wheedles and cajoles where she should command, and whose influence over Macbeth's rugged nature is exercised not by means of masculine force but of feminine blandishment'. Added to this are the accusations that her conception of the role is 'wholly at variance with stage tradition', and thus 'wholly un-Shakespearean'. Ristori was felt at least to have engaged with a discernible tradition. Bernhardt threatened to overturn it completely for the sake of originality and the fulfilment of that 'character' of serpentine sexuality which was her trademark, and which would determine reception of her performances in England, no matter what her motivations.

Her first Shakespearean, or pseudo-Shakespearean, performance in England in the 1890s was in the leading role in Sardou's *Cléopâtre*, which opened at the Royal English Opera House in May 1892. She clearly looked splendid in a part which, visually, was made for her. Indeed the *Times* reviewer notes amongst the production's few successes two 'pictorially effective' scenes: 'namely, Cleopatra's arrival in her barge, with its poop of beaten gold and its purple sails, and a view of the valley of the Nile with the pyramids in the distance'.[35] Shakespeare's play is the 'basis' of what seems to have been a fairly loose adaptation, which contained passing reference to *Antony and Cleopatra*, but which 'resolve[d] itself into a duet of passion between the queen and Antony with the variations incidental to such a theme'. The production seemed tired, determined on milking Bernhardt's reputation for serpentine sensuality, with little for her to act with. She was, then, no more successful than Duse in this role.

In June 1899, however, Bernhardt opened to huge critical and popular interest as Hamlet at the Adelphi Theatre. In doing so, she was amalgamating two well-established theatre traditions: of the foreign actress appearing in Shakespeare on the London stage, and the travesti Hamlet. Gerda Taranow cites sources suggesting that there had been upwards of fifty female Hamlets before Bernhardt took to the stage (Taranow, p. 89), and articles in *The Sketch* and *The Illustrated London News* just before Bernhardt opened made sure that spectators were aware of the often distinguished actresses who preceded her; or, as the *Sketch* writer put it, 'she is not the first Dame to assume the role of the Dane'.[36] The most recent female Hamlet had been Janette Steer who appeared at the Crystal Palace theatre in April 1899. *The Times* found hers an intelligent performance, but 'one cannot forget that she is a woman, nor can her performance be regarded as much more than a tour de force'.[37] As the *Daily Telegraph* reviewer put it, 'It is hard to remember a time when the female Hamlet has not been with us.'[38] This was also a thoroughly international tradition, with English, French, American, Australian, Irish and Italian women amongst the names cited by the *Illustrated London News*.[39] So there was nothing in itself new in Bernhardt's choice of role, which was one she had been interested in for years, but which she had felt was impossible until she came across what she describes as 'the admirable translation by Marcel Schwob'.[40]

There are of course numerous translations being attempted here, as the English Renaissance play is performed by a nineteenth-century French company; the hero is played by an actress; and one of the most pre-eminent plays of Shakespeare is rendered into intelligible modern French. Many critics questioned the felicity of Schwob's rendering, and none more fiercely than Max Beerbohm, who wrote that the translation

carries in it no faintest echo nor most shadowy reflection of the original magic. It is thin, dry, cold – in a word, excruciating. The fact is that the French language, limpid and exquisite though it is, affords no scope for phrases which … are charged with a dim significance beyond their meaning and with reverberations beyond their sound. The French language, like the French genius, can give no hint of things beyond those which it definitely expresses.[41]

He concluded that 'The only tribute a French translator can pay Shakespeare is not to translate him – even to please Sarah' (p. 35). Other critics concurred, whilst some were defensive of the play as an English standard: the *Daily Telegraph* suggests that 'At the first sight the French cast of characters causes a slight shiver to run through Anglican limbs' (p. 9).[42] But, even within this review, that shudder is preceded with a very minute dissection of the terms of the play's Englishness, and the difficulties attending upon its production by a French performer. 'Hamlet was a Dane, drawn by an Englishman with English ideas. Sarah Bernhardt's Hamlet is a Dane, pictured through French glasses,' writes the *Daily Telegraph* reviewer, and goes on of this essentially youthful rendering: 'Sarah Bernhardt is impulsive and irrepressible – a torrent that must be let loose. The student and the philosopher are rarely suggested – at least, to Englishmen' (p. 10). However, this comment occurs within a lengthy and carefully considered review, which is far from casually xenophobic, and which indeed embeds this response within a history of international, female Hamlets and an impressively detailed account of Bernhardt's own rendering of the part.

Though this particular reviewer eventually comes out as critical overall of the Bernhardt Hamlet, despite, as he acknowledges, the enthusiastic response she garnered from her audience, the review generously acknowledges its strengths ('She has given us a picturesque, and earnest, and a boyish Hamlet. That it is one of soul and thoughtfulness, that it is impressive and thoroughly imaginative, is open to doubt' (p. 10)) in the context of taking Bernhardt seriously on her own terms as a Shakespearean performer. Particularly interesting in this, as in some other reviews, is the lack of attention being paid to Bernhardt's gender, beyond the initial location of her performance within its context of travesti Hamlets. Clement Scott goes further in making no mention at all of Bernhardt's femaleness in his entirely laudatory opening chapter on her in his *Some Notable Hamlets of the Present Time* (1900):

> In Hamlet we do not want only new readings, new ideas, change for the sake of change. We want the actor or actress Hamlet to have genius and the gift of inspiration. These things belong to Sarah Bernhardt … As Hamlet I see her a greater artist than ever, because her task was heroic in its significance and importance.[43]

With this role, Bernhardt achieves the recognition of a critical seriousness, a gravity which had not been hers before, and which is conferred, I would argue, by Shakespeare and the 'male brains' she cites as the great attraction of the role for her (Bernhardt, p. 137). In this context, *Punch*'s cartoon of her and Henry Irving in *Hamlet* is curiously self-defeating: it shows a robust, rather beautiful, slim, but nonetheless powerful and vigorous Bernhardt dressed in the traditional Hamlet black, gesturing – perhaps slightly threateningly, and certainly impatiently – to a cowering Ophelia, whose face is that of Henry Irving, but whose body curiously resembles nothing more than the snake-like poses of the younger Bernhardt, and whose hair and dress recall those of Ellen Terry's 1888 Lady Macbeth (illustration 4).[44] The caption beneath the cartoon reads: 'Now that Madame Bernhardt has made so conspicuous a success as *Hamlet*, why should not she and our leading tragedian join forces when she comes to London! Sir Henry's *Ophelia* would be sure to attract more than passing notice.' The parodic impulse behind the cartoon would seem to be to ridicule Bernhardt's appropriation of a male role, but in fact the semiotics of the piece are extremely unstable. Bernhardt's is a fine and flattering image of a commanding performance which appears far from ridiculous. And the figure of ridicule is not really Henry Irving, but the conventions of stage femininity which had so enmeshed Terry during her career, and which meant that Bernhardt would not have been satisfied to play the role: she writes, 'Ophelia brought nothing new to me in the study of character' (Bernhardt, p. 139). Bernhardt's success has rendered deeply insecure the grounds of the gendered parody that was a stock attribute of *Punch* humour throughout the period.

To a large extent, Bernhardt was benefiting also from the challenge to gender stereotypes both on- and offstage, and specifically contemporary viewing practices of Shakespeare, that had been effected during the rest of the decade. We can see the effect of this challenge in another *Punch* cartoon, this time from 1897, the full impact of which rests upon a two-stage response, which is based initially in the cartoon's immediate humour of

" GREET ATTRACTION ! "

4 'Great Attraction', *Punch*, 31 May 1899, p. 258.

visual incongruity, and then followed up by a qualifying recognition of its textual dimensions. The cartoon appeared in the number for 11 September 1897, and is entitled 'Fashion à la Shakspeare' (illustration 5). It is a rather striking full-page cartoon whose tag line, 'I have a suit wherein I mean to touch your love indeed', is taken from *Othello* III.iii.80–1, where the lines are spoken by Desdemona to Othello as she pleads for Cassio to be restored to his favour. At first sight, the cartoon appears to be perfectly in line with *Punch*'s usual familiar and familiarly punning use of Shakespeare, instances

FASHION À LA SHAKSPEARE.

" I HAVE A SUIT WHEREIN I MEAN TO TOUCH YOUR LOVE INDEED."—*Othello*, Act III., Scene 3.

5 'Fashion à la Shakspeare', *Punch*, 11 September 1897, p. 110.

of which can be found strewn throughout the periodical in the 1890s. Just a couple of months in 1898 find the following tags: 'Shakspeare on Mr John Hare in the part of Mr Goldfinch. "What 'a pair of spectacles' is here!" *Troilus and Cressida* IV.iv' (9 July, p. 1); 'A Question of Hospitality at Henley. "Unbidden guests are often welcomest when they are gone." – Shakspeare' (16 July , p. 15); and 'Shakspearian motto for August 12th. "Now will I hence to seek my lovely Moor!" *Titus Andronicus*, II.iii' (13 August, p. 63). The magazine appropriates Shakespeare for its own jokes, exploiting the gap between the quotation's original context and the context of its appropriation as part of the joke, the lack of a fit an integral part of the predominantly punning mode in which Shakespeare is used.

The same strategy might at first sight seem to apply here in an apparently anti-New Woman cartoon which sends up the rational dress of the cyclist first by its prominence, and secondly perhaps by an implied contrast with the modesties of Desdemona. However, the cartoon also seems to be self-parodying: the figure of the bewildered male is rather dwarfed and unsure of himself, a slightly preposterous figure with his monocle, and his cane raised uncertainly and a little defensively to his lips. By contrast the figure of the New Woman, still enjoying some prominence and success even post-Wilde, is rather splendid in her Amazonian mode. She is dashing and vital, she has poise, and is full of fun and wit, for the joke here, the cartoon's tag, can be read as her joke, rather than simply a comment on the cartoon. Sufficiently confident in her self-knowing to be self-mocking, she is a rather impressive figure, and is not unlike Desdemona in III.iii of the play, as the speech from which the tag is taken demonstrates. When Othello grudgingly concedes to her pleading on Cassio's behalf she teases him thus:

> Why this is not a boon;
> 'Tis as I should entreat you wear your gloves,
> Or feed on nourishing dishes, or keep you warm,
> Or sue to you to do a peculiar profit
> To your own person: nay, when I have a suit
> Wherein I mean to touch your love indeed,
> It shall be full of poise and difficult weight
> And fearful to be granted.   (*Othello*, III.iii.76–83)

In the light of the rest of the play of course, the lines take on an ominous colour, but spoken innocently, in the moment of utterance, they show Desdemona to be charming and challenging, entreating Othello in a knowing manner which acknowledges her power within the dimensions of their marriage. Before Iago's evil begins to do its work, Desdemona is confident and sure both of herself and of Othello.

While it cannot be argued that Desdemona is in any way a New Woman, there is nonetheless a strength and impressiveness about her which the cartoon – read alongside the tag line's original context – perhaps unintentionally captures, and which tended to be overlooked in the Victorian theatre, and by some nineteenth-century readers. Desdemona's champions often celebrate her more passive qualities: in 1894, Helen Zimmern's translation of Louis Lewes's *The Women of Shakespeare* declared that Desdemona's 'gentleness, her patience, her resignation are inexhaustible … In this dove there is no contradiction, not one drop of gall' (p. 286). This is also the year in which Elizabeth Wordsworth declared that a 'well-educated girl ought to be, at 12 or 15 years old, in love with Miranda, Cordelia,

Desdemona, Portia, and Perdita … she ought to catch some of their beautiful feeling, their dignity'.[45]

However, in her lectures on Shakespeare, Ellen Terry writes of Desdemona that she gives an actress 'difficult problems to solve', and goes on:

> I know no character in Shakespeare which has suffered from so much misconception. The general idea seems to be that Desdemona is a ninny, a pathetic figure chiefly because she is half-baked. It is certainly the idea of those who think an actress of the dolly type, a pretty young thing with a vapid innocent expression, is well suited to the part. I shall perhaps surprise you by telling you that a great tragic actress, with a strong personality and a strong method, is far better suited to it, for Desdemona is strong, not weak. (Terry, *Lectures*, pp. 128–9)

In her letter on Desdemona Helen Faucit anticipates Terry's position, and her suspicion of stage tradition when she writes:

> In the gallery of heroes and heroines which my young imagination had fitted up for my daily and nightly reveries, Desdemona filled a prominent place. How could it be otherwise? A being so bright, so pure, so unselfish, generous, courageous – so devoted in her love, unconquerable in her allegiance to her 'kind lord', even while dying by his hand … Of course I did not know in those days that Desdemona is usually considered a merely amiable, simpering, yielding creature, and is also generally so represented on the stage. This is the last idea that would have entered my head. (Faucit, p. 47)

Faucit and Terry's responses are part of the revisionist aesthetic which was evident in responses to Shakespeare's women, and actresses in Shakespeare, in the 1890s and which ran alongside, and indeed perhaps necessitated, the collapse of Terry's relationship with Irving and the emergence on-stage of a new breed of 'Shakespearean actress', whose remit was to persist in the ever-evolving, ever-regenerative acts of translation upon which were founded the relationships between Shakespeare and Victorian women.

Notes

INTRODUCTION

1. Kathleen Knox, 'On the Study of Shakespeare for Girls', *Journal of Education*, n.s. 17 (1895), 222–3 (p. 222). I was first made aware of this article by the work of Linda Rozmovits in her book *Shakespeare and the Politics of Culture in Late-Victorian England* (Baltimore and London: Johns Hopkins University Press, 1998).

2. Matthew Arnold, *Culture and Anarchy*, ed. Stefan Collini (Cambridge University Press, 1993), p. 190.

3. John Ruskin, 'Of Queens' Gardens', in *Sesame and Lilies* (London: George Allen, 1911).

4. Helena Faucit, Lady Martin, *On Some of Shakespeare's Female Characters* (Edinburgh and London: Blackwood, 1885).

5. Adrian Poole, 'Introduction', in Gail Marshall and Adrian Poole (eds.), *Victorian Shakespeare*, ii: *Literature and Culture* (Basingstoke: Palgrave Macmillan, 2003), pp. 1–13 (p. 12).

6. See Martha Tuck Rozett, *Talking Back to Shakespeare* (Newark: University of Delaware Press; London and Toronto: Associated University Press, 1994).

7. Christy Desmet, 'Introduction', in Christy Desmet and Robert Sawyer (eds.), *Shakespeare and Appropriation* (London: Routledge, 1999), pp. 1–12 (p. 2).

8. See for instance Clare Pettitt, 'Shakespeare at the Great Exhibition of 1851', in Marshall and Poole (eds.), pp. 61–83.

9. Russell writes of Jameson's social aim in this work as being 'a critique of her own culture's conception of womanliness, though not of the conception of womanliness as an ideal. The title of the first edition, *Characteristics of Women, Moral, Poetical, and Historical*, suggests which aim was more important to Jameson, while the later title, *Shakespeare's Heroines*, indicates the way in which the work was understood' ('"History and Real Life": Anna Jameson, Shakespeare's Heroines and Victorian Women', *Victorian Review*, 17 (1991), 35–49 (p. 36)).

10. Anna Jameson, *Shakespeare's Heroines: Characteristics of Women, Moral, Poetical, and Historical*, ed. Cheri L. Larsen Hoeckley (Ontario: Broadview, 2005), p. 79.

11. See Marianne Novy, *Engaging with Shakespeare: Responses of George Eliot and other Women Novelists* (Athens and London: University of Georgia Press, 1994).

12. See for instance, as examples of texts which have grappled with ways of speaking of Shakespeare's cultural and literary afterlives, Graham Holderness (ed.), *The Shakespeare Myth* (Manchester University Press, 1988); Marianne Novy (ed.), *Women's Re-visions of Shakespeare* (Urbana and Chicago: University of Illinois Press, 1990); Gary Taylor, *Reinventing Shakespeare: A Cultural History from the Restoration to the Present* (London: Hogarth Press, 1990); and Brian Vickers, *Appropriating Shakespeare: Contemporary Critical Quarrels* (New Haven and London: Yale University Press, 1993).

13. See Christopher Smith, 'Shakespeare on French Stages in the Nineteenth Century', in Richard Foulkes (ed.), *Shakespeare and the Victorian Stage* (Cambridge University Press, 1986), pp. 223–39; Kenneth Richards, 'Shakespeare and the Italian Players in Victorian London', in Foulkes (ed.), pp. 240–54; and Gail Marshall, 'Cultural Formations: The Nineteenth-century Touring Actress and Her International Audiences', in John Stokes and Maggie B. Gale (eds.), *The Cambridge Companion to the Actress* (Cambridge University Press, 2007), pp. 52–73.

14. George Steiner, *After Babel: Aspects of Language and Translation* (Oxford University Press, 1975), p. 17.

15. Jacques Derrida, 'Des Tours de Babel', in Joseph F. Graham (ed.), *Difference in Translation* (Ithaca and London: Cornell University Press, 1985), pp. 165–207 (p. 188).

16. Kurt Mueller-Vollmer and Michael Irmscher, 'Introduction', in Kurt Mueller-Vollmer and Michael Irmscher (eds.), *Translating Literatures, Translating Cultures: New Vistas and Approaches in Literary Studies* (Berlin: Erich Schmidt Verlag, 1998), pp. ix–xviii (p. xii).

17. *Derrida, Writing and Difference*, trans. Alan Bass (Chicago University Press, 1978); quoted in Barbara Godard, 'Theorizing Feminist Discourse/Translation', in Susan Bassnett and Andre Lefevere (eds.), *Translation, History and Culture* (London: Pinter, 1990), pp. 87–96 (p. 87).

18. See Gerda Taranow, *The Bernhardt Hamlet* (New York: Peter Lang, 1996).

1 SHAKESPEARE AND VICTORIAN GIRLS' EDUCATION

1. 'Female Education', *Quarterly Review*, 119 (1866), 499–515 (p. 501).

2. Isaiah Berlin, *Karl Marx: His Life and Environment* (Oxford University Press, 1959), p. 262.

3. Yvonne Kapp, *Eleanor Marx*, i: *Family Life (1855–1883)* (London: Lawrence & Wishart), p. 58.

4. Chushichi Tsuzuki, *The Life of Eleanor Marx 1855–1898: A Socialist Tragedy* (Oxford: Clarendon Press, 1967), p. 17.

5. Annie S. Swan, *My Life: An Autobiography* (London: Ivor, Nicholson & Watson, 1934), p. 24.

6. M. Vivian Hughes, *A London Family, 1870–1900* (Oxford University Press, 1946), p. 75. Neither of Hughes's parents were very scrupulous observers of

the Sabbath. *The Pickwick Papers* were read on Sundays too, as, 'by some blessed workings of mother's conscience, [they] did not come under the head of novels. They were "papers"' (pp. 75–6).

7. Sarah Stickney Ellis, *The Young ladies' reader, or, Extracts from modern authors: adapted for educational or family use: with observations on reading aloud, as connected with social improvement, and remarks prefixed to the divisions of the work* (London: Grant and Griffith, 1845), pp. 289–90.

8. Harriet Martineau, *Autobiography* (1877); quoted in Valerie Sanders, *Records of Girlhood: An Anthology of Nineteenth-century Women's Childhoods* (Aldershot: Ashgate, 2000), p. 143.

9. Charlotte Elizabeth Tonna, *Personal Recollections* (London: Seeley & Burnside, 1841); quoted in Sanders, pp. 67–8.

10. See Ann Thompson and Sasha Roberts (eds.), *Women Reading Shakespeare: An Anthology of Criticism, 1660–1900* (Manchester University Press, 1997), p. 49.

11. Mary Lamb, 'Preface', in *Tales from Shakespeare* (Harmondsworth: Penguin, 2003), vii–ix (p. viii).

12. A 'Preface' to Mary Cowden Clarke, *The Complete Concordance to Shakspere: being a verbal index to all the passages in the dramatic works of the poet* (London: Knight, 1845), pp. v–vii (p. v).

13. This was an influential publication which, according to Edward G. Salmon, in 1884 was said to have attained 'a circulation equalled by no other English illustrated magazine published in the country'. See Salmon, 'What Girls Read', *Nineteenth Century*, 20 (1886), 515–29 (p. 520).

14. Mary Cowden Clarke, 'Shakespeare as the Girl's Friend', *Girls' Own Paper*, 8 (1886–87), 562–4 (p. 562).

15. George C. Gross, 'Mary Cowden Clarke, "The Girlhood of Shakespeare's Heroines", and the Sex Education of Victorian Women', *Victorian Studies*, 16 (1972), 37–58 (p. 43).

16. These will be discussed further below in chapter 2 on Elizabeth Barrett Browning.

17. *Phoebe's Shakespeare, arranged for children*, by Adelaide C. Gordon Sim (London: Bickers, 1894), p. 79.

18. E. Nesbit, *The Children's Shakespeare* (London: Tuck, 1897), p. 18.

19. David Vincent, 'The Domestic and the Official Curriculum in Nineteenth-century England', in Mary Hilton, Morag Styles and Victor Watson (eds.), *Opening the Nursery Door: Reading, Writing and Childhood, 1600–1900* (London and New York: Routledge, 1997), pp. 161–79 (p. 175).

20. Annette Peile, 'Instruction by Correspondence', *Journal of the Women's Education Union*, 1 (1873), 19–20; 'The Liverpool Ladies' Educational Society', *Journal of the Women's Education Union*, 1 (1873), 39.

21. 'Minutes of the Liverpool Ladies' Educational Society, and of the Windsor and Eton Association for the Education of Women', *Journal of the Women's Education Union*, 1 (1873), 39, 55.

22. Rosemary O'Day, 'Women and Education in Nineteenth-century England', in Joan Bellamy, Anne Lawrence and Gill Perry (eds.), *Women, Scholarship and*

Criticism: Gender and Knowledge, c. 1790–1900 (Manchester University Press, 2000), pp. 91–109 (p. 94).

23. Emily Shirreff, *Intellectual Education, and its Influence on the Character and Happiness of Women* (London: Parker, 1858), p. 184; and Lucy H. M. Soulsby, *The Use of Leisure,* i: *Some Thoughts on the Education of Girls*; ii: *Our Duty to our Neighbour* (London: Longmans, Green, 1900), p. 4.

24. Isabella M. S. Tod, 'On the Education of Girls of the Middle Classes' (London: Ridgway, 1873), p. 4.

25. Lucy H. M. Soulsby, *Stray Thoughts on Reading* (London: Longmans, Green, 1897), p. 19.

26. Mrs William Grey, 'On the Special Requirements for Improving the Education of Girls' (London: Ridgway, 1872), p. 4. This paper, and that by Isabella Tod, were part of a series published under the 'Sanction of the National Union for Improving the Education of Woman of all Classes'. Grey's is one of the few papers which genuinely tries to address its remarks to women of all stations of life.

27. Dorothea Beale, *On the Education of Girls* (London: Bell and Daldy, 1866), p. 1.

28. Dorothea Beale, 'Rocks and Quicksands – No. II. Home Difficulties', *Journal of the Women's Education Union,* 1 (1873), 85–7 (p. 87).

29. Kate Flint, *The Woman Reader, 1837–1914* (Oxford: Clarendon Press, 1993), p. 204.

30. Amy Lumby, 'English Literature', in *Work and Play in Girls' Schools*, ed. Dorothea Beale, Lucy H. M. Soulsby and Jane Frances Dove (London: Longmans Green, 1898), pp. 192–201 (pp. 200–1).

31. See for instance Soulsby, *The Use of Leisure*, p. 28.

32. Dorothea Beale, 'On the Organisation of Schools', *Journal of the Women's Education Union,* 1 (1873), 177–90 (p. 183).

33. Raikes, *Dorothea Beale of Cheltenham* (1908), p. 226; quoted in Flint, p. 205.

34. *Girls' Own Paper,* 8 (1886–7), 239.

35. Dorothea Beale, 'King Lear: a Study', *Cheltenham Ladies' Magazine* (1881), pp. 33–51 (p. 34).

36. Alice Greenwood, 'The Ladies in "Coriolanus"', *Cheltenham College Magazine* (1880), pp. 116–19 (p. 116).

37. James Mason, 'How to Form a Small Library', *Girls' Own Paper,* 2 (1881), 7–8 (p. 7); quoted in Catherine J. Golden, *Images of the Woman Reader in Victorian British and American Fiction* (Florida: University Press of Florida, 2003), p. 22.

38. See Regina Barreca (ed.), *Sex and Death in Victorian Literature* (Basingstoke: Macmillan, 1990).

39. Marlon B. Ross, *The Contours of Masculine Desire: Romanticism and the Rise of Women's Poetry* (Oxford University Press, 1989), p. 260; cited in Judith Johnston, *Anna Jameson: Victorian, Feminist, Woman of Letters* (London: Scolar Press, 1997), p. 79.

40. See for instance Christy Desmet, '"Intercepting the Dew-Drop": Female Readers and Readings in Anna Jameson's Shakespeare Criticism', in Marianne Novy (ed.),

Women's Re-visions of Shakespeare, pp. 41–57; Judith Johnston, *Anna Jameson: Victorian, Feminist, Woman of Letters* (Aldershot: Scolar Press, 1997), especially ch. 3, 'Writing Romeo Out: Rereading Shakespeare's Women', pp. 73–99; and Anne E. Russell, '"History and Real Life": Anna Jameson, Shakespeare's Heroines and Victorian Women', *Victorian Review*, 17:2 (1991), 35–49.

41. Review of Jameson in *The Monthly Review* (1832); quoted in *Shakespeare's Heroines*, pp. 419–27 (p. 419).

42. *The Shakespeare Gallery, containing the Principal Female Characters in the Plays of the Great Poet. Engraved in the most highly-finished manner, from drawings by the first artists, under the direction and superintendence of Mr. Charles Heath* (London: Heath, n.d.), n.p.

43. John Christian, 'Shakespeare in Victorian Art', in Jane Martineau (ed.), *Shakespeare in Art* (London: Merrell, 2003), pp. 217–21 (p. 217). According to Christian, the Academy shows regularly displayed between five and ten Shakespearean subjects each year between 1768 and 1828. Interestingly, that figure doubled in the 1830s.

44. 'Our Prize Competition. Essay Writing on a Great English Author – My Favourite Heroine from Shakespeare', *The Girls' Own Paper*, 10 March 1888, 380–1.

2 ELIZABETH BARRETT BROWNING AND SHAKESPEARE: TRANSLATING THE LANGUAGE OF INTIMACY

1. Elizabeth Barrett Browning, 'The Book of the Poets', in *The Greek Christian Poets and The English Poets* (London: Chapman and Hall, 1863; the essay was originally published in 1842), pp. 105–211 (p. 150).

2. Barrett Browning is hereafter referred to as EBB, the initials she used for herself.

3. Elizabeth Barrett Browning, *Aurora Leigh*, ed. Margaret Reynolds (New York and London: Norton, 1996; 1856), I, 881–7.

4. Caroline Norton, *The Dream, and other poems* (London: Colburn, 1840), p. 36.

5. Bessie Rayner Belloc, *Poems* (London: Chapman, 1852), pp. 33, 38.

6. Eliza Cook, 'Shakspeare', in *The Poetical Works* (s.l: Warne, n.d.), p. 570.

7. Mary Colborne-Veel, *A Little Anthology of Mary Colborne-Veel*, ed. Jessie Mackay (Christchurch, NZ: Whitcombe & Tombs, 1924), p. 35.

8. Marian Evans, 'Silly Novels by Lady Novelists', in *George Eliot: Selected Essays, Poems and other writings*, ed. A. S. Byatt and Nicholas Warren (Harmondsworth: Penguin, 1990), pp. 140–63 (pp. 148, 151).

9. 'Look on this picture and on this', in *The Complete Poems of Christina Rossetti*, 3 vols., ed. R. W. Crump (Baton Rouge and London: Louisiana State University Press, 1979–90), III, 255–6.

10. See Kathleen Jones, *Learning Not to be First: The Life of Christina Rossetti* (Moreton-in-Marsh: Windrush, 1991), p. 76.

11. Letter of March 1855; quoted in *Aurora Leigh*, p. 331.

12. Alice Falk, 'Lady's Greek without the Accents: Aurora Leigh and Authority', *Studies in Browning and His Circle*, 19 (1991), 84–92 (p. 86).
13. I am grateful to Dr Jane Wood for this insight.
14. Dorothy Mermin, *Elizabeth Barrett Browning: The Origins of a New Poetry* (Chicago and London: University of Chicago Press, 1989), p. 138.
15. See Angela Leighton, *Elizabeth Barrett Browning* (Brighton: Harvester, 1986), pp. 95–113.
16. *Sonnets from the Portuguese*, in Elizabeth Barrett Browning, *Aurora Leigh, and other poems* (Harmondsworth: Penguin, 1995), Sonnet 2, ll. 10–14.
17. Erik Gray, 'Sonnet Kisses: Sidney to Barrett Browning', *Essays in Criticism*, 52 (2002), 126–42 (p. 137). Despite this apparently unsympathetic phrase, however, Gray also pays important attention to the 'self-conscious physicality of her sonnet-kisses' (p. 139).
18. Richard Halpern, *Shakespeare Among the Moderns* (Ithaca and London: Cornell University Press, 1997), p. 7.
19. 'Poems. By Elizabeth Barrett Browning', *North American Review*, 94 (1862), 338–56 (p. 353).
20. 'Elizabeth Barrett Browning', *Dublin University Magazine*, 60 (1862), 157–62 (p. 158).
21. Mary Russell Mitford, *Recollections of a Literary Life; or, Books, Places, and People*, 3 vols. (London: Bentley, 1852), I, 282; *North American Review*, p. 353.
22. Tricia Lootens, *Lost Saints: Silence, Gender, and Victorian Literary Canonisation* (Charlottesville and London: University of Virginia Press, 1996), pp. 116–57.
23. G. B. S[mith], 'Elizabeth Barrett Browning', *Cornhill Magazine*, 29 (1874), 469–90 (p. 486).
24. Edmund Gosse, 'The Sonnets from the Portuguese', in *Critical Kit-Kats* (London: Heinemann, 1913; essay first published in 1894), p. 6.
25. [W. H. Smith], *British Quarterly Review*, 34 (1861), 350–81 (p. 353).
26. E. C. Stedman, *Victorian Poets* (London: Chatto & Windus, 1876), pp. 120, 132.
27. See Lagretta Tallent Lenker, *Fathers and Daughters in Shakespeare and Shaw* (Westport, CT and London: Greenwood Press, 2001).
28. William Black, *Judith Shakespeare*, 3 vols. (London: Macmillan, 1884), II, 210.
29. Mary Cowden Clarke, *The Girlhood of Shakespeare's Heroines*, 3 vols. (London: Smith, 1850–51), I, 278.
30. John Gross (ed.), *After Shakespeare: Writing Inspired by the World's Greatest Author* (Oxford University Press, 2002), pp. 105–09. See also *The Brantwood Diary of John Ruskin*, ed. Helen Gill Vilhoen (New Haven and London: Yale University Press, 1971), pp. 92–100.
31. *The Brownings' Correspondence*, ed. Philip Kelley, Ronald Hudson and Scott Lewis, 14 vols. (Winfield, KS: Wedgestone Press, 1984–98), I, 54; c. January 1818.
32. Cordelia: 'What shall Cordelia do? Love, and be silent.'
33. Notably, after her departure for Italy with Browning, EBB's sisters, Henrietta and Arabella, become the most frequent recipients of her Shakespeare references and quotations.

34. The quotation is one which EBB used frequently in her letters, including a later letter to Boyd, on (10?) August 1837 (*Correspondence*, III, 266) and a letter to Mary Russell Mitford on 18 November 1841 (*Correspondence*, V, 172) in which very varying uses are made of the quotation. To Mitford, for instance, she writes somewhat testily: 'There are more things in Heaven & earth than are in other people's philosophy just now.'

35. Margaret Forster, *Elizabeth Barrett Browning: A Biography* (London: Chatto & Windus, 1988), p. 56.

36. EBB writes slightingly to Mitford of Joseph Hunter's *A Disquisition on the Scene, Origin, Date, etc. of Shakespeare's Tempest* (1839): 'I do hate all those geographical statistical historical yea, & natural-historical illustrators of a great poet. I hate them & excommunicate them! I dont care a grain of sand on the shore whether Prospero's island was Bermuda or Lampedusa' (1–6 January 1842; *Correspondence*, V, 199).

37. EBB used the same analogy in letters to Mary Russell Mitford on 3–5 October 1843 (*Correspondence*, VII, 350) and to Mary Minto on 30 June–1 July 1846 (*Correspondence*, XIII, 100). The analogy is less fully developed in these letters, however, where the comparison is rather between not reading Shakespeare and not travelling.

38. Daniel Karlin, *The Courtship of Robert Browning and Elizabeth Barrett* (Oxford: Clarendon Press, 1985), p. 68.

39. Yopie Prins, 'Elizabeth Barrett, Robert Browning, and the Différance of Translation', *Victorian Poetry*, 29 (1991), 435–51 (p. 436).

40. 'Preface to Prometheus Bound', in *The Complete Works of Elizabeth Barrett Browning*, ed. Charlotte Porter and Helen A. Clarke, 6 vols. (New York: Crowell, 1900; repr. New York: AMS Press, 1973), I, 82.

3 'SHE HAD MADE HIM, AS IT WERE, THE AIR SHE LIVED IN': SHAKESPEARE, HELEN FAUCIT AND FANNY KEMBLE

1. Quoted in Sir Theodore Martin, *Helena Faucit (Lady Martin)* (London: Blackwood, 1900), p. 405.

2. Faucit's entrée into court life was effected by her husband, who was the biographer of the Prince Consort. However, after her first visit to the Queen at Osborne in 1868, Faucit seems to have generated a genuine affection in Queen Victoria. She and her husband were even visited by the Queen at their home in Wales when Victoria visited the country in 1889. Faucit spent much of her time at court in reading to the Queen and in helping the Royal children with amateur dramatics.

3. Fanny Kemble, *Records of Later Life* (London: Bentley, 1882); quoted in Eleanor Ransome (ed.), *The Terrific Kemble: A Victorian Self-Portrait from the Writings of Fanny Kemble* (London: Hamish Hamilton, 1978), p. 215.

4. Information is taken from Gerald Kahan, 'Fanny Kemble Reads Shakespeare: Her First American Tour, 1849–50', *Theatre Survey*, 24 (1983), 77–98 (p. 78).

5. Henry James, 'Frances Anne Kemble', in *Essays in London and Elsewhere* (London: Osgood, McIlvaine, 1893, pp. 86–127 (p. 107).

6. Diary of Philip Hone, 13 March 1849; quoted in Dorothy Marshall, *Fanny Kemble* (London: Weidenfeld & Nicolson, 1977), p. 220.

7. Carol Jones Carlisle, *Helen Faucit: Fire and Ice on the Victorian Stage* (London: Society for Theatre Research, 2000), p. 7.

8. Helena Faucit, Lady Martin, *On Some of Shakespeare's Female Characters* (Edinburgh and London: Blackwood, 1887), p. 5. Subsequent page references are to this edition, and are included in parentheses in the text. The book is made up of eight essays, originally published for private circulation as letters to a number of friends including Geraldine Jewsbury, John Ruskin and Robert Browning.

9. Rebecca Jenkins, *Fanny Kemble: Reluctant Celebrity* (London: Simon & Schuster, 2005), p. 47.

10. *Records of a Girlhood*, 3 vols. (London: Bentley, 1878), I, 3.

11. Monica Gough (ed.), *Fanny Kemble: Journal of a Young Actress* (New York: Columbia University Press, 1990), pp. 56–7.

12. 29 December 1893, in *Henry James Letters*, ed. Leon Edel, 4 vols. (London: Macmillan, 1974–84), III, 452.

13. Francis Anne Kemble, *Notes Upon Some of Shakespeare's Plays* (London: Bentley, 1882), p. 3.

14. Unbeknownst to Fanny, there was in fact another member of her audience, a Major Dawkins, a friend of her father's who advised Charles that Fanny was ready for her first public appearance.

15. Charles gave up his usual role of Romeo, perhaps fearing to create an impression of impropriety in acting such a romantic and passionate role with his daughter. Fanny, however, regretted this, writing: 'My father not acting Romeo with me deprived me of the most poetical and graceful stage lover of his day' (*Records of a Girlhood*, II, 16).

16. Fanny Kemble to George Combe, 7 September 1830; quoted in Owen Wister.

17. Fanny Kemble, *Journal*, 2 vols. (Philadelphia: Carey, Lea & Blanchard), II, 125.

18. [Margaret Stokes and Georgina Colmache], 'Helen Faucit', *Blackwood's*, 138 (1885), 741–60 (p. 741).

19. Lewes's review appeared in the *Pall Mall Gazette* of 10 March 1865 and is quoted in Jones Carlisle, p. 215.

20. G. H. Lewes to Mr and Mrs Charles Lee Lewes, 25 March 1865, in *The George Eliot Letters*, ed. Gordon S. Haight, 9 vols. (New Haven and London: Yale University Press, 1954–78), IV, 186.

21. George Fletcher, *Studies of Shakespeare* (London: Longman, 1847), p. 237.

22. Stanley Wells, *Shakespeare for All Time* (London: Macmillan, 2002), p. 259.

23. Entry for 11 January 1836, in *The Journal of William Charles Macready, 1832–51*, abridged and ed. J. C. Trewin (London: Longmans, 1967), p. 50.

24. In *On Some of Shakespeare's Female Characters*, Faucit gives a brief appendix on Lady Macbeth (pp. 344–7), most of which is taken up with a letter on the subject of her Lady Macbeth by Dr William Stokes of Dublin.

25. Charles H. Shattuck, *Mr Macready Produces 'As You Like It'; A Prompt-Book Study* (Urbana, IL: Beta Phi Mu, 1962), n. p.
26. Juliet Dusinberre, *Shakespeare and the Nature of Women*, 2nd edn (Basingstoke: Macmillan, 1996), p. 250.
27. See Jean Howard, 'Crossdressing, The Theatre, and Gender Struggle in Early Modern England', *Shakespeare Quarterly*, 38 (1988), 418–40 (p. 435).
28. This goes some way to explaining the difficulties Faucit had in giving the epilogue of *As You Like It*, which explicitly acknowledges the boy-player originally responsible for acting Rosalind.
29. Alison Booth, 'From Miranda to Prospero: the Works of Fanny Kemble', *Victorian Studies*, 38 (1994–95), 227–54 (p. 238).
30. Lady [Anne Thackeray] Ritchie, *From Friend to Friend* (London: Murray, 1919), p. 87.
31. Frances Anne Kemble, *Poems* (London: Bentley, 1883), p. 201.
32. Ellen Terry, *The Story of My Life* (London: Hutchinson, 1908), p. 176.

4 GEORGE ELIOT AND SHAKESPEARE: DEFAMILIARISING 'SECOND NATURE'

1. 3 April 1859, *GE Letters*, III, 42.
2. For further details, see Marianne Novy, *Engaging with Shakespeare*, p. 118.
3. Henry James, 'Daniel Deronda: a Conversation' (1876); reprinted in F. R. Leavis, *The Great Tradition* (Harmondsworth: Penguin, 1993), pp. 284–304 (pp. 288–9).
4. 23 November 1873; *GE Letters*, V, 465. Fiske (1842–1901) was assistant librarian at Harvard from 1872 to 1879. He was also author of *Myths and Myth-Makers* (1872), a copy of which he sent to George Eliot. He was previously known to her as a contributor to the *Fortnightly Review*.
5. Alexander Main, *Wise, Witty and Tender Sayings in Prose and Verse, selected from the Works of George Eliot* (Edinburgh and London: Blackwood, 1872), p. vii.
6. Oscar Browning, *George Eliot* (London: Scott, 1890), p. 142.
7. Julia Wedgwood, 'The Moral Influence of George Eliot', *Contemporary Review*, 39 (1881), 173–85 (pp. 174, 175).
8. John Lyon, 'Shakespearian Margins in George Eliot's "working-day world"', *Shakespeare Survey*, 53 (2000), 114–26 (p. 116).
9. Adrian Poole, *Shakespeare and the Victorians* (London: Arden, 2004), pp. 132, 133.
10. See Poole, *Shakespeare and the Victorians*, pp. 130–31, and Novy, *Engaging with Shakespeare*, p. 107.
11. George Eliot, *Middlemarch* (Harmondsworth: Penguin, 1994), p. 194, ch. 20.
12. The quotation is from *As You Like It*, I. iii.12. The letter is to Maria Lewis, 30 March 1840; *GE Letters* I, 44. The 'working-day world' phrase is also used in relation to Adam Bede and to Caleb Garth, two of Eliot's least equivocally presented characters.
13. 22 December 1873; *GE Letters*, V, 472. The reference is to *Macbeth*, V.iii.40.

14. 27 November 1851; *GE Letters*, I, 377. Lewes remembered the evening less fondly in print in the *Leader* two days later, where he calls the play 'one of the worst plays, if not altogether the worst, that Shakespeare has left us' (*GE Letters*, I, 377, n. 2).
15. 'Recollections of Berlin, 1854–55', in *The Journals of George Eliot*, ed. Margaret Harris and Judith Johnston (Cambridge University Press, 1998), pp. 241–58 (p. 255).
16. After Lewes's death, Shakespeare references appear much less frequently in her notebooks, with one of her last notebooks, dated around 1879, containing nothing from or about Shakespeare but these lines from *Titus Andronicus*: 'The Eagle suffers little birds to sing / And is not careful what they mean thereby' (IV.iv.84–5) and Dryden's comment on Shakespeare that 'He is many times flat and insipid; his comick wit degenerating into clenches, his serious swelling into bombast' (from *Of Dramatic Poesy: An Essay* (1668)) (Folger manuscript M.a.14).
17. This is held at the Folger Shakespeare Library, Washington DC.
18. Eliot finds eleven instances of 'tender', eight of 'remorse', four of 'ecstasy' and seven of 'secure'.
19. These parallel usages are: *Othello*, I.iii.10 and IV.i.72, *Richard II*, II.i.267 and III.ii.34, *The Merry Wives of Windsor*, II.i.239, and *Henry V*, IV.17. Each usage contains its own contradiction or insecurity.
20. William Hazlitt, from *Characters of Shakespear's Plays* (1817); quoted in Novy, p. 38.
21. Charlotte Brontë, *Shirley* (Harmondsworth: Penguin, 1985), pp. 116–17.
22. Margaret J. Arnold, '*Coriolanus* Transformed: Charlotte Brontë's Use of Shakespeare in Shirley', in Marianne Novy (ed.), *Women's Re-visions of Shakespeare* (Urbana and Chicago: University of Chicago Press, 1990), pp. 76–88 (p. 86).
23. George Eliot, *Felix Holt* (Harmondsworth: Penguin, 1995) [1866], ch. 46, p. 447.
24. Gillian Beer, *George Eliot* (Brighton: Harvester, 1986), p. 201.
25. Quoted in Martin Harries, *Scare Quotes from Shakespeare: Marx, Keynes, and the Language of Reenchantment* (Stanford, CA: Stanford University Press, 2000), p. 3.
26. Hannah Lawrance, 'Shakespeare in Domestic Life', *British Quarterly Review*, 45 (1867), 81–110 (pp. 85, 93).
27. 'The Sonnets of Shakspeare', *Westminster Review*, 68 o.s./12 n.s. (1857), 116–37 (p. 128). The early to mid-1860s saw a marked increase in publications on the Sonnets, as witnessed by reviews and articles in the *Fortnightly Review* (1860), *Temple Bar* (1862), *Quarterly Review* (1862) which reviewed thirteen recent publications on Shakespeare, mainly concerning the Sonnets, and another review in the *Fortnightly Review* in 1866.
28. Taylor, who became John Stuart Mill's stepdaughter, wrote in an essay of 28 March 1848, when she was sixteen, that 'we think it most likely that [the Sonnets] were written on various occasions and are almost as dramatic as

his plays', though she concedes that Sonnets 135 and 136 may be about himself as they play on the word 'will'. The essay is in the commonplace books and essays of Helen Taylor which are held at the Folger Shakespeare Library, Washington DC.

29. Carol Thomas Neely notes that 'women's responses to and appropriations of Shakespeare' are enabled by his 'personal anonymity combined with the powerful myths which he generates both as a person and as a Foucauldian author-function' ('Epilogue: Remembering Shakespeare, Revising Ourselves', in Novy (ed.), pp. 242–52 (p. 247)).

30. Intriguingly, during speculation about the authorship of *Scenes of Clerical Life*, Charles Bray made the suggestion that such thoughts found parallels in the speculation surrounding Shakespeare's authorship. George Eliot responds with a put-down whose obliqueness might mask an enjoyment of the connection made: 'I entirely differ from you in your view of such conduct as Mr Bracebridge's and fail to see any parallel between it and that of the investigators in the personal history of Shakspear: I am not yet an "archaeological" subject' (to Charles Bray, 26 September 1859; *GE Letters*, III, 163).

31. George Elliot's *Middlemarch Notebooks: A Transcription*, ed. John Clark Pratt and Victor A. Neufeldt (Berkeley CA: University of California Press, 1979), p. 209.

32. *George Eliot's Middlemarch Notebooks*, p. 213. The final two sentences are a later addition. The other Sonnets which Eliot most admired are 22, 23, 29, 30, 33, 54, 64, 66, 68, 71, 73, 75, 90, 91, 93, 94, 97, 98, 102, 104, 106, 10, and 116.

33. Otice C. Sircy, '"The Fashion of Sentiment": Allusive Technique and the Sonnets of Middlemarch', *Studies in Philology*, 84 (1987), 219–44 (p. 225).

34. *King John*, II.i.436–40. The same concept is also used of Esther Lyon in *Felix Holt* (p. 429, ch. 44).

35. Where it is rendered 'To hear with eyes is part of love's rare wit'.

36. 'Mr Gilfil's Love Story' in *Scenes of Clerical Life* (Harmondsworth: Penguin, 1998), p. 116, ch. 4.

37. The review is reproduced in Joseph Wiesenfarth (ed.), *George Eliot: A Writer's Notebook, 1854–1879, and Uncollected Writings* (Charlottesville VA: University of Virginia Press, 1981), pp. 253–55 (pp. 253–54).

38. Carol Siegel, '"This thing I like my sister may not do": Shakespearean Erotics and a Clash of Wills in Middlemarch', *Style*, 32 (1998), 36–59 (p. 44).

39. [Peter Bayne], 'George Eliot', *British Quarterly Review*, 45 (1867), 141–78 (p. 142).

40. Peter Bayne, 'Shakespeare and George Eliot', *Blackwood's*, 133 (1883), 524–38 (p. 525).

5 SOCIALISM, NATIONALISM AND STRATFORD: SHAKESPEARE AND THE NEW WOMAN AT THE *FIN DE SIÈCLE*

1. Henry James, 'The Birthplace', in *The Better Sort* (London: Methuen, 1903), p. 193.
2. Quoted in Leon Edel, *Henry James: A Life* (London: Collins, 1987), p. 562.

3. Preface to *The Tempest*; quoted in Edel, p. 562.

4. Mathilde Blind, *Birds of Passage: Songs of the Orient and Occident* (London: Chatto and Windus, 1895), pp. 109–10.

5. Philip Dodd, 'Englishness and the National Culture', in Robert Colls and Philip Dodd (eds.), *Englishness: Politics and Culture, 1880–1920* (London: Croom Helm, 1986), pp. 1–28 (p. 22).

6. Simon Avery, 'Eleanor Marx and Karl Blind', in John Stokes (ed.), *Eleanor Marx (1855–1898): Life, Work, Contacts* (Aldershot: Ashgate, 2000), pp. 173–87 (p. 175).

7. 'Introduction', in *The Journal of Marie Bashkirtseff*, trans. Mathilde Blind (London: Virago, 1985; 1890), pp. 695–716 (p. 716).

8. Letter from Mathilde Blind to Richard Garnett, 21 September 1894; quoted in Garnett's memoir of Blind in *The Poetical Works of Mathilde Blind*, ed. Arthur Symons (London: T. Fisher Unwin, 1900), p. 40.

9. Mathilde Blind, Commonplace book, Bodleian manuscript, Walpole collection, p. 22.

10. Letter of 14 September 1894; quoted in *The Poetical Works of Mathilde Blind*, p. 40.

11. John Lucas, *England and Englishness: Ideas of Nationhood in English Poetry, 1688–1900* (London: Hogarth, 1990), p. 204.

12. Robert Blatchford (Nunquam), *Merrie England* (London: Scott, 1894), p. 21.

13. Laurence Irving, *Henry Irving: The Actor and His World* (London: Faber & Faber, 1951), pp. 242–3.

14. The letter is dated 25 October 1875, and is quoted in full in Chushichi Tsuzuki, 'Japanese Archives Relating to British Labour History (2)', *Society for the Study of Labour History*, Bulletin 8 (1964), 18–22 (p. 19).

15. Mrs Comyn, 'My Recollections of Karl Marx', *Nineteenth Century and After*, 91 (1922), 161–9 (p. 166).

16. Both letters are quoted in Yvonne Kapp, *Eleanor Marx*, ii: *The Crowded Years (1884–1898)* (London: Lawrence & Wishart, 1976), pp. 441, 443.

17. Opening Speech of the Director, in 'Notices of Meetings. Opening Meeting, Friday 13th March, 1874', in *New Shakspere Society's Transactions*, 1874 (London: Trubner, n.d.), p. vi.

18. 'Monthly Abstract of Proceedings', 10 March 1882, in the *New Shakspere Society's Transactions, 1880–86* (London: Trubner, n.d.), pp. 25–31 (p. 30).

19. 25 March 1882; quoted in Kapp I, 234.

20. 5 July 1881; quoted in Kapp I, 222.

21. Introduction to Gustave Flaubert, *Madame Bovary*, trans. Eleanor Marx-Aveling (London: Vizetelly, 1886), pp. vii–xxii (p. x). Picking up on the popular image of Flaubert's fastidiousness, his 'weary striving after the heaven of the artist – ideal perfection', she writes that Shakespeare too 'had his hours of doubt and despair … when life seems but too often a striving and a striving, and an ending in nothing'. But she goes on to note: 'It is only we who come after them who know how much that striving has achieved.'

22. S. S. Prawer, *Karl Marx and World Literature* (Oxford: Clarendon Press, 1976), p. 85.

23. Karl Marx, *Werke*, XV, 464; quoted in Prawer, p. 268.
24. *The Letters of Olive Schreiner, 1876–1920*, ed. S. C. Cronwright-Schreiner (London: T. Fisher Unwin, 1924), pp. 298, 302.
25. Edward and Eleanor Marx Aveling, *The Woman Question* (London: Swan Sonnenschein, Le Bas & Lowrey, 1886), pp. 8, 9.
26. See E. B. A. and E. M. A., 'Dramatic Notes', *Tinsley's Magazine*, 46 (1890–1), 276–80.
27. Edward B. Aveling, DSc, 'Shakespeare the Dramatist', *Our Corner*, 1 (1883), 147–52, 218–22, 272–6, 345–9; 2 (1883) 33–6, 89–93, 207–12, 267–70, 343–6.
28. Edward B. Aveling, DSc, FLS, 'Works of Shakespeare', *Hall of Science Thursday lectures* (London: Freethought, 1882), Lecture 1, p. 1. Sadly none of Marx's teaching notes have been passed down to us. She taught evening classes on Shakespeare at the Hampstead and Highgate Institute.
29. Havelock Ellis, 'Eleanor Marx', *Adelphi*, 10 (1935), 342–52 (p. 352). Ellis wrote a second article on Marx in the next volume of the *Adelphi*, 11 (1935), 33–41.
30. *The New Shakspere Society's Transactions*, 1874, 1880–6, 1887–92 (London: Trubner, n.d.), pp. 14–15.
31. The Countess of Charlemont, 'Gruach (Lady Macbeth)', *NSS Transactions*, 1875–6, pp. 194–9.
32. 'Monthly Abstract of Proceedings', 3 March 1889, p. 43.
33. Quoted in Teresa Ransom, *The Mysterious Miss Marie Corelli: Queen of Victorian Best-Sellers* (Stroud: Sutton, 1999), p. 98.
34. Marie Corelli, et al., *The Modern Marriage Market* (London: Hutchinson, 1898), pp. 19–20. The other authors contributing to this collection of essays are Lady Jeune, Flora Annie Steel and Susan, Countess of Malmesbury.
35. Marie Corelli, *The Sorrows of Satan* (Oxford: World's Classics, 1998), p. 306.
36. Though the sentiment is unaltered, it is possible that Corelli may have got muddled here, as although *Othello* unquestionably is profoundly concerned with honour, the quotation comes from *Julius Caesar* and refers to Brutus. It occurs in Mark Antony's 'Friends, Romans, Countrymen' speech in III.ii.88.
37. Jonathan Bate, *The Genius of Shakespeare* (London: Picador, 1997), p. 161.
38. This was published in 1903 by Methuen.
39. Letter by Marie Corelli, which appeared in the *Morning Post* on 11 February 1903; quoted in *The Plain Truth*.
40. Gordon McMullan, *Shakespeare and the Idea of Late Writing: Authorship in the Proximity of Death* (Cambridge University Press, 2007), p. 315.

6 SHAKESPEARE AND THE ACTRESS IN THE 1890S

1. Nina Auerbach, *Ellen Terry: Player in her Time* (London: Dent, 1987); Roger Manvell, *Ellen Terry* (London: Heinemann, 1968); and Michael R. Booth, 'Ellen Terry', in John Stokes, Michael R. Booth and Susan Bassnett, *Bernhardt, Terry, Duse: The Actress In Her Time* (Cambridge University Press, 1988), pp. 65–117.
2. Ellen Terry, *Four Lectures on Shakespeare* (London: Hopkinson, 1932), p. 16.
3. 'At the Play. In London. Cymbeline', *The Theatre*, n.s. 28 (1896), 212–15 (p. 213).

4. 'Lyceum Theatre. Production of Cymbeline', *The Times*, 23 September 1896, p. 4

5. William Archer, 'Cymbeline' in *The Theatrical 'World' for 1896* (London: Scott, 1897), pp. 260–77 (p. 270).

6. George Bernard Shaw, 'Poor Shakespear!', in *Our Theatres in the Nineties*, 3 vols. (London: Constable, 1932), I, 24–30 (p. 25). The review covered a production of *All's Well That Ends Well* by the Irving Dramatic Club at St George's Hall.

7. *Ellen Terry and Bernard Shaw: A Correspondence*, ed. Christopher St. John (London: Reinhardt & Evans, 1931), p. 42.

8. Edwin Wilson (ed.), *Shaw on Shakespeare: An Anthology of Bernard Shaw's Writings on the Plays and Productions of Shakespeare* (London: Cassell, 1962), pp. 97–8.

9. She is referring to Georg Brandes, *William Shakespeare* (London: Heinemann, 1896).

10. The comment is found in Terry's copy of Jameson's book which is in her library at Smallhythe.

11. Laurent Mayali, 'For a Political Economy of Annotation', in Stephen Barney (ed.), *Annotation and its Texts* (Oxford University Press, 1991), pp. 185–91 (p. 185).

12. Ralph Mama III, 'Annotation as Social Practice', in Barney (ed.), pp. 178–84 (p. 178).

13. William Archer, 'All's Well That Ends Well', in *The Theatrical 'World' for 1895* (London: Scott, 1896), pp 37–41 (pp. 38–9).

14. Peter Whitebrook, Archer's biographer, cites this visit as crucial also in introducing Archer to European forms of naturalism on the stage (Peter Whitebrook, *William Archer: A Biography* (London: Methuen, 1993), p. 82).

15. As Archer goes on to note, he thus opposes the view of Helena put forward in a recent translation of Louis Lewes's *The Women of Shakespeare* (London: Heinemann, 1894). Archer writes: 'She simply made up her sincere and noble mind to marry him willy-nilly, and she carried her point by methods which, if used by a man towards a woman, would brand him as a villain of the deepest dye, and earn him the execrations of every gallery in Christendom' (Archer, 'All's Well That Ends Well', p. 40). Lewes's book was first published the previous year as *Shakespeares Frauengestalten*.

16. 'Romeo and Juliet', in *The Theatrical 'World' for 1895*, pp. 284–95 (p. 294).

17. 'As You Like It – Mrs Dexter', in *The Theatrical 'World' for 1894* (London: Scott, 1895), pp. 69–73 (p. 69).

18. Letter of 14 June 1899, in the Bram Stoker Collection, Brotherton Library, University of Leeds. Previously quoted in Gail Marshall, *Actresses on the Victorian Stage* (Cambridge University Press, 1998), p. 176.

19. Elizabeth Robins, *Theatre and Friendship: Some Henry James Letters* (London: Cape, 1932), p. 151.

20. Quoted in Giovanni Pontiero, *Eleanora Duse: In Life and Art* (Frankfurt, Bern and New York: Lang, 1986), p. 218.

21. 'Dramatic Notes', *Pall Mall Gazette*, 30 May 1893, p. 4.

22. William Archer, 'A Doll's House – A Scrap of Paper', in *The Theatrical 'World' for 1893* (London: Scott, 1894), pp. 155–62 (pp. 156, 160).

23. Quoted in Susan Bassnett, 'Eleanora Duse', in Stokes, Booth and Bassnett, pp. 119–70 (p. 147).

24. William Archer, 'Antony and Cleopatra – The Comédie Française', in *The Theatrical 'World' for 1893*, pp. 172–9 (p. 172).

25. 'Shakespear in Manchester', in *Our Theatres in the Nineties*, III, 76–83 (pp. 76–77).

26. William Archer, 'Antony and Cleopatra in Manchester', in *The Theatrical 'World' for 1897* (London: Scott, 1898), pp. 66–71 (p. 71).

27. 'Romeo and Juliet again – Cheer, Boys, Cheer – In a Locket', in *The Theatrical 'World' for 1895*, pp. 295–303 (p. 297).

28. Henry James, 'The Comédie Française in London', in *The Scenic Art*, ed. Allan Wade (London: Hart-Davis, 1949), pp. 125–32 (p. 128).

29. The performances of Ristori and Bernhardt in particular may have helped to inspire the Lyceum production of Macbeth in 1888, when Ellen Terry gave a performance which is usually read in comparison to Sarah Siddons' innovations in the part, but which may just as well have been responding to recent European and American performances.

30. 'Lady Macbeth', *Saturday Review*, 11 July 1857, p. 37. It should perhaps be noted that Ristori's performances were the only theatrical productions being noticed by the *Saturday Review* at this period.

31. Adelaide Ristori, *Memoirs and Artistic Studies of Adelaide Ristori* (London: Doubleday, Page, 1907), p. 44.

32. See Ristori, p. 44, and *Memories and Impressions of Helena Modjeska: An Autobiography* (New York and London: Blom, 1969; 1910), p. 446. Modjeska writes of the English lack of respect for Shakespeare's birthplace.

33. 'Madame Bernhardt's Lady Macbeth', *The Times*, 25 June 1884, p. 10.

34. 'Gaiety Theatre: Madame Sarah Bernhardt in "Macbeth"', *The Times*, 5 July 1884, p. 7.

35. 'Royal English Opera-House. Mme Sarah Bernhardt as Cléopâtre', *The Times*, 30 May 1892, p. 8.

36. 'Some Women Hamlets', *The Sketch*, 31 May 1899, p. 244.

37. '*Hamlet* at Crystal Palace', *The Times*, 14 April 1899, p. 13.

38. 'Bernhardt as Hamlet. Enthusiastic Reception', *Daily Telegraph*, 13 June 1899, pp. 9–10.

39. 'Some Women Players of Hamlet', *Illustrated London News*, 17 June 1899, p. 874.

40. Sarah Bernhardt, *The Art of the Theatre*, trans. H. J. Stenning (London: Bles, n.d.), p. 139.

41. Max Beerbohm, 'Hamlet, Princess of Denmark', in *Around Theatres* (London: Rupert Hart-Davis, 1953), pp. 34–7 (p. 35).

42. An anonymous review in the *Daily Telegraph*, entitled 'Bernhardt as Hamlet. Enthusiastic Reception', 13 June 1899, p. 9.

43. Clement Scott, *Some Notable Hamlets of the Present Time* (London: Greening, 1900), p. 50.
44. "Great Attraction", *Punch*, 31 May 1899, p. 258.
45. Elizabeth Wordsworth, *First Principles in Women's Education* (Oxford: Parker, 1894), p. 9; quoted in Flint, p. 76.

Bibliography

PRIMARY TEXTS

Barrett Browning, Elizabeth, *The Greek Christian Poets and the English Poets* (London: Chapman & Hall, 1863)

    The Complete Works of Elizabeth Barrett Browning, ed. Charlotte Porter and Helen A. Clarke, 6 vols. (New York: Crowell, 1900; repr. New York: AMS Press, 1973)

    Aurora Leigh, ed. Margaret Reynolds (New York and London: Norton, 1996)

Bashkirtseff, Marie, *The Journal of Marie Bashkirtseff*, trans. Mathilde Blind (London: Virago, 1985), pp. 695–716

Baughan, Rosa, *Shakespeare's Plays, abridged and revised for the use of girls* (London: Allman, 1863)

Black, William, *Judith Shakespeare: A Romance*, 3 vols. (London: Macmillan, 1884)

Blind, Mathilde, *Birds of Passage: Songs of the Orient and Occident* (London: Chatto and Windus, 1895)

    Commonplace book, in dummy copy of *The Ascent of Man* (Walpole Collection, Bodleian)

    The Poetical Works of Mathilde Blind, ed. Arthur Symons, with a memoir by Richard Garnett, CB, LLD (London: T. Fisher Unwin, 1900)

Brontë, Charlotte, *Shirley* (Harmondsworth: Penguin, 1985)

Brownings' Correspondence, ed. Philip Kelley, Ronald Hudson and Scott Lewis, 14 vols. (Winfield, KS: Wedgestone, 1984–98)

Corelli, Marie, *The Sorrows of Satan* (Oxford: World's Classics, 1998)

    Poems (London: Hutchinson, n.d. [1925])

Cowden Clarke, Mary, *The Complete Concordance to Shakspere: being a verbal index to all the passages in the dramatic works of the poet* (London: Knight, 1845)

    The Girlhood of Shakespeare's Heroines, 3 vols. (London: Smith, 1850–1)

Eliot, George, *Scenes of Clerical Life* (Harmondsworth: Penguin, 1998)

    Felix Holt (Harmondsworth: Penguin, 1995)

    Middlemarch (Harmondsworth: Penguin, 1994)

    Daniel Deronda (Harmondsworth: Penguin, 1995)

    The George Eliot Letters, ed. Gordon S. Haight, 9 vols. (New Haven and London: Yale University Press, 1954–78)

Essays of George Eliot, ed. Thomas Pinney (London: Routledge and Kegan Paul, 1968)

George Eliot: Selected Essays, Poems and Other Writings, ed. A. S. Byatt and Nicholas Warren (Harmondsworth: Penguin, 1990)

George Eliot's Middlemarch Notebooks: A Transcription, ed. John Clark Pratt and Victor A. Neufeldt (Berkeley CA and London: University of California Press, 1979)

George Eliot: A Writer's Notebook, 1854–1879, and Uncollected Writings, ed. Joseph Wiesenfarth (Charlottesville, VA: University Press of Virginia, 1981)

George Eliot's Daniel Deronda Notebooks, ed. Jane Irwin (Cambridge University Press, 1998)

The Journals of George Eliot, ed. Margaret Harris and Judith Johnston (Cambridge University Press, 1998)

Flaubert, Gustave, *Madame Bovary: Provincial Manners*, trans. from the French Edition Definitive by Eleanor Marx Aveling (London: Vizetelly, 1886)

Gordon Sim, Adelaide C., *Phoebe's Shakespeare arranged for Children* (London: Bickers, 1894)

Heath, Charles, *The Shakespeare Gallery, containing The Principal Female Characters in the Plays of the Great poet. Engraved in the most highly-finished manner, from drawings by the first artists, under the direction and Superintendence of Mr. Charles Heath* (London: Tilt, n.d.)

The Heroines of Shakespeare: Comprising The Principal Female Characters in the Plays of the Great Poet. Engraved under the Direction of Mr Charles Heath, from Drawings by Eminent Artists (London: Bogue: 1848)

James, Henry, 'The Birthplace', in *The Better Sort* (London: Methuen, 1903)

Hughes, Molly V., *A London Family, 1870–1900* (Oxford University Press, 1946)

Fanny Kemble: *Journal of a Young Actress*, ed. Monica Gough (New York: Columbia University Press, 1990)

Records of a Girlhood, 3 vols. (London: Bentley, 1878)

Records of Later Life (London: Bentley, 1882)

Lamb, Charles and Mary Lamb, *Tales from Shakespeare* (Harmondsworth: Penguin, 2003)

Macready, William Charles, *The Journal of William Charles Macready, 1832–51*, abridged and ed. J. C. Trewin (London: Longmans, 1967)

Nesbit, E., *The Children's Shakespeare* (London: Tuck, n.d.)

Rossetti, Christina, *The Complete Poems of Christina Rossetti*, 3 vols., ed. R. W. Crump (Baton Rouge and London: Louisiana State University Press, 1979–90)

Ruskin, John, *The Diaries of John Ruskin*, 3 vols., selected and ed. Joan Evans and John Howard Whitehouse (Oxford: Clarendon Press, 1959)

Schreiner, Olive, *The Letters of Olive Schreiner, 1876–1920*, ed. S. C. Cronwright Schreiner (London: T. Fisher Unwin, 1924)

Shakespeare, William, *Complete Works* (Oxford University Press, 1980)

Terry, Ellen, *The Story of My Life* (London: Hutchinson, 1908)

Ellen Terry's Memoirs, with Preface, Notes and Additional Biographical Chapters by Edith Craig and Christopher St John (London: Gollancz, 1933)

Ellen Terry and Bernard Shaw: A Correspondence, ed. Christopher St John (London: Reinhardt & Evans, 1931)

SECONDARY TEXTS

Archer, William, *The Theatrical 'World' for 1893* (London: Scott, 1894)
The Theatrical 'World' for 1894 (London: Scott, 1895)
The Theatrical 'World' for 1895 (London: Scott, 1896)
The Theatrical 'World' for 1896 (London: Scott, 1897)
The Theatrical 'World' for 1897 (London: Scott, 1898)
Ardis, L. Ann, '"Shakespeare" and Mrs Grundy: Redefining Literary Value in the 1890s', in Nikki Lee Manos and Meri-Jane Rochelson (eds.), *Transforming Genres: New Appropaches to British Fiction of the 1890s* (London: Macmillan, 1994)
Arnold, Margaret J., 'Coriolanus Transformed: Charlotte Brontë's Use of Shakespeare in *Shirley*', in Marianne Novy (ed.), *Women's Re-visions of Shakespeare* (Urbana and Chicago: University of Illinois Press, 1990)
Auerbach, Nina, *Woman and the Demon* (Cambridge MA and London: Harvard University Press, 1982)
Ellen Terry: Player in Her Time (London: Dent, 1987)
Aveling, Edward B., 'Works of Shakespeare', in *Hall of Science Thursday Lectures* (London: Freethought, 1882)
'Shakespeare the Dramatist', *Our Corner*, 1 (1883), 147–52, 218–22, 272–6, 345–9; 2 (1883) 33–6, 89–93, 207–12, 267–70, 343–6
Avery, Simon, 'Eleanor Marx and Karl Blind', in John Stokes (ed.), *Eleanor Marx (1855–1898): Life, Work, Contacts* (Aldershot: Ashgate, 2000)
Barney, Stephen (ed.), *Annotation and its Texts* (Oxford University Press, 1991)
Barreca, Regina (ed.), *Sex and Death in Victorian Literature* (Basingstoke: Macmillan, 1990)
Bate, Jonathan, *Shakespearean Constitutions: Politics, Theatre, Criticism, 1730–1830* (Oxford: Clarendon Press, 1989)
The Genius of Shakespeare (London: Picador, 1997)
Bayne, Peter, 'Shakespeare and George Eliot', *Blackwood's Edinburgh Magazine*, 133 (1883), 524–38
'George Eliot', *British Quarterly Review*, 45 (1867), 141–78
Beale, Dorothea, *On the Education of Girls* (London: Bell & Daldy, 1866)
'Rocks and Quicksands – No. II. Home Difficulties', *Journal of the Women's Education Union*, 1 (1873), 85–7
'On the Organisation of Schools', *Journal of the Women's Education Union*, 1 (1873), pp. 177–90
'King Lear: A Study', *Cheltenham Ladies' College Magazine* (1881), 33–51
Treasure that Faileth Not (Abingdon: Hooke, 1907)
Beerbohm, Max, 'Hamlet, Princess of Denmark', in *Around Theatres* (London: Rupert Hart-Davis, s 1953), pp. 34–7
Bell, Robert, 'Shakespeare's Sonnets', *Fortnightly Review*, 5 (1866), 734–41

Berlin, Isaiah, *Karl Marx: His Life and Environment* (Oxford University Press, 1959)

Bernhardt, Sarah, *The Art of the Theatre*, trans. H. J. Stenning (London: Bles, n.d.)

Blatchford, Robert (Nunquam), *Merrie England* (London: Scott, 1894)

Booth, Alison, 'From Miranda to Prospero: The Works of Fanny Kemble', *Victorian Studies*, 38 (1994–5), 227–54

    'The Lessons of the Medusa: Anna Jameson and Collective Biographies of Women', *Victorian Studies*, 42 (1999–2000), 257–88

Brown, John Russell, *Focus on Macbeth* (London: Routledge & Kegan Paul, 1982)

Browning, Oscar, *George Eliot* (London: Scott, 1890)

Chew, Shirley and Alistair Stead (eds.), *Translating Life: Studies in Transpositional Aesthetics* (Liverpool University Press, 1999)

Christ, Carol, 'Painting the Dead: Portraiture and Necrophilia in Victorian Art and Poetry', in Sarah Webster and Elizabeth Bronfen (eds.), *Death and Representation* (Baltimore and London: Johns Hopkins University press, 1993), pp. 133–51

Clinton, Catherine, *Fanny Kemble's Civil Wars* (New York: Simon & Schuster, 2000)

Comyn, Marian, 'My Recollections of Karl Marx', *Nineteenth Century and After*, 91 (1922), 161–9

Corelli, Marie, *The Plain Truth of the Stratford-on-Avon Controversy* (London: Methuen, 1903)

Corelli, Marie, et al., *The Modern Marriage Market* (London: Hutchinson, 1898)

Cowden Clarke, Mary, 'Shakespeare as the Girl's Friend', *The Girl's Own Paper*, 8 (1886–7), 562–4

Derrida, Jacques, 'Des Tours de Babel', in Joseph F. Graham (ed.), *Difference in Translation* (Ithaca and London: Cornell University Press, 1985)

Desmet, Christy, '"Intercepting the Dew-Drop": Female Readers and Readings in Anna Jameson's Shakespearean Criticism', in Marianne Novy (ed.), *Women's Re-visions of Shakespeare* (Urbana and Chicago: University of Illinois Press, 1990), pp. 41–57

Desmet, Christy, and Robert Sawyer (eds.), *Shakespeare and Appropriation* (London: Routledge, 1999)

Dodd, Philip, 'Englishness and the National Culture', in Robert Colls and Philip Dodd (eds.), *Englishness: Politics and Culture, 1880–1920* (London: Croom Helm, 1986), pp. 1–28

Dowden, Edward, 'Shakespeare's Portraiture of Women', *Contemporary Review*, 47 (1885), 517–35

Driver, Leota S., *Fanny Kemble* (Chapel Hill: University of North Carolina Press, 1933)

Dusinberre, Juliet, *Shakespeare and the Nature of Women*, 2nd edn (Basingstoke: Macmillan, 1996)

Eckert, Georg, *Wilhelm Liebknecht: Briefwechsel mit Karl Marx und Friedrich Engels* (The Hague: Mouton, 1963)

Edel, Leon, *Henry James: A Life* (London: Collins, 1987)

    'Elizabeth Barrett Browning', *Dublin University Magazine*, 60 (1862), 157–62

Ellis, Havelock, 'Eleanor Marx', *Adelphi*, 10 (1935), 342–52; 11 (1935), 33–41

Ellis, Sarah Stickney, *The Young ladies' reader, or, Extracts from modern authors: adapted for educational or family use: with observations on reading aloud, as connected with social improvement, and remarks prefixed to the divisions of the work* (London: Grant and Griffith, 1845)

Ewbank, Inga-Stina, 'Transmutations of the Green World: Re-writing *As You Like It*', in M. T. Jones-Davies (ed.), *Shakespeare et le monde vert* (Paris, 1994)

  'Shakespeare Translation as Cultural Exchange', *Shakespeare Survey*, 48 (1995), 1–12

Falk, Alice, 'Lady's Greek without the Accents: Aurora Leigh and Authority', *Studies in Browning and His Circle*, 19 (1991), 84–92

Faucit, Helena, Lady Martin, *On Some of Shakespeare's Female Characters* (Edinburgh and London: Blackwood, 1885)

'Female Education', *Quarterly Review*, 119 (1866), 499–515

Fletcher, George, *Studies of Shakespeare* (London: Longman, Brown, Green and Longman, 1847)

Flint, Kate, *The Woman Reader, 1837–1914* (Oxford University Press, 1993)

Follini, Tamara, 'The Friendship of Fanny Kemble and Henry James', *Cambridge Quarterly*, 19 (1990), 230–42

Forster, Margaret, *Elizabeth Barrett Browning: A Biography* (London: Chatto & Windus, 1988)

Foulkes, Richard (ed.), *Shakespeare and the Victorian Stage* (Cambridge University Press, 1986)

Glavin, John, ''Caught in the Act: Or, the Prosing of Juliet', in Jean Marsden (ed.), *The Appropriation of Shakespeare: Post-Renaissance Reconstructions of the Works and the Myth* (London: Harvester Wheatsheaf, 1991), pp. 93–110

Godard, Barbara, 'Theorizing Feminist Discourse/Translation', in Susan Bassnett and Andre Lefevere (eds.), *Translation, History and Culture* (London: Pinter, 1990), pp. 87–96

Golden, Catherine J., *Images of the Woman Reader in Victorian British and American Fiction* (Gainesville: University of Florida Press, 2003)

Gosse, Edmund, 'The Sonnets from the Portuguese', in *Critical Kit-Kats* (London: Heinemann, 1913)

Gray, Erik, 'Sonnet Kisses: Sidney to Barrett Browning', *Essays in Criticism*, 52 (2002), 126–42

Greenwood, Alice, 'The Ladies in "Coriolanus"', *Cheltenham Ladies' College Magazine* (1880), 116–19

Grey, Mrs William [Maria], 'On the Special Requirements for Improving the Education of Girls', Paper read at the Social Science Congress, October 1871 (London: Ridgway, 1872)

Grey, Mrs William [Maria] and Emily Shirreff, *Thoughts on Self-Culture, Addressed to Women*, 2 vols. (London: Moxon, 1850)

Gross, George C., and Mary Cowden Clarke, ''The Girlhood of Shakespeare's Heroines", and the Sex Education of Victorian Women', *Victorian Studies*, 16 (1972), 37–58

Gross, John (ed.), *After Shakespeare: Writing Inspired by the World's Greatest Author* (Oxford University Press, 2002)

Halpern, Richard, *Shakespeare Among the Moderns* (Ithaca and London: Cornell University Press, 1997)

Hamer, Mary, 'Shakespeare's Rosalind and Her Public Image', *Theatre Research International*, 11 (1986), 105–18

Hankey, Julie, 'Helen Faucit and Shakespeare: Womanly Theater', in Marianne Novy (ed.), *Cross-Cultural Performances: Differences in Women's Re-Visions of Shakespeare* (Urbana and Chicago: University of Illinois Press, 1993)

'Victorian Portias: Shakespeare's Borderline Heroine', *Shakespeare Quarterly*, 45 (1994), 426–48

Hardwick, Lorna, 'Women, Translation and Empowerment', in Joan Bellamy, Anne Lawrence and Gill Perry (eds.), *Women, Scholarship and Criticism: Gendered Knowledge, c. 1790–1900* (Manchester University Press, 2000), pp. 180–203

Harries, Martin, *Scare Quotes from Shakespeare: Marx, Keynes, and the Language of Reenchantment* (Stanford, CA: Stanford University Press, 2000)

Holderness, Graham (ed.), *The Shakespeare Myth* (Manchester University Press, 1988)

Howard, Jean, 'Crossdressing, The Theatre, and Gender Struggle in Early Modern England', *Shakespeare Quarterly*, 38 (1988), 418–40

Howard, Tony, *Women as Hamlet: Performance and Interpretation in Theatre, Film and Fiction* (Cambridge University Press, 2007)

Irving, Laurence, *Henry Irving: The Actor and His World* (London: Faber & Faber, 1951)

Jackson, Russell, '"Perfect Types of Womanhood": Rosalind, Beatrice and Viola in Victorian Criticism and Performance', *Shakespeare Survey*, 32 (1979), 15–26

James, Henry, 'Frances Anne Kemble', in *Essays in London and Elsewhere* (London: Osgood, McIlvaine, 1893), pp. 86–127

The Scenic Art, ed. Allan Wade (London: Hart-Davis, 1949)

Jameson, Anna, *Shakespeare's Heroines: Characteristics of Women, Moral, Poetical, and Historical*, ed. Cheri L. Larsen Hoeckley (Ontario: Broadview, 2005)

Jenkins, Rebecca, *Fanny Kemble: A Reluctant Celebrity* (London: Simon & Schuster, 2005)

Johnston, Judith, *Anna Jameson: Victorian, Feminist, Woman of Letters* (Aldershot: Scolar Press, 1997)

Jones, Kathleen, *Learning Not to be First: The Life of Christina Rossetti* (Moreton-in-Marsh: Windrush, 1991)

Jones Carlisle, Carol, *Helen Faucit: Fire and Ice on the Victorian Stage* (London: Society for Theatre Research, 2000)

Kahan, Gerald, 'Fanny Kemble Reads Shakespeare: Her First American Tour, 1849–50', *Theatre Survey*, 24 (1983), 77–98

Kapp, Yvonne, *Eleanor Marx, i: Family Life (1855–1883)* (London: Lawrence and Wishart, 1972)

Eleanor Marx, ii: *The Crowded years (1884–1898)* (London: Lawrence and Wishart, 1976)

Karlin, Daniel, *The Courtship of Robert Browning and Elizabeh Barrett* (Oxford: Clarendon Press, 1985)

Fanny Kemble, *Notes Upon Some of Shakespeare's Plays* (London: Bentley, 1882)

Knox, Kathleen, 'On the Study of Shakespeare for Girls', *Journal of Education*, n.s. 17 (1895), 222–3

'Last Poems and Other Works of Mrs Browning', *North British Review*, 36 (1862), 514–34.

Lawrance, Hannah, 'Shakespeare in Domestic Life', *British Quarterly Review*, 45 (1867), 81–110

Leighton, Angela, *Elizabeth Barrett Browning* (Brighton: Harvester, 1986)

Lenker, Lagretta Tallent, *Fathers and Daughters in Shakespeare and Shaw* (Westport, CT and London: Greenwood Press, 2001)

Lewes, Louis, *The Women of Shakespeare*, trans. Helen Zimmern (London: Hodder, 1894)

The Liverpool Ladies' Educational Society', *Journal of the Women's Education Union*, 1 (1873), 39

Lootens, Tricia, *Lost Saints: Silence, Gender, and Victorian Literary Canonisation* (Charlottesville and London: University of Virginia Press, 1996)

Lucas, John, *England and Englishness: Ideas of Nationhood in English Poetry, 1688–1900* (London: Hogarth Press, 1990)

Lumby, Amy, 'English Literature', in *Work and Play in Girls' Schools*, ed. Dorothea Beale, Lucy H. M. Soulsby and Jane Frances Dove (London: Longmans Green, 1898), pp. 192–201

Lyon, John, 'Shakespearian Margins in George Eliot's "working-day world"', *Shakespeare Survey*, 53 (2000), 114–26

Main, Alexander, *Wise, Witty and Tender Sayings in Prose and Verse, selected from the Works of George Eliot* (Edinburgh and London: Blackwood, 1872)

Manvell, Roger, *Ellen Terry* (London: Heinemann, 1968)

Marsden, Jean (ed.), *The Appropriation of Shakespeare: Post-Renaissance Reconstructions of the Works and the Myth* (London: Harvester Wheatsheaf, 1991)

Marshall, Dorothy, *Fanny Kemble* (London: Weidenfeld and Nicolson, 1977)

Marshall, Gail and Adrian Poole (eds.), *Victorian Shakespeare,* i: *Theatre, Drama and Performance* (Basingstoke: Palgrave Macmillan, 2003)

Victorian Shakespeare, ii: *Literature and Culture* (Basingstoke: Palgrave Macmillan, 2003)

Martin, Sir Theodore, *Helena Faucit (Lady Martin)* (Edinburgh and London: Blackwood, 1900)

Martineau, Jane (ed.), *Shakespeare in Art* (London: Merrell, 2003)

Marx Aveling, Edward and Eleanor Marx Aveling, *The Woman Question* (London: Swan, Sonnenschein, 1886)

Mason, James, 'How to Form a Small Library', *The Girl's Own Paper*, 2 (1880–81), 7–8, 122–23

McLellan, David, *Karl Marx: His Life and Thought* (London: Macmillan, 1973)

Mermin, Dorothy, *Elizabeth Barrett Browning: the Origins of a New Poetry* (Chicago and London: University of Chicago Press, 1989)

Modjeska, Helena, *Memories and Impressions of Helena Modjeska: An Autobiography* (New York and London: Blom, 1969; 1910)

Mueller-Vollmer, Kurt, and Michael Irmscher (eds.), *Translating Literatures, Translating Cultures: New Vistas and Approaches in Literary Studies* (Berlin: Erich Schmidt Verlag, 1998)

New Shakspere Society's Transactions, 1874 – (London: Trubner, n.d.)

Novy, Marianne (ed.), *Women's Re-visions of Shakespeare* (Urbana and Chicago: University of Illinois Press, 1990)

Engaging with Shakespeare: Responses of George Eliot and other Women Novelists (Athens and London: University of Georgia Press, 1994)

O'Day, Rosemary, 'Women and Education in Nineteenth-Century England', in Joan Bellamy, Anne Lawrence and Gill Perry (eds.), *Women, Scholarship and Criticism: Gendered Knowledge, c. 1790–1900* (Manchester University Press, 2000), pp. 91–109

'Our Prize Competition: Essay Writing on a Great English Author. – My Favourite Heroine from Shakespeare', *The Girl's Own Paper*, 10 March 1888, pp. 380–2

Palser Havely, Cicely, 'Mary Cowden Clarke's Labours of Love', in Joan Bellamy, Anne Lawrence and Gill Perry (eds.), *Women, Scholarship and Criticism: Gendered Knowledge, c. 1790–1900* (Manchester University Press, 2000), pp. 110–24

Peile, Annette, 'Instruction by Correspondence', *Journal of the Women's Education Union*, 1 (1873), 19–20

'Poems. By Elizabeth Barrett Browning', *North American Review*, 94 (1862), 338–56

Poole, Adrian, *Shakespeare and the Victorians* (London: Arden, 2004)

Prawer, S. S., *Karl Marx and World Literature* (Oxford: Clarendon Press, 1976)

Prins, Yopie, 'Elizabeth Browning, Robert Browning, and the Differance of Translation', *Victorian Poetry*, 29 (1991), 435–51

Raikes, Elizabeth, *Dorothea Beale of Cheltenham* (London: Constable, 1910)

Ransom, Teresa, *The Mysterious Miss Marie Corelli: Queen of Victorian Best-sellers* (Stroud: Sutton, 1999)

Ransome, Eleanor (ed.), *The Terrific Kemble: A Victorian Self-Portrait from the Writings of Fanny Kemble* (London: Hamish Hamilton, 1978)

Ristori, Adelaide, *Memoirs and Artistic Studies of Adelaide Ristori* (London: Doubleday, Page, 1907)

Ritchie, Anne Thackeray, *From Friend to Friend* (London: Murray, 1919)

Robins, Elizabeth, 'On Seeing Madame Bernhardt's Hamlet', *North Amercian Review*, 171 (1900), 908–19

Theatre and Friendship: Some Henry James Letters (London: Cape, 1932)

Royal Readers (London: Nelson, 1882), vol. 5

Rozett, Martha Tuck, *Talking Back to Shakespeare* (Newark: University of Delaware Press; London and Toronto: Associated University Press, 1994)

Rozmovits, Linda, *Shakespeare and the Politics of Culture in Late-Victorian England* (Baltimore and London: Johns Hopkins University Press, 1998)

Ruskin, John, 'Of Queens' Gardens', in *Sesame and Lilies* (London: George Allen, 1911)

Russell, Anne E., '"History and Real Life": Anna Jameson, Shakespeare's Heroines and Victorian Women', *Victorian Review*, 17 (1991), 35–49

Russell Mitford, Mary, *Recollections of a Literary Life; or, Books, Places, and People*, 3 vols. (London: Bentley, 1852)

Salmon, Edward G., 'What Girls Read', *Nineteenth Century*, 20 (1886), 515–29

Sanders, Valerie (ed.), *Records of Girlhood: An Anthology of Nineteenth-Century Women's Childhoods* (Aldershot: Ashgate, 2000)

Sawyer, Robert, *Victorian Appropriations of Shakespeare: George Eliot, A. C. Swinburne, Robert Browning, and Charles Dickens* (Madison and London: Fairleigh Dickinson University Press, 2003)

Scott, Clement, *Some Notable Hamlets of the Present Time* (London: Greening, 1900)

Shattuck, Charles H., *Mr Macready Produces 'As You Like It'; A Prompt-Book Study* (Urbana, IL: Beta Phi Mu, 1962)

Shaughnessy, Robert, *Representing Shakespeare: England, History and the Royal Shakespeare Company* (Hemel Hempstead: Harvester Wheatsheaf, 1994)

(ed.) *The Cambridge Companion to Shakespeare and Popular Culture* (Cambridge University Press, 2007)

Shaw, George Bernard, *Our Theatres in the Nineties*, 3 vols. (London: Constable, 1932)

Shirreff, Emily, *Intellectual Education, and its Influence on the Character and Happiness of Women* (London: Parker, 1858)

Siegel, Carol, '"This thing I like my sister may not do": Shakespearean Erotics and a Clash of Wills in *Middlemarch*', *Style*, 32 (1998), 36–59

Sircy, Otice C., '"The Fashion of Sentiment": Allusive Technique and the Sonnets of *Middlemarch*', *Studies in Philology*, 84 (1987), 219–44

Slights, Jessica, 'Historical Shakespeare: Anna Jameson and Womanliness', *English Studies in Canada*, 19 (1993), 387–400

Slinn, E. Warwick, 'Elizabeth Barrett Browning and the Problem of Female Agency', in Barbara Garlick (ed.), *Tradition and the Poetics of Self in Nineteenth-Century Women's Poetry* (Amsterdam, NL: Rodopi, 2002), pp. 43–55

Smith, G. B., 'Elizabeth Barrett Browning', *Cornhill Magazine*, 29 (1874), 469–90

Smith, W. H., 'Elizabeth Barrett Browning', *British Quarterly Review*, 34 (1861), 350–81

'The Sonnets of Shakespeare', *Westminster Review*, 12 n.s. (1857), 116–37

Soulsby, Lucy H. M., *Stray Thoughts on Reading* (London: Longmans, Green, 1897)

The Use of Leisure, i: *Some Thoughts on the Education of Girls* (London: Longmans, Green, 1900)

Stavisky, Aron Y., *Shakespeare and the Victorians: Roots of Modern Criticism* (Norman: University of Oklahoma Press, 1969)

Steiner, George, *After Babel: Aspects of Language and Translation* (Oxford University Press, 1975)

Stokes, John, Michael R. Booth and Susan Bassnett, *Bernhardt, Terry, Duse: The Actress in Her Time* (Cambridge University Press, 1988)

Stokes, Margaret and Georgina Colmache, 'Helen Faucit', *Blackwood's Edinburgh Magazine*, 138 (1885), 741–60

Swan, Annie S., *My Life: An Autobiography* (London: Ivor, Nicholson & Watson, 1934)

Taranow, Gerda, *The Bernhardt Hamlet* (New York: Peter Lang, 1996)

Taylor, Gary, *Reinventing Shakespeare: A Cultural History from the Restoration to the Present* (London: Hogarth Press, 1990)

Terry, Ellen, *Four Lectures on Shakespeare*, ed. and intro. Christopher St John (London: Hopkinson, 1932)

Thompson, Ann and Sasha Roberts (eds.), *Women Reading Shakespeare: An Anthology of Criticism, 1660–1900* (Manchester University Press, 1997)

Tod, Isabella M. S., *On the Education of Girls of the Middle Classes* (London: Ridgway, 1874)

Tsuzuki, Chushichi, 'Japanese Archives Relating to British Labour History (2)', *Society for the Study of Labour History, Bulletin* 8 (1964), 18–22

  The Life of Eleanor Marx, 1855–1898, A Socialist Tragedy (Oxford: Clarendon Press, 1967)

van den Broek, A. G., 'Shakespeare at the Heart of George Eliot's England', *George Eliot–George Henry Lewes Studies*, 24/25 (1993), 36–64

Vaughan, Alden T., and Virginia Mason Vaughan, *Shakespeare's Caliban: A Cultural History* (Cambridge University Press, 1991)

Vincent, David, 'The Domestic and the Official Curriculum in Nineteenth-Century England', in Mary Hilton, Morag Styles and Victor Watson (eds.), *Opening the Nursery Door: Reading, Writing and Childhood, 1600–1900* (London and New York: Routledge, 1997), pp. 161–79

Vyver, Bertha, *Memoirs of Marie Corelli* (London: Alston Rivers, 1930)

'L. W.', 'Our Shakespeare Society', *The Girl's Own Paper*, 6 (1884–5), 507–8

Watson, Nicola J., *The Literary Tourist: Readers and Places in Romantic and Victorian Britain* (Basingstoke: Palgrave Macmillan, 2006)

Wedgwood, Julia, 'The Moral Influence of George Eliot', *Contemporary Review*, 39 (1881), 173–85

  'The "Midsummer Night's Dream"', *Contemporary Review*, 57 (1890), 580–7

  'Shakespere's "Julius Caesar"', *Contemporary Review*, 63 (1893), 356–68

Wells, Stanley, *Shakespeare for All Time* (London: Macmillan, 2002)

White, Richard Grant, *Studies in Shakespeare* (Boston and New York: Houghton, Mifflin, 1886)

Whitebrook, Peter, *William Archer: A Biography* (London: Methuen, 1993)

Ziegler, Georgianna, *Shakespeare's Unruly Women* (Seattle and London: University of Washington Press, 1997)

Index

Achurch, Janet, 166–7
Anderson, Mary, 31
annotation, 160–1
Archer, William, 156, 161–3
Arnold, Matthew, 1, 2, 57, 106, 178, 187, 196
Aveling, Edward, 132, 137, 139

Barrett Browning, Elizabeth, 10, 12, 49–70, 99,
    100, 152, 180
    Aurora Leigh, 45, 49–52, 54, 55, 56, 58, 60
    Correspondence, 63–70
    Sonnets from the Portuguese, 49, 52, 54, 57,
        63–70, 71
Bayne, Peter, 124–5
Beale, Dorothea, 25, 26, 28, 29, 30, 39
Beerbohm Tree, Herbert, 154, 166
Beerbohm, Max, 172
Belloc, Bessie Rayner, 46
Bernard Shaw, George, 132, 154, 156–8,
    166–7
Bernhardt, Sarah, 9, 11, 159, 163, 165, 169–73
Besant, Annie, 132, 140
Black, William, *Judith Shakespeare*, 59–60
Blackwood, John, 111
Blatchford, Robert, 134
Blind, Karl, 132
Blind, Mathilde, 8, 10, 47, 130–4, 147, 151
Booth, Edwin, 135
Bowdler, Henrietta, 19, 38
Boyd, Hugh Stuart, 46, 65
Brandes, Georg, 158, 191
Bronte, Charlotte, *Shirley*, 106–7
Browning, Oscar, 100
Browning, Robert, 46, 52, 56, 59, 65, 67, 70, 73
Butler, Pierce, 75, 77, 93
Byron, George Gordon, Lord, 46

Campbell, Stella (Mrs Patrick), 165, 167–8
Carlyle, Thomas, 4, 27
Cheltenham Ladies' College, 4, 28, 29, 38
Colborne-Veel, Mary, 47

Coleridge, Samuel Taylor, 29, 104, 140
Cook, Eliza, 47
Corelli, Marie, 7, 8, 144–52
    'The Modern Marriage Market', 145
    The Sorrows of Satan, 145–7, 150
Cowden Clarke, Mary, 19, 61
    'My Favourite Shakespeare Heroine', 20–1
    Complete Concordance to Shakspere, 19
    The Girlhood of Shakespeare's Heroines, 20, 21
cross-dressing, 163, *see also* travesti
Cushman, Charlotte, 169

Daly, Augustin, 154, 166
daughters, 58–62, *see also* father and mother
Dickens, Charles, 49
Duke of Saxe Meiningen, 9
Duse, Eleanora, 9, 163, 165–6, 168, 171

education, 13–44
Eliot, George, vii, 5, 7, 8, 10, 12, 29, 79, 87,
    99–127, 128, 132, 138
    'Love in the Drama', 122
    'Brother and Sister' sonnets, 111
    Daniel Deronda, 79, 99, 123
    Felix Holt, 105, 107–8, 115, 124, 187
    Middlemarch, 100, 102, 108, 109, 112–27
    writing as Marian Evans, 47
Ellis, Havelock, 139
Ellis, Sarah Stickney, 16

father, 14, 15, 17, 19, 22, 26, 29, 39, 40, 42, 45, 48,
    55, 58, 59, 60, 61, 62, 63, 64, 74, 76, 78, 79,
    80, 82, 94, 95, 96, 97, 121, 138, 116
Faucit, Helen, vii, 4, 5, 7, 8, 31, 37, 38, 61, 72, 73,
    74, 75–7, 80, 83–93, 94, 96, 97, 98, 100,
    120, 121, 145, 149, 153, 154, 156, 157, 165, 177
    On Some of Shakespeare's Female Characters, 76,
    83–5
Fechter, Charles, 9
Feuerbach, Anselm, 31
Fiske, John, 99

Flaubert, Gustave, 137, 138, 142, 189, *see also* Eleanor Marx, translation of Madame Bovary
friendship, 1, 12, 20, 40, 48, 60, 65, 70, 75, 77, 84, 85, 90, 102, 110, 133, 140, 144, 145, 159
Furnivall, F. J., 136

Garnett, Richard, 132, 133
Gilbert, Sir John, 31
Girls' Own Paper, 20, 29, 30, 40, 42
Girls' Public Day School company, 24
Gordon Sim, Adelaide C., 21–2
Gosse, Edmund, 56, 57
Grey, Maria G., 25

Hathaway, Anne, 130, 141
Hayez, Francesco, 31
Hazlitt, William, 88, 105
Heath, Charles, 5, 15, 36–8
Homer, 45, 49, 146
    Iliad, 52
Hughes, Molly Vivian, 15–16, 22

Ibsen, Henrik, 8, 128, 142, 154, 157, 161, 162, 164, 165, 167, 169
Irving, Henry, 31, 97, 134, 135, 145, 155, 159, 160, 161, 163, 164, 166, 167, 169, 173, 177

James, Henry, 74–5, 96, 99, 169
    'The Birthplace', 128–9, 151–2
Jameson, Anna, 6, 7, 34, 35, 36, 37, 38, 39, 40, 44, 59, 85, 86, 120, 143, 144, 158

Kean, Charles, 155
Kemble, Charles , 74, 78, 79
Kemble, Fanny, 8, 31, 72, 73–6, 77–83, 93–6, 97
    Further Records, 1848–1883, 77
    Journal of a Residence on a Georgian Plantation, 77, 93
    Journal of a Young Actress, 77, 185
    Notes Upon Some of Shakespeare's Plays, 77, 79, 82–3
    Poems, 95
    Records of a Girlhood, 77, 78, 80, 81
    Records of Later Life, 77, 94
Kemble, John Philip, 77, 78, 79
Kenyon, John, 49
Knox, Kathleen, 1, 2, 3, 4, 5, 6, 8, 12, 30, 122

Lamb, Mary and Charles
    Tales from Shakespear, 18, 19, 21
Langtry, Lillie, 140
Leighton, Lord Frederic, 33–4

Lewes G. H., 8, 87, 99, 100, 103–5, 109, 112
Lumby, Amy, 27–8

Macmillan, Alexander, 110
Macready, William, 67, 88–9
Madox Brown, Ford, 32, 132
Madox Brown, Lucy, 42, 43, 132
Main, Alexander, 99
Martin, Theodore, 73, 77, 96, 99, 115, 145
Martineau, Harriet, 16–17
Marx, Eleanor, 8, 10, 14, 44, 132, 134–44, 147, 151, 165
    translation of *Madame Bovary*, 137, 139
    The Woman Question, 139, 190
Marx, Karl, 14, 22, 132, 135, 138, 141
Maxwell, Caroline, 19, 38
Milton, John, 24, 26, 27, 29, 30, 49, 52, 77
Modjeska, Helena, 9, 170
mother, 14, 15, 16, 19, 21, 23, 33, 48, 61, 63, 68, 76, 77, 78, 79, 80, 107, 115, 144

National Union for Improving the Education of Women of All Classes, 23–4
Nesbit, Edith, 21–2
New Shakspere Society, 136–7
new woman, vii, 2, 21, 128, 147, 153, 157, 158, 165, 176

Pinero, A. W., *The Second Mrs Tanqueray*, 165, 168
Poel, William, 154, 161
Punch, 173, 174, 175

Rehan, Ada, 154, 161
Ristori, Adelaide, 9, 169, 170, 171
Roberts, Sarah Margaret, 38–40
Robins, Elizabeth, 162, 163–5
Rossetti, Christina, 48–9
Rossetti, William Michael, 132
Rossi, Ernesto, 9
Ruskin, John, 4, 5, 6, 7, 8, 11, 23, 27, 62, 72, 86, 108, 120, 122, 137
    'The Brantwood Diaries', 62
Russell Mitford, Mary, 56, 64, 65, 66, 68, 69

Salvini, Tommaso, 9, 100
Sand, George, 46, 49, 138
Schreiner, Olive, 139, 165
Scott, Clement, 34, 173
Scott, Walter, 29, 102
Shakespeare
    Parts
        Ariel, 59
        Beatrice, 72, 86, 114, 143
        Bianca, 21, 22
        Caliban, 59, 93, 135

Shakespeare (cont.)
  Cordelia, 3, 29, 64, 68, 137, 176
  Cassio, 147, 174, 176
  Celia, 12, 95, 123
  Cleopatra, 38, 117, 140, 142, 158, 165–7, 168,
    170, 171
  Coriolanus, 107
  Desdemona, 3, 28, 38, 61, 62, 63, 86, 118, 122,
    131, 159, 174–7
  Duke Senior, 48, 49, 95, 101
  Edgar, 29
  Emilia, 159
  Falstaff, 15
  Ferdinand, 59, 140
  Gertrude, 48
  Goneril, 4, 29
  Hamlet, 2, 9, 11, 14, 18, 19, 27, 28, 38, 39, 48,
    49, 50, 51, 62, 63, 64, 68, 78, 94, 99, 102,
    103, 104, 110, 123, 135, 138, 147, 159, 162,
    171–3
  Helena (*All's Well That Ends Well*), 3,
    139–40
  Helena (*A Midsummer Night's Dream*),
    12, 110
  Henry V, 159
  Hermia, 12, 110
  Hermione, 3, 96
  Imogen, 3, 36, 62, 86, 90, 118–22, 155, 156,
    157, 158, 168
  Isabella, 3, 181
  Juliet, 9, 31, 32, 33, 34, 38, 42, 70, 79, 80, 81, 83,
    84, 90, 91, 118, 122, 123, 137, 167, 169
  Katharine, 21
  King Lear, 138
  Lady Macbeth, 4, 9, 38, 49, 51, 61, 89, 90, 91,
    142–4, 159, 169–70, 173
  Macbeth, 135, 159, 170
  Mariana, 48, 67
  Miranda, 36, 55, 58, 59, 60, 82, 93, 97, 139,
    140, 176
  Ophelia, 4, 28, 36, 39, 40, 42, 48, 53, 62, 77,
    85, 86, 123, 130, 142, 173
  Orlando, 95, 123
  Othello, 63, 100
  Perdita, 3, 36, 177
  Portia, 3, 6, 7, 15, 39, 40, 41, 43, 79, 86, 87,
    122, 158, 164, 177
  Prospero, 55, 58, 59, 60, 82, 83, 93, 94, 97, 135
  Queen Catherine, 3
  Regan, 4, 29
  Richard III, 14, 103, 142
  Rosalind, 3, 12, 86, 87, 88, 89–91, 95, 96, 122,
    141, 159
  Shylock, 15, 17, 19, 38, 39, 40
  Sylvia, 3, 122

  Titania, 12, 130, 133, 141
  Virgilia, 3, 37, 107, 108
  Volumnia, 30, 107
  Plays
    A Midsummer Night's Dream, 12, 19, 27, 74,
      94, 103, 105, 133
    All's Well That Ends Well, 3, 124, 125, 139, 161,
      162, 191
    Antony and Cleopatra, 74, 103, 166, 171
    As You Like It, 12, 19, 27, 40, 48, 74, 89,
      90, 100, 101, 102, 103, 104, 133, 162, 163
    Coriolanus, 3, 30, 74, 103, 105, 106, 107, 108
    Cymbeline, 3, 19, 94, 120, 121, 155, 157
    Hamlet, 2, 38, 48, 50, 63, 64, 65, 66, 74,
      133, 146
    Henry IV, part 1, 19, 74, 103, 162
    Henry IV, part 2, 19, 74, 103, 162
    Henry V, 19, 27, 64, 74, 103, 105, 162
    Henry VIII, 19, 74, 103
    Julius Caesar, 2, 19, 27, 69, 74, 103, 162
    King John, 19, 74, 103, 113
    King Lear, 2, 3, 12, 18, 19, 29, 30, 64, 68, 69,
      74, 103, 104
    Macbeth, 2, 18, 19, 27, 68, 74, 90, 91, 94, 103,
      142, 143, 170, 192
    Measure for Measure, 3, 74, 103, 126, 139
    Much Ado About Nothing, 3, 19, 74, 92, 140
    Othello, 3, 18, 19, 51, 61, 63, 74, 174, 176
    Richard II, 19, 74, 103, 147, 162
    Richard III, 19, 74
    Romeo and Juliet, 3, 18, 31, 32, 33, 34, 42, 43,
      53, 61, 70, 74, 83, 89, 94, 103, 110, 114,
      162, 168
    The Merchant of Venice, 3, 17, 19, 27, 38, 41,
      43, 74, 94, 103, 105
    The Merry Wives of Windsor, 74, 103
    The Taming of the Shrew, 21, 37, 103, 162
    The Tempest, 19, 59, 60, 70, 74, 77, 82, 93,
      103, 129, 162
    The Winter's Tale, 19, 74, 96, 103, 104,
      155, 162
    Troilus and Cressida, 104, 149, 175
    Twelfth Night, 19, 37, 74, 103, 162
    Two Gentlemen of Verona, 103, 123
  Sonnets, 52–5, 110–17
Shelley, Percy Bysshe, 40, 132, 136
Shirreff, Emily, 24, 25, 26, 27
Siddons, Sarah, 77, 78, 91, 153, 169
Soulsby, Lucy, 24, 25
Spencer, Herbert, 99
Staunton, Howard, 31
Stedman, E. C., 58
Steer, Janette, 171
Steiner, George, 46
Stickney Ellis, Sarah, 38

Stratford, 8, 92, 128, 129, 132, 133, 136, 141–2,
        144–5, 147–52
    Carnegie Library, 148–51
Suicide, 142
Swan, Annie S., 14–15

Taylor, Helen, 110
Tennyson, Alfred, Lord, 49
Terry, Ben, 77
Terry, Ellen , 8, 12, 34, 77, 97, 135, 137, 143, 144,
        145, 153, 154–61, 164, 165, 167, 168, 169,
        173, 177
    Four Lectures on Shakespeare, 155, 159–60, 177
    The Story of My Life, 77
Thackeray Ritchie, Anne, 95
The Girls' Own Paper, 40–2
theatre, 66–7, 72–98, 153–77
theatres
    Covent Garden, 76, 79, 80, 88
    Drury Lane, 88, 170
    Haymarket, 154, 165

Her Majesty's, 154
Independent Theatre, 165, 166
Lyceum, 34, 135, 137, 140, 154, 155, 156, 157, 158,
        164, 167
Opéra Comique, 165
Princess's Theatre, 155
Tod, Isabella, 26
Tonna, Charlotte Elizabeth, 17
translation, 9–12, 46, 66, 67, 70–1, 92,
        99, 108, 121, 138, 139, 161, 166, 170,
        172, 176, 177
travesti, 154, 171, 173, *see also* cross-dressing

Vestris, Eliza 90
visual arts 7, 31–4

Wedgwood, Julia 100, 109
Wilde, Oscar
    The Picture of Dorian Gray 142
Wordsworth, Elizabeth 176
Wordsworth, William 27, 57

CAMBRIDGE STUDIES IN NINETEENTH-CENTURY
LITERATURE AND CULTURE

General editor

Gillian Beer, *University of Cambridge*

Titles published

1 The Sickroom in Victorian Fiction: The Art of Being Ill
   Miriam Bailin, *Washington University*

2 Muscular Christianity: Embodying the Victorian Age
   edited by Donald E. Hall, *California State University, Northridge*

3 Victorian Masculinities: Manhood and Masculine Poetics in Early Victorian
   Literature and Art
   Herbert Sussman, *Northeastern University, Boston*

4 Byron and the Victorians
   Andrew Elfenbein, *University of Minnesota*

5 Literature in the Marketplace: Nineteenth-Century British Publishing and the
   Circulation of Books
   edited by John O. Jordan, *University of California, Santa Cruz* and Robert L.
   Patten, *Rice University, Houston*

6 Victorian Photography, Painting and Poetry
   Lindsay Smith, *University of Sussex*

7 Charlotte Brontë and Victorian Psychology
   Sally Shuttleworth, *University of Sheffield*

8 The Gothic Body: Sexuality, Materialism and Degeneration at the Fin de Siècle
   Kelly Hurley, *University of Colorado at Boulder*

9 Rereading Walter Pater
   William F. Shuter, *Eastern Michigan University*

10 Remaking Queen Victoria
   edited by Margaret Homans, *Yale University* and Adrienne Munich, *State
   University of New York, Stony Brook*

11 Disease, Desire, and the Body in Victorian Women's Popular Novels
Pamela K. Gilbert, *University of Florida*

12 Realism, Representation, and the Arts in Nineteenth-Century Literature
Alison Byerly, *Middlebury College, Vermont*

13 Literary Culture and the Pacific
Vanessa Smith, *University of Sydney*

14 Professional Domesticity in the Victorian Novel: Women, Work and Home
Monica F. Cohen

15 Victorian Renovations of the Novel: Narrative Annexes and the Boundaries of Representation
Suzanne Keen, *Washington and Lee University, Virginia*

16 Actresses on the Victorian Stage: Feminine Performance and the Galatea Myth
Gail Marshall, *University of Leeds*

17 Death and the Mother from Dickens to Freud: Victorian Fiction and the Anxiety of Origin
Carolyn Dever, *Vanderbilt University, Tennessee*

18 Ancestry and Narrative in Nineteenth-Century British Literature: Blood Relations from Edgeworth to Hardy
Sophie Gilmartin, *Royal Holloway, University of London*

19 Dickens, Novel Reading, and the Victorian Popular Theatre
Deborah Vlock

20 After Dickens: Reading, Adaptation and Performance
John Glavin, *Georgetown University, Washington D C*

21 Victorian Women Writers and the Woman Question
edited by Nicola Diane Thompson, *Kingston University, London*

22 Rhythm and Will in Victorian Poetry
Matthew Campbell, *University of Sheffield*

23 Gender, Race, and the Writing of Empire: Public Discourse and the Boer War
Paula M. Krebs, *Wheaton College, Massachusetts*

24 Ruskin's God
Michael Wheeler, *University of Southampton*

25 Dickens and the Daughter of the House
   Hilary M. Schor, *University of Southern California*

26 Detective Fiction and the Rise of Forensic Science
   Ronald R. Thomas, *Trinity College, Hartford, Connecticut*

27 Testimony and Advocacy in Victorian Law, Literature, and Theology
   Jan-Melissa Schramm, *Trinity Hall, Cambridge*

28 Victorian Writing about Risk: Imagining a Safe England in a Dangerous World
   Elaine Freedgood, *University of Pennsylvania*

29 Physiognomy and the Meaning of Expression in Nineteenth-Century Culture
   Lucy Hartley, *University of Southampton*

30 The Victorian Parlour: A Cultural Study
   Thad Logan, *Rice University, Houston*

31 Aestheticism and Sexual Parody 1840–1940
   Dennis Denisoff, *Ryerson University, Toronto*

32 Literature, Technology and Magical Thinking, 1880–1920
   Pamela Thurschwell, *University College London*

33 Fairies in Nineteenth-Century Art and Literature
   Nicola Bown, Birkbeck, *University of London*

34 George Eliot and the British Empire
   Nancy Henry *The State University of New York, Binghamton*

35 Women's Poetry and Religion in Victorian England: Jewish Identity
   and Christian Culture
   Cynthia Scheinberg, *Mills College, California*

36 Victorian Literature and the Anorexic Body
   Anna Krugovoy Silver, *Mercer University, Georgia*

37 Eavesdropping in the Novel from Austen to Proust
   Ann Gaylin, *Yale University*

38 Missionary Writing and Empire, 1800–1860
   Anna Johnston, *University of Tasmania*

39 London and the Culture of Homosexuality, 1885–1914
   Matt Cook, *Keele University*

40 Fiction, Famine, and the Rise of Economics in Victorian Britain and Ireland
Gordon Bigelow, *Rhodes College, Tennessee*

41 Gender and the Victorian Periodical
Hilary Fraser, Birkbeck, *University of London,* Judith Johnston and Stephanie
Green, *University of Western Australia*

42 The Victorian Supernatural
edited by Nicola Bown, *Birkbeck College, London* Carolyn Burdett, *London
Metropolitan University* and Pamela Thurschwell, *University College London*

43 The Indian Mutiny and the British Imagination
Gautam Chakravarty, *University of Delhi*

44 The Revolution in Popular Literature: Print, Politics and the People
Ian Haywood, *Roehampton University of Surrey*

45 Science in the Nineteenth-Century Periodical: Reading the Magazine of
Nature
Geoffrey Cantor, *University of Leeds,*
Gowan Dawson, *University of Leicester,*
Graeme Gooday, *University of Leeds,*
Richard Noakes, *University of Cambridge,*
Sally Shuttleworth, *University of Sheffield,*
and Jonathan R. Topham, *University of Leeds*

46 Literature and Medicine in Nineteenth-Century Britain From Mary Shelley to
George Eliot
Janis McLarren Caldwell, *Wake Forest University*

47 The Child Writer from Austen to Woolf
edited by Christine Alexander, *University of New South Wales* and Juliet
McMaster, *University of Alberta*

48 From Dickens to Dracula: Gothic, Economics, and Victorian Fiction
Gail Turley Houston, *University of New Mexico*

49 Voice and the Victorian Storyteller
Ivan Kreilkamp, *University of Indiana*

50 Charles Darwin and Victorian Visual Culture
Jonathan Smith, *University of Michigan-Dearborn*

51 Catholicism, Sexual Deviance, and Victorian Gothic Culture
Patrick R. O'Malley, *Georgetown University*

52 Epic and Empire in Nineteenth-Century Britain
    Simon Dentith, *University of Gloucestershire*

53 Victorian Honeymoons: Journeys to the Conjugal
    Helena Michie, *Rice University*

54 The Jewess in Nineteenth-Century British Literary Culture
    Nadia Valman, *University of Southampton*

55 Ireland, India and Nationalism in Nineteenth-Century Literature
    Julia Wright, *Dalhousie University*

56 Dickens and the Popular Radical Imagination
    Sally Ledger, Birkbeck, *University of London*

57 Darwin, Literature and Victorian Respectability
    Gowan Dawson, *University of Leicester*

58 'Michael Field': Poetry, Aestheticism and the *Fin de Siècle*
    Marion Thain, *University of Birmingham*

59 Colonies, Cults and Evolution Literature: Science and Culture in Nineteenth-
    Century Writing
    David Amigoni, *Keele University*

60 Realism, Photography and Nineteenth-Century Fiction
    Daniel A. Novak, *Lousiana State University*

61 Caribbean Culture and British Fiction in the Nineteenth Century
    Tim Watson, *University of Miami*

62 The Poetry of Chartism: Aesthetics, Politics, History
    Michael Sanders, *University of Manchester*

63 Literature and Dance in Nineteenth-Century Britain: Jane Austen to the New
    Woman
    Cheryl Wilson, *Indiana University*

64 Shakespeare and Victorian Women
    Gail Marshall, *Oxford Brookes University*